BOLLINGEN SERIES XLV·A

PAUL VALÉRY

An Anthology

Selected, with an Introduction,
by James R. Lawler

from
The Collected Works of Paul Valéry
edited by Jackson Mathews

BOLLINGEN SERIES XLV · A

PRINCETON UNIVERSITY PRESS

THIS ANTHOLOGY IS TAKEN FROM THE COLLECTED WORKS
OF PAUL VALÉRY CONSTITUTING NUMBER XLV IN BOLLINGEN
SERIES
SPONSORED BY BOLLINGEN FOUNDATION

LIBRARY OF CONGRESS CATALOGING IN PUBLICATION DATA
VALÉRY, PAUL, 1871-1945.
PAUL VALÉRY, AN ANTHOLOGY.
(BOLLINGEN SERIES; 45-A)
INCLUDES BIBLIOGRAPHICAL REFERENCES.
I. TITLE.   II. SERIES.
PQ2643.A26A23   1976   848'.9'1209   76-3026
ISBN 0-691-09928-6
ISBN 0-691-01814-6 PBK.

TEXT DESIGNED BY ANDOR BRAUN
COVER DESIGNED BY MARGARET DAVIS
COVER ILLUSTRATION: *PORTRAIT OF VALÉRY*
BY D'ESPAGNAT, FROM THE GIRAUDON
"CÉLÉBRITÉS FRANÇAISES"
COLLECTION, REPRODUCED WITH THE PERMISSION·OF
ART RESOURCE, NEW YORK
PRINTED IN THE UNITED STATES OF AMERICA

9 8 7 6 5 4 3

CONTENTS

Two Dialogues

Introduction

It was Monsieur Teste, the arch cynic, who knew
well that the mind which consents to fame is a mind flawed.
Valéry's own ambition at twenty, as at forty, was to avoid
this error, to safeguard his secrets, to choose anonymity.
He was the bourgeois from the provinces leading a life
without events and conforming in exterior things to the
general face of his age; not for him the voyages to the East,
the various wanderings of a Claudel or a Gide. At the same
time he sought to inhabit an island of the spirit of which he
was the Robinson, a domain his alone that he could codify
and control. "My desire was for life as simple, and for
thought as complex, as possible," he wrote; again: "Events
are the froth of things, but my true interest is the sea."

One hardly needs to recall the major shift in his position
shortly prior to, and during, the First World War; how,
by a singular concourse of circumstances—his revision of
adolescent verse at Gide's urging, his rediscovery of Racine
and Mallarmé—he became engrossed in the composition of
a poem that he intended to be 30 to 40 lines in length but
expanded into the 512 alexandrines of *La Jeune Parque*. Its
publication in April 1917, when he was forty-five, marked
the end of his so-called silence: not a period in which he
abandoned writing—far from it—but one in which he
eschewed publication, and was appreciated by only a handful of readers as the erstwhile poet, by fewer still as the

author of *Monsieur Teste* and the essay on Leonardo da Vinci. Yet, almost from *La Jeune Parque* on, he went into print in several genres, pronounced himself on any number of issues, and served as a kind of spokesman for the French intelligentsia. He accepted prominence with much good grace, although he was prone to express tedium to family and friends, whom he once asked to inscribe upon his grave: "Here lie I, done in by my fellow-men."

Quite early he was the subject of studies in France and abroad, being promoted, as Claudel wryly put it, to the rank of "professorial idol." It was inevitable that his audience should be first of all among intellectuals despite attacks by Benda and others, which make curious reading today, on his supposed byzantinism. But his celebrity was not restricted to academic circles, and for many the first acquaintance with his work was a revelation. In France there were several such cases, not the least touching of which concerns the banker Julien P. Monod, who, seeing the newly published *La Jeune Parque* displayed in Gallimard's bookshop, procured a copy and became a little thereafter Valéry's companion and honorary secretary—"minister of the quill," "shadow," "conscience"—loyal to a relationship that lasted until Valéry's death. Elsewhere kindred attachments were formed; one thinks of Rainer Maria Rilke, who wrote: "I was alone, I was waiting, my whole heart was waiting. One day, I read Valéry. I knew my waiting was over." Rilke was drawn by what he termed the "composure" and "finality" of Valéry's language, and he devoted himself without stinting to his translations of *Charmes* and the dialogues, which offer no doubt a Valéry having suffered a sea-change, but are nonetheless admirable.

There are other signal examples of his influence. Whereas in France the most active currents of poetry were set, and Breton and Eluard would publish a cheekily reworded version of Valéry's 1929 text *Littérature* (for instance, "A poem must be a festivity of the intellect" was corrected to read "A poem must be the debacle of the intellect"), foreign poets were not so much concerned with the quarrels of schools. Several of the more prominent—Eliot, Ungaretti, Stevens, Guillén—greeted the work with an enthusiasm parallel to Rilke's. Eleven years after Valéry's death, the 1956 Exhibition at the Bibliothèque Nationale assembled a surprising array of translations published in the twenties and thirties, ranging from a version of "Narcisse" in Chinese to a Czech translation of "Aurore." The man who had lived what we would consider to be a homely existence, in no way comparable to the globe-trotting of Claudel or even Gide, had received wide recognition. But then of course we remember that a particular sort of humanism had been his lifelong ambition, the strategy of his mind, and that, eagerly, obstinately, he had sought to echo Leonardo's words: "Facil cosa è farsi universale" (It is easy to make oneself universal).

* * *

Notwithstanding this acclaim, Valéry was seldom well understood. The reception given to *La Jeune Parque* may be taken as particularly instructive in this regard. On its appearance, the critics of the day quickly assessed its manner: it was a Symbolist poem that recalled—for some, all too transparently—his apprenticeship to Mallarmé. At a time when *Alcools* had made an impression, and Cendrars and Reverdy were publishing, it seemed to a great number of these first influential commentators a kind of relic, the belated testimony of a coterie dead if not forgotten. In May 1921 the poet protested in vain: "I cannot stand to be compared to Mallarmé nor to be opposed to him. Nothing displeases me more, nor is more harmful to me. You must not use the workman against his master." If we look back today to the major critical studies that followed, we find remarkable consistency of interpretation. Approached with greater or less subtlety, in words of praise or disparagement, he was seen essentially in the perspective already established—that is, by and large in Mallarméan terms—and catalogued as a tardy epigone of Symbolism.

We now realize, however, that he had long been considering poetry in a different light, analyzing its elements and designs from a rigorous viewpoint, even when, according to a myth he willingly fostered, he was most hostile to such pursuits. His attitude, tirelessly put during the years of retreat, is that the poetic state—the state in which poetry would become as it were the natural language of its creator—can be isolated from other states with which too often it is confused and that, by means of the close definition of this idea, particular applications, or poems, can be deduced. He seeks to move from the general to the particular, from notion to object: "Poetry until now," he writes, "has thought of itself as an accident. The subject or a certain detail is given—and this lights a match. . . . *People have believed that this capricious lighting was essential to vision.* But I believe the contrary." Such a point of view displaces the Symbolist cult of art for art, the quest for the single supreme work, and postulates instead a resource that would imply all poems both accomplished and yet to be. So we find among the earliest jottings in his notebooks: "It is not one image that I seek, but the marvelous group of all possible images."

To envisage more clearly the idea of poetry reduced to its essence, from which everything alien has been expunged, he calls on certain key metaphors: the exactness of mathematics, the purity of chemistry. He also makes much of the comparison of poetry to the sexual act, the organicity of the tree, the freedom of the dance, and the richness of music—especially that of Wagner. Behind these analogies, however, we find a pivotal reference to Mallarmé, on the occasion of whose death he wrote a remarkable homage intended for himself alone:

> *J'ai de ton pur esprit bu le feu le plus beau*
>
> (Of your pure spirit I have drunk the fairest fire)

and again:

> *Je serai la tombe de ton ombre pensive*
>
> (I shall be the tomb of your pensive shade).

Moving as they are, these lines contain a manifest pride, an egocentricity that invites a moment's reflection. For if the relationship with Mallarmé is patently established, it is not a simple one; it partakes of the complexity of a filial struggle in which the unlike emerges from a fascinated exploration of the like ("an adversary link," "the ever more accurate groping of signs that reach towards one another until they attain the point of pure difference"). The artist becomes, not imitator or follower, but a rival and intimate enemy; and it is this struggle with a phantom that Valéry's early writings trace out with unique detail as he strives again and again to distance and define the qualities of the other, and comes regularly to personal terms with them. "I adored that extraordinary man," he said, "at the very same time as I considered his head to be the only one—a head beyond price!—to cut off so as to decapitate Rome." Mallarmé substituted consciousness for that which was unconscious, seeking to know language as none had known it before, minutely determining its functions and elements, seeing words as previous to ideas. ("Thought expresses the word," is the way he paraphrased Mallarmé's project. "All that the scholastics said of being etc.—power, chance, act, essences, form, etc.—applies only to language.") Yet throughout Valéry's remarks one basic criticism prevails: Mallarmé was not ruthless enough, for he continued to worship the clay idol of

xi

poetry, drew from it a conception of the world, turned his sonnets into a sort of "Marivaudage with the absolute." Valéry could admire the discipline and the finesse, the devotion to a view of language diametrically opposed to the ends of prose, but he could not be bound to the *religion* of art. This was his fundamental criticism, a vital and liberating one as we recognize, which allowed him in 1892 or shortly thereafter to grasp as never before his own identity. Via Mallarmé he made the discovery of a focus of thought, an ultimate and personal violence, a fervent identity. Realizing that he must slough off poetry as a goal in itself, he concerned himself with mental functioning and, in poetry, with the creative art. He had drunk the potion that induced a necessary reaction: "I loved Mallarmé, hated him, and looked in myself to find something else." This same thought was put in many forms but nowhere more strikingly than in a notation penciled on a page bearing the date 1906: "To have known Mallarmé is the distinction of my chance; to have fought him, Jacob matched with the angel, is the honor of my law." Through the soul's resistance, an apparently fortuitous encounter became a rule of life, and Valéry emerged a man fortified.

Fortified, and not weakened. His loyalty to Mallarmé is the loyalty of one who scrutinizes in a new frame. Like others of his generation, he spoke of Symbolism in the past tense: "that which was baptized Symbolism . . .," "Symbolism had other enemies . . .," "Symbolism was. . . ." Indeed, it is this very pastness by which he defines it: "The word Symbolism is the verbal symbol for the intellectual qualities and conditions most opposed to those which reign, and even govern, today." His ambition was different, his observances changed. The poetry of the past, including that of Mallarmé, was to be an instrument he could adopt and fashion, but it clearly was not his own. "I could not," he said, "ignore Mallarmé's technique. If my verse at times recalls it, that does me honor, but one does not think of reproaching the musicians who came after Bach for having studied the fugue."

The test of such a transformation lies, of course, not so much in what Valéry said of it himself, but in what his poems reveal, above all in what is revealed by *La Jeune Parque*, around which his other verse is gathered as around a single feature commanding a landscape, or as Mallarmé's entire work turns on *Hérodiade*. He had long been developing the theme of his prose-poem *Agathe*, the abstract pre-Parque begun in 1898 that proposes the sequence of moods, thoughts, and emotions within an individual sensibility over a given period of time, a strange ascesis of the senses and the will; he had also referred to, and described, a haunting musical continuity, a deeply moving contralto that suggested an ideal—"the real, necessary, absolute thing"—to which his life and language aspired. On the one hand, then, a recitative, a warm solo sung by a woman; on the other, the cycle of transformations within a mind: by virtue of these two elements he held, unwittingly, the nub of his grand endeavor.

The fictional character he finally created is a virginal heroine who calls to mind several Mediterranean myths. A true sister of Hérodiade in her vulnerability, she stands, like her, at the limits of life and death, "on the golden edge of the universe." Yet her monologue, far from being a "mystery" in the way of *Les Noces d'Hérodiade*, is an "opera," which she sings in several voices and without external drama. Valéry might well have named her Eve, or Psyche, or Helen, or Pandora, as he thought of doing: each is the image of a fatal error and a portentous discovery; he chose instead the "Jeune Parque," which, freed from any traditional affabulation, signifies man's Fate—his body and mind—struggling with the dawning knowledge of its own mortality.

In the beginning a strangely intimate self is heard as it weeps and sings its ageless elegy, which corresponds to a keening of the moist wind. The Parque remembers days of translucent pleasure before the fault of self-awareness, she foretells light reborn; but every time she momentarily escapes in thought, she is brought back again to the central equation of consciousness and body, "as a sea anemone is restricted to its stone." She resolves at last, no longer to combat her anxiety, but to accept the passage of tears, this flaw, like a salutary thread of knowledge. Her poem ends on the grace of dawn, the transformation of tears into a dance of spray and light, or a splendid integration of the self.

Valéry's intention becomes manifest, and decidedly un-Mallarméan, when we look further than the line of discourse. For *La Jeune Parque* is not a vignette, however nobly evocative, but the portrayal of a sensibility. We are offered a sequence of psychological states, from the first prick of sorrow and the stirring of consciousness, through a cycle of sensations, memories, and aspirations. Each section might bear an abstract subtitle such as grief, pleasure, nostalgia, desire: emotions, affective movements, but not ideas like those we find as the basis of *L'Après-midi d'un faune* or *Hérodiade*, which offer, each in its way, a shimmering *mise-en scène* of Mallarmé's aesthetics. On the contrary, Valéry is not so much presenting a philosophy as a mode of being, which can be deciphered from the particularized monologue of his persona. The poem is therefore not symbolic except insofar as the Parque's drama is also our own. Its difficulty results from the need to learn a system of images that are pre-eminently images of the body ("a course in physiology," as he put it), and not from any one idiosyncratic meaning in, or behind, the text.

The creative process may be illustrated by reference to a few lines from one of the manuscripts. Referring to the passage that will evoke the Parque's confrontation with the Serpent ("Quel repli de désirs, sa traîne! . . . Quel désordre / De trésors s'arrachant à mon avidité / Et quelle sombre soif de la limpidité!"), Valéry writes: "I must paint at this point of the poem—a death modulated by insensible, painless substitutions as a musical change, as a passage from double to single, a subterranean retreat—by an irreversible process. So that one cannot say to oneself at any moment that something has changed. Sensations become images, the present merges with the past . . ., knowledge gives way to existence, the other gives way to the self, and this is death." He then takes up again the whole question: "How can I give this substance and detail? I need to go back from what I have just written to what I thought in the rough, between each one of the thoughts I noted down." Here we have, not poetry, but a manner of preparing for poetry, after which will come a cluster of images translating, as he says, thought "in the rough," then lists of rhymes, sounds, rhythmical patterns, sometimes even accompanied by a stave bearing crotchets and minims. Analysis is linked to music, psychological description ("the identical or permanent, the fluid, the substitutions, the reductions to images, the sequences") to imagination. From these disparate beginnings at far remove from the actual poem, a sequence, a bodily and psychological "fate" evolves.

The originality of project and procedure is evident. Yet one of the most interesting aspects of La Jeune Parque is Valéry's conscious use of a poetic tradition. He enumerates the authors who were his familiar spirits when writing it: Mallarmé, of course, but also Euripides, Virgil, Petrarch, Racine, Chénier, Hugo, Baudelaire, Rimbaud, Claudel: poets lyrical, tragic, elegiac, visionary. The list may appear incongruous; nevertheless he plainly associated each author with certain specific effects, a language and rhythm he could employ as a model within the structure of his poem. Thus Racine played a vital role in proposing, beyond a particular impassioned tone, what Valéry calls "Racinian mimetism," the intimate correlation of body and mind, the intermingling of vertigo and lucidity, knowledge and guilt, thirst and poison in order to portray a quasi-Jansenist passion. The Parque becomes Phaedra:

> Je n'attendais pas moins de mes riches déserts
> Qu'un tel enfantement de fureur et de tresse :
> Leurs fonds passionnés brillent de sécheresse
> Si loin que je m'avance et m'altère pour voir
> De mes enfers pensifs les confins sans espoir.

> (I expected no less from my rich deserts
> Than such a pregnancy of violence and tresses;
> Their passionate distances glare with barrenness
> The further I press, dry with thirst to see
> The hopeless confines of my thought's inferno.)

But there is also the recognizable echo of Baudelaire, warm and bitter ("Souvenir, ô bûcher, dont le vent d'or m'affronte" [Memory, bonfire whose golden wind assaults me]), of Chénier, in the elegiac passages of nostalgia ("O paupières qu'opprime une nuit de trésor, / Je priais à tâtons dans vos ténèbres d'or !" [Eyelids overborne by a night of riches, / Gropingly I was praying in your golden glooms!]), of other poets. And present is Mallarmé, his work occasionally begetting an awkward phrase, a patent calque, but predominantly lending strength as it is transformed into an uncompromising elevation of thought and language:

> L'ennui, le clair ennui de mirer leur nuance
> Me donnait sur ma vie une funeste avance :
> L'aube me dévoilait tout le jour ennemi.

> (The clear-eyed tedium of mirroring their changes
> Gave me a mournful prospect of my life:
> Dawn unveiled to me the whole hostile day.)

Mallarmé was thus a voice among the several that composed the Parque's individual drama: voices that did not impose themselves in spite of their author, for they were his conscious means, at a time when Europe was tearing itself asunder in war, of paying tribute to a living tradition in a spirit not dissimilar to that of Eliot five years later in *The Waste Land*; of creating a poem that has the fullness of many registers but the controlling mode, the characteristic self-awareness, of its author alone. Valéry accomplished his masterpiece in his forties, when he could look back on Symbolism and bend it to his ends, appropriating what he needed, rejecting the dogma. The verdict of many of his contemporaries was too hasty and oversimple: his work was an art practiced when he no longer believed in the absolute of art, but only in the analytical precision with which his poetics could be plied and to which his theme and method lent themselves.

*   *   *

It is hardly necessary to say that most interpreters outside France in the thirties and forties found *La Jeune Parque*, and the poems of *Charmes*, which followed in 1922, no less difficult to define and situate than did their French colleagues. Indeed, the majority of foreign critiques published before the 1950's did not aspire to rival in scholarship or daring the best known French analyses. From this general rule one would except a few studies whose merit is pointed up by the passage of time. One thinks, for example, of the exegesis of *La Jeune Parque* published in 1938 by the Australian A. R. Chisholm, who saw the poem with personal insight and a philosophical bent in the wake of Thibaudet and Alain; of the much more exhaustive approach to the language of the same poem by the Danish scholar Hans Sørensen in 1944; of the commentaries on the poetry by the Belgian Jacques Duchesne-Guillemin (1947), and the Swiss Pierre-Olivier

Walzer (1952), and of the precise research into the origin and meaning of "Le Cimetière marin" by the Australian Lloyd J. Austin (1954).

This was the first phase, and the initial fruit, of Valéry's international reputation. Nevertheless, we observe that the growth of his fame since 1955 has been almost unique; for to a work already held to be among the most important in French literature, a volume of writings of much vaster dimensions was added a decade after his death. The 26,000-odd pages of his *Cahiers* were published in facsimile by the Centre National de la Recherche Scientifique between 1957 and 1961. We understand today that they were the main-spring of his creative life, of comparable, but more oblique, importance for the origins of his work than were *Jean Santeuil* and *Contre Sainte-Beuve* for Proust's masterpiece. Begun in 1894 in imitation of Leonardo's notebooks and not as a private diary, they were added to each day in the early morning hours over a period of fifty years. Valéry saw them as the record of his mental exercises, his logbook compiled in the name of self-control, the disport of his detachment, clarity, precision. They were a personal enterprise, which he yet acknowledged to have been brought about by his apprenticeship as an adolescent Symbolist poet, literary creation having shown him the intimate connection between verbal maneuver and thought. "All literature is contained in the curve of words. Try to see, try to exhaust the greatest possible number of them." That was the lesson he read into Mallarmé; but in his *Cahiers* he applied it to the curvature of mental functioning. For, as against his master in poetry who put his end in the artifact, he centered his quest on the prospection of the mind—a distinction that he formulated succinctly in these terms: "For him [that is, Mallarmé], the work; for me, the self." His project reminds us of research much closer to us in time into the nature of creativity.

The publication of the *Cahiers* was an event of considerable note that showed as never before the unity of a practice
that had appeared highly diverse, if not self-contradictory.
We possess the key, unique in its constant application;
among the ocean currents of the sensibility we can follow
the accompanying scrutiny of reason, with its ironic distance
not always kept but constantly reasserted. We observe, however, that France has been curiously slow to approach these
pages with the seriousness they deserve. French critics have
not as yet devoted a study of real depth to them, although
some more cursory appraisals have appeared. On the other
hand, the last fifteen or so years have seen a number of
important essays by foreign authors that have brought about
significant progress in our understanding of Valéry. The
phenomenon may be ascribed to several factors: a temporary disaffection for him among French critics, who have
preferred to turn to other fields; the difficulty of consulting
and utilizing documents that were unedited; the very size
of the *Cahiers*.

The volumes seem to have appeared less daunting when
approached from abroad. The pioneering book *L'Analyse de
l'esprit dans les 'Cahiers' de Valéry* by the Australian Judith
Robinson (1963) isolated some of the main orientations of
the notebooks and showed in particular Valéry's radical
approach to language. Professor Robinson followed up her
work with admirable care and skill by publishing a version
of the *Cahiers* in which she grouped Valéry's writings, not
chronologically, but according to the headings that in later
years he himself considered as a possible way of ordering the
vast assemblage of notes. Other important research on the
Cahiers has been done by the Canadian Pierre Laurette in his
Le Thème de l'arbre chez Paul Valéry (1967), which raises
much more central issues than its title suggests; and in a
study of 1972, "Paul Valéry: Consciousness and Nature,"

by the English scholar Christine M. Crow. One might also refer to work of a different tenor and reach by two Polish-born academics: Edouard Gaède, who drew extensively on the *Cahiers* in his *Nietzsche et Valéry*, a book which he subtitled "Essay on the Comedy of the Mind" (1962); and Leon Tauman, who adopted a moral and religious viewpoint in his *Paul Valéry et le mal de l'art* (1969).

It may seem curious that I have so far made no mention of research done in the United States. It would not be far wrong to say that in this country Valéry has by and large enjoyed little more than a *succès d'estime*. Some research of a fundamental kind has, however, been carried out by scholars such as Charles Whiting on the early poems and Jeanine Parisier-Plottel on the dialogues. But two enterprises stand out. The first is the Pléiade edition of the *Œuvres*, which was prepared with exemplary taste by Jean Hytier. The other is the monumental achievement of Jackson Mathews, who for twenty years devoted himself, with a fidelity that must win our admiration, to the formidable task of producing a Valéry in English. Like almost all such publications, the Bollingen *Collected Works* is the triumph of one man's determination and vision.

I shall not speak of the translations themselves, nor of the careful groupings and annotations; it is to the introductions, done by a variety of critics from several countries, that I should like to draw particular attention. Doubtless the most valuable is T. S. Eliot's essay on the art of poetry, the last of five in which Eliot came to grips with the work of his contemporary. As early as 1920 he had taken issue with a statement concerning philosophical poetry as Valéry formulated it in the "Avant-propos à la *Connaissance de la Déesse*"; four years later, in 1924, he wrote his "Brief Introduction to the Method of Paul Valéry," which, now in appreciative fashion, looked at tradition and the individual talent in

Valéry's own work, seeing him as the "completion" and "explanation" of Symbolism; in 1946, a year after the French poet's death, he composed a homage entitled "Leçon de Valéry," his tribute to an intelligence that, despite what Eliot terms its "nihilistic" climate, continued to create by way of personal daring and courage, by a "desperate heroism which is a triumph of character"; then, in 1948, his "From Poe to Valéry" discussed the tradition of poetic consciousness in the late nineteenth and early twentieth centuries that culminates in Valéry's extreme awareness of language. "Valéry will remain for posterity," he writes, "the representative poet, the symbol of the poet of the first half of the twentieth century—not Yeats, not Rilke, not anyone else." The comments in the 1958 Bollingen volume entitled *The Art of Poetry* show the will to take Valéry's measure one last time. In praising him as the epitome of the European poet of his age Eliot does not refrain from criticism; he warns of the dangers inherent in a sharp distinction between poetry and prose, which involve Valéry in the dilemma of separating the idiom of poetry from that of ordinary speech. Even more central is a reference to the fact that Valéry never offers in his theoretical writings any criterion of seriousness, any penetration of the special relationship that exists between poetry and life. Valéry might have answered by saying that the reader's experience is essentially a matter of digestion, for he profits in relation to his alimentary needs, his capacity to do justice to what is set before him; on another occasion, he might have referred to the essential complexity of a good poem, which calls on the whole reader—intellect, emotion, sensuousness—in order to state a complete thought, a rounded apprehension. Yet even if such answers fail to satisfy us—for they must—Eliot in no way imputes a lack of seriousness to Valéry's own poems.

These pages, both economical and probing, are one of

the minor glories of the *Collected Works* in English. Yet much still remains to be taken up and examined. With the *Cahiers*, and also the published writings, in hand, we have the exceptional testimony of a poet and thinker who sought to spell out for himself, in its consequences and, hence, its contradictions, his myth of "purity." One is reminded of Gide's early statement: "When the world is not in accord with your dream, you must dream it in accord with your desire." The next years will no doubt be a fertile period for Valéry criticism. We await, for instance, the biography that demands to be done; we shall examine the system of the mind articulated in the *Cahiers*. We shall also no doubt come to see with greater acuteness the drama of sensibility, the pathos never cultivated in a Symbolist mode but rejected, explored, stated with intensity. This he expressed most often in indirect fashion; but it is easy to forget that in 1939 he published a deeply personal poem that was drafted in 1892 or thereabouts, elaborated in 1908, revised in 1917, and placed in *Mélange* alongside fragments written fifty years later. I am thinking of his "Sinistre," a ballad depicting the despair incurred by loss of faith, in respect of which the rest of his work can be viewed as an opposite response. It begins with the naming of an hour of crisis:

> Quelle heure cogne aux membres de la coque
> Ce grand coup d'ombre où craque notre sort?
> Quelle puissance impalpable entre-choque
> Dans nos agrès des ossements de mort?

> (What hour hurtles at the staves of the hull
> That knock of darkness on which our fate cracks?
> What force untouchable plays the castanets
> In our tackle with a dead man's bones?)

The Valéry who had been an avid reader of "Bateau ivre" adapts certain of Rimbaud's images to a narrative of tempest, Satanic revolt, shipwreck, his decasyllables faithful to a sense of foreboding. The last lines, however, show the figure of Christ drowning in some horrendous death at sea, bearing with him a familiar world:

Je vois le Christ amarré sur la vergue! . . .
Il crie à mort, sombrant avec les siens;
Son œil sanglant m'éclaire cet exergue:
UN GRAND NAVIRE A PÉRI CORPS ET BIENS! . . .

(I see Christ roped to the yardarm!
Dancing to death, foundering with his herd;
His bloodshot eye lights me to this exergue:
A GREAT SHIP GONE DOWN WITH ALL ON BOARD!)

It is not the tone and imagery of a detached cynic but of a poet who, as dramatically as the young Mallarmé or—perhaps no less near—the Claudel of a wartime "Ballade," wrested his vision from an imaginary shipwreck.

We recall a few laconic words he wrote in a notebook shortly posterior to *Monsieur Teste*: "For having once foolishly skirted the abysses of the mind . . ."; forty years later, after he had long since emerged from reclusion, his Apollo likened poetry to a thunderbolt that implacably sears a mountain—"as a summit is elected by the bolt." He appears to us today in more than one regard to resemble his Parque: "bitten by the marvel" of self-awareness, he suffered the flash and knew the marine depths of which his sensibility bore the trace. Formalist he sought to be, and was, in noble if poignant fashion—to quell a turmoil too much with him. So we follow, against a primal division within the self, the lucid adventure that French Symbolism alone could inform yet whose crystalline expression is rightly the reserve of no single time or place.

JAMES R. LAWLER

From *Monsieur Teste*

The Evening with Monsieur Teste

Vita Cartesii res est simplicissima

STUPIDITY is not my strong point. I have seen many persons; I have visited several countries; I have taken part in various enterprises without liking them; I have eaten nearly every day; I have had women. I can now recall a few hundred faces, two or three great spectacles, and the substance of perhaps twenty books. I have not retained the best nor the worst of these things: what could stay with me did.

Such arithmetic spares me any surprise at growing old. I could also count up the victorious moments of my mind and imagine them joined and blended, composing a *happy* life. . . . But I think I have always been a good judge of myself. I have rarely lost sight of myself; I have detested and adored myself; so, we have grown old together.

Often I have supposed that all was over for me, and I would begin ending with all my strength, anxious to drain and clarify some painful situation. This made me aware that we appraise our own thought too nearly as others *express* theirs! From that moment, the billions of words that have buzzed in my ears have rarely stirred me with what they were meant to mean; and all those I have myself spoken to others, I have always felt them become distinct from my thought—for they were becoming *invariable*.

If I had decided like most men, not only should I have felt superior to them but should have appeared so. I pre-

3

ferred myself. What they call a superior man is a man who has deceived himself. To be astonished at him, one must see him—and to be seen, he must show himself. And he shows me that he is possessed by an inane infatuation with his own name. So every great man is flawed with an error. Every mind said to be powerful begins with the mistake that makes it known. In exchange for the public's dime, he gives the time required to make himself noticeable, the energy spent in conveying himself, preparing to satisfy someone else. He goes even so far as to compare the crude sport of fame with the joy of feeling unique—the great private pleasure.

At that time I dreamed that the most vigorous minds, the canniest inventors, the most precise connoisseurs of thought, must be unknown men, misers, or those who die without confessing. Their existence was revealed to me precisely by those brilliant individuals a bit less *solid*.

This conclusion was so easy that I could see it taking shape from moment to moment. All that was needed was to imagine the usual sort of great men free of their first error, or even to base oneself on that error in order to conceive a higher degree of consciousness, a less crude sense of the mind's freedom. So simple an operation opened curious perspectives before me, as if I had gone down under sea. Along with the neglected creations produced every day by commerce, fear, boredom, or poverty, I thought I could make out certain *inner* masterpieces, lost amid the brilliance of published discoveries. It amused me to extinguish known history beneath the annals of anonymity.

Invisible in their limpid lives, they were solitaries who knew before all the rest. It seemed to me that in their obscurity they were twice, three times, many times greater than any famous person—they, in their disdain for revealing their

4

luck and their personal discoveries. They would have refused, I believe, to consider themselves anything more than things.

These ideas came to me during October of '93, at those moments of repose when thought takes pleasure simply in existing.

I was beginning to think no more about them, when I made the acquaintance of Monsieur Teste. (I am thinking now of the traces a man leaves in the little space he moves in every day.) Before I came to know Monsieur Teste, I was attracted by his special ways. I studied his eyes, his clothes, his slightest muffled words to the waiter at the café where I used to see him. I wondered whether he felt observed. I would turn my eyes quickly away from his, so as to catch his following me. I would take up the newspapers he had just been reading, I would rehearse in my mind the sober gestures he made unawares; I noticed that no one paid him any attention.

I had nothing more of this kind to learn when our relations began. I never saw him except at night. Once in a sort of...house; often at the theater. I was told that he lived by frugal weekly speculations on the stock market. He took his meals in a small restaurant in the Rue Vivienne. There he would eat as if he were taking a purgative, with the same quick gestures. Occasionally he would allow himself a fine leisurely meal elsewhere.

Monsieur Teste was perhaps forty years old. His speech was extraordinarily rapid, and his voice low. Everything about him was unobtrusive, his eyes, his hands. Yet his shoulders were military and his step had an astonishing regularity. When he spoke he never lifted an arm or a finger; he had *killed his puppet*. He never smiled, nor said good morning or goodnight; he seemed not to hear a "How are you?"

5

His memory gave me much thought. The signs by which I could judge led me to imagine incomparable intellectual gymnastics. This was not, in him, an excessive trait but rather a trained and transformed faculty. Here are his own words: "I gave up books twenty years ago. I have burned my papers also. I scrape the quick....I keep what I want. But that is not the difficulty. *It is rather to keep what I shall want tomorrow....* I have tried to invent a mechanical sieve...."

After a good deal of thought, I came to believe that Monsieur Teste had managed to discover laws of the mind we know nothing of. Certainly he must have devoted years to this research; even more certainly, other years and many more years had been set aside for maturing his inventions, making them his instincts. Finding is nothing. The difficulty is in acquiring what has been found.

The delicate art of duration, time, its distribution and regulation—using it on well-chosen things to give them special nourishment—this was one of Monsieur Teste's great experiments. He watched for the repetition of certain ideas; he sprinkled them with numbers. This served to make the application of his conscious studies in the end mechanical. He even sought to summarize this labor. He would often say: "Maturare!..."

Certainly his singular memory must have retained for him almost solely those impressions which our imagination, by itself, is powerless to construct. If we imagine an ascent in a balloon, we may with shrewdness and force produce many of the probable sensations of an aeronaut; but there will always remain something peculiar to the real ascent, and that difference from what we imagine expresses the value of the methods of an Edmond Teste.

This man had known quite early the importance of what

might be called human *plasticity*. He had investigated its mechanics and its limits. How deeply he must have reflected on his own malleability!

I had a glimpse of feelings in him that made me shudder, a terrible obstinacy in his delirious experiments. He was a man absorbed in his own variations, one who becomes his own system, who commits himself without reservation to the frightening discipline of the free mind, and sets his pleasures to killing his pleasures, the stronger killing the weaker —the mildest, the transitory, the pleasure of the moment and the hour just begun, destroyed by the fundamental—by hope for the fundamental.

And I felt that he was master of his thought: I record this absurdity here. The expression of feeling is always absurd.

Monsieur Teste had no opinions. I believe he stirred his passions when he willed, and to attain a definite end. What had he done with his personality? What was his view of himself?...He never laughed, there was never a look of distress on his face. He hated sadness.

He would talk and one felt included among things in his mind: one felt remote, mingled with the houses, the magnitudes of space, the shifting colors of the street, the street corners.... And the most artfully touching words—the very ones that bring their author closer to us than any other man, those that make us believe the eternal wall between minds is falling—would occur to him.... He was wonderfully aware that they would have moved *anyone else*. He would talk and one realized, though unable to discern the motives or the extent of the taboo, that a large number of words had been banished from his discourse. Those he used were at times so curiously sustained by his voice or lighted by his phrasing that their weight was altered and their meaning renewed.

7

At times they would lose all sense, seeming merely to fill a blank for which the appropriate term was still in doubt, or not provided by the language. I have heard him designate a concrete object by a group of abstract words and proper names.

To what he said there was no reply. He killed polite assent. Conversations were kept going by leaps that were no surprise to him.

If this man had changed the object of his inner meditations, if he had turned upon the world the controlled power of his mind, nothing could have resisted him. I am sorry to speak of him as we speak of those of whom statues are made. I am sure that between "genius" and him there is a quantity of weakness. He, so real! So new! So free of all deception, of all wonders! So hard! My own enthusiasm spoils him for me. . . .

How can one not feel enthusiasm for the man who never said anything *vague*? For the man who calmly remarked: "In all things I am interested only in the *ease* or the *difficulty* of knowing them and doing them. I take extreme care in measuring the degree of each, and in remaining detached. . . . And what do I care for what I know all too well?"

How can one not be won over by a man whose mind seemed to transform for itself alone every existing thing, a mind that *performed* everything that occurred to it? I imagined it handling, combining, transforming, connecting, and, within the field of its knowledge, able to cut off and deviate, illuminate, freeze this or heat that, suppress, heighten, name the unnamed, forget at will, subdue or brighten this or that. . . .

I am grossly simplifying his impenetrable powers. I don't dare say all that my subject suggests. Logic stops me. But in myself, every time the problem of Teste arises, curious formations appear.

8

On certain days I recover him quite clearly. He reappears in my memory, sitting beside me. I breathe the smoke of our cigars, I listen to him, I am *wary*. At times, reading a newspaper brings me up against some thought of his now justified by an event. And again I try a few of those experiments in illusion that used to delight me when we spent our evenings together. That is, I imagine him doing something I never saw him do. What is Monsieur Teste like when he is sick? In love, how does he reason? Is he ever sad? What would frighten him? What could make him tremble? ...I wondered. I held the complete image of this rigorous man before me, trying to make it answer my questions.... It kept on fading.

He loves, he suffers, he is bored—like everyone else. But when he sighs, or heaves an elemental groan, I want him to bring into play the rules and forms of his whole mind.

Exactly two years and three months ago this evening I was with him at the theater, in a box lent to him. I have been thinking about this all day.

I can still see him standing beside the golden column at the Opéra; together.

He looked only at the audience. He was breathing the great burst of brilliance at the edge of the pit. He was red.

An immense copper girl separated us from a group murmuring beyond the dazzlement. Deep in the vapor glittered a naked bit of woman, smooth as a pebble. Numerous ladies' fans were independently alive over the audience, dark and bright, foaming up to the top lamps. My glance picked out dozens of small faces, alighted on a sad head, rippled over bare arms, over people, and finally flickered out.

Everyone was in his seat, free to make a slight movement.

I liked the system of classification, the almost theoretical simplicity of the audience, the social order. I had the delightful sensation that all who breathed in that cube would follow its laws, flare up in great circles of laughter, grow excited in sections; feel in *groups* things *intimate—unique*—secret stirrings, rising to the unavowable! I strayed over those layers of people row by row, in orbits, fancying that I could bring together ideally all those having the same illness or the same theory or the same vice....One music touched us all; it swelled to abundance, then became quite small.

It vanished. Monsieur Teste was murmuring: "One is handsome or extraordinary only to others. *They* are eaten by others!"

The last word arose from the silence created by the orchestra. Teste drew his breath.

His face, flushed with heat and color, his broad shoulders, his dark figure splashed with light, the shape of the whole clothed block of him propped against the heavy column, struck me again. Not an atom escaped him of all that was becoming perceptible, momentarily, in that grandeur of red and gold.

I watched his skull making acquaintance with the angles of the capital, the right hand cooling itself among the gilt cornices; and in the purple shadow his large feet. From the far reaches of the theater, his eyes turned toward me; his mouth said: "Discipline is not bad....It's at least a beginning...."

I found nothing to reply. He said in his low quick voice: "Let them enjoy and obey!"

His eyes were fixed for a long moment on a young man seated facing us, then on a woman, then on a whole group in the upper galleries—overflowing the balcony in five or six glowing faces—then on the whole audience, the whole theater filled like the heavens, tense, fascinated by the stage we could not see. The stupor that held all the others told us that something or other sublime was going on. We watched the dying light reflected from all the faces in the audience. And when it was quite faint, when the light no longer shone, all that was left was the vast phosphorescence of those thousand faces. I saw that the twilight was making all these souls passive. Their attention and the darkness, both increasing, formed a continuous equilibrium. I was myself attentive *inevitably*—to all that attention.

Monsieur Teste said: "The supreme simplifies *them*. I wager they are all thinking, more and more, *toward* the same thing. They will be equal at the climax or common limit. Yet the law is not so simple...since it does not include me; and—here I am."

He added: "The lights hold them."

I said, laughing: "You too?"

He replied: "You too."

"What a dramatist you would make!" I said. "You seem to be watching some experiment on the frontiers of all the sciences! I would like to see a theater inspired by your meditations...."

He said: "No one meditates."

The applause and the house-lights drove us out. We circled and went down. The people passing seemed free. Monsieur Teste complained mildly of the midnight chill. He alluded to old pains.

As we walked along, he was muttering almost incoherent phrases. Although I tried, I could barely follow his words, and in the end merely recalled them. The incoherence of speech depends on the one listening to it. The mind seems to me so made that it cannot be incoherent to itself. That is why I was careful not to classify Teste among the mad. Besides, I could vaguely make out the thread of his ideas, and I noticed no contradiction in them; also, I should have feared too simple a solution.

We were going through streets made quiet by the darkness, turning corners in the void, finding our way by instinct—wider, narrower, wider. His military step dominated mine.

"And yet," I replied, "how can we escape music of such power! And why should we? I find a special excitement in it; must I reject it? I find in it the illusion of a tremendous work that might suddenly become possible for me...an illusion that gives me *abstract sensations*, delightful images of everything I love—change, movement, mixture, flow, transformation. ...Will you deny that certain things are anaesthetic? Trees that make us drunk, men who give us strength, girls who paralyze us, skies that strike us dumb?"

Monsieur Teste raised his voice in reply:

"But, Monsieur! What does the 'talent' of your trees—or anybody's—matter to me? I am at home in MYSELF, I speak my own language, I hate extraordinary things. Only weak minds need them. Believe me literally: genius is *easy*, *divinity* is *easy*....I mean simply...that I know how it is to be conceived. It is *easy*.

"In the past—some twenty years ago—anything above the ordinary achieved by another man was for me a personal defeat. At that time, I could see nothing but ideas stolen from me! How stupid!...To say that our own image is not a matter of indifference to us! In our imaginary battles, we treat it either *too well* or *too badly*!..."

He coughed. He said to himself: "*Que peut un homme?*
...What is a man's potential?" He said to me: "You know
a man who knows that he doesn't know what he is saying!"

We were at his door. He invited me to come in and
smoke a cigar with him.

At the top floor of the house, we went into a very small
"furnished" apartment. There was not a book in sight. Nothing indicated the usual sort of work at a table, beneath a
lamp, amongst pens and papers. In the greenish room smell-
ing of mint, there around the candle was nothing but the
dull abstract furniture—a bed, a clock, a wardrobe with a
mirror, two armchairs—like creations of the mind. On the
mantelpiece a few newspapers, a dozen calling cards covered
with numbers, and a medicine bottle. I have never had a
stronger impression of the *ordinary*. This was any room, like
"any point" in geometry—and perhaps as useful. My host
existed in lodgings of the most usual sort. I thought of the
hours he would spend in that armchair. I was terrified by the
infinite dreariness possible in that abstract and banal place.
I have lived in such rooms—I could never believe, without a
shudder, that they were my final destination.

Monsieur Teste talked about money. I cannot reproduce
his special eloquence: it seemed to me less precise than usual.
Fatigue, the silence deeper by the hour, the bitter cigars, the
relaxation of night, seemed to overtake him. I still hear his
voice, softer and slower, fluttering the flame of the single
candle burning between us, while he cited very large
numbers, wearily. Eight hundred ten million seventy-five
thousand five hundred fifty....I listened to that extraordinary music without following the calculation. He was reciting
for me the fluctuations of the stock market, and the long
sequences of the names of numbers held me like a poem. He

would compare events of the day, industrial phenomena, public taste and the passions, and still more numbers, one with another. He would say: "Gold is somehow the mind of society."

Suddenly, he was silent. He was in pain.

Again I looked around the chill room at the nullity of the furniture, not to look at him. He took his flask and drank. I stood up to leave.

"Stay on," he said, "you don't mind. I'm going to bed. In a few moments I'll be asleep. You'll take the candle to go down."

He undressed quietly. His gaunt body slid beneath the covers and lay still. Later he turned over and sank deeper into the bed—it was too short.

He said with a smile. "I'm a plank...floating!...I feel an imperceptible rolling under me—a vast movement? I sleep for an hour or two at most....I'm fond of navigating the night. Often I can't distinguish my thought from sleep. I don't know whether I have been asleep. In the past, whenever I drowsed I would think of all that had given me pleasure—faces, things, moments. I would bring them to mind so that thinking would be as pleasant as possible, smooth as the bed....I'm old. I can show you that I feel old.... Remember! Whan we are children we *discover* ourselves, we learn little by little the extent of our body, we express our body's particularity by a series of movements, I suppose? We twist and discover or rediscover ourselves, and are amazed! We touch our heel, or hold the right foot in the left hand, we take a cold foot into a warm palm!...Now, I know myself by heart. My heart included. Bah! The whole earth is staked off, all the flags are flying over all territories. ...My bed remains. I'm fond of this flow of sleep and linen;

the sheet stretched and folded, or crumpled—falling over me like sand when I lie 'dead' still, it curdles around me in sleep.... A very complex bit of mechanics. Along the warp or the woof, the slightest deviation.... Ah-h-h!"

He was in pain.

"What's the matter?" I said. "I can...."

"It's nothing...much," he said. "It's...a tenth of a second appearing.... Wait.... At certain moments my body lights up.... This is very odd. Suddenly, I can see into my-self....I can make out the depths of the layers of my flesh; I feel zones of pain...rings, poles, plumes of pain. Do you see these living forms, this geometry of my suffering? There are certain flashes that are exactly like ideas. They make me understand—from here, to there.... Yet they leave me un-certain. 'Uncertain' is not the word.... When *it* is coming on, I find something confused or diffused in me. Inside my *self*...foggy places arise, there are open expanses that come into view. Then I pick out a question from my memory, some problem or other...and plunge into it. I count grains of sand...and so long as I can see them.... My increasing pain forces me to notice it. I think about it! Waiting only to hear my cry...and the moment I hear it, the *object*, the terrible *object*, smaller and still smaller, vanishes from my inner sight....

"What is a man's potential? I fight against everything—except the suffering of my body, beyond a certain intensity. Yet, it is there I should begin. Because...to suffer is to give supreme attention to something, and I am somewhat a man of attention.... Let me tell you that I foresaw my future illness. I had thought with precision about something every-one else knows. I believe that such a look at an obvious por-tion of the future should be a part of one's education. Yes, I had foreseen what is now beginning. At the time, it was an idea like any other. So I was able to pursue it."

He was calm now.

He turned on his side, closed his eyes; and a moment later was talking again. He was beginning to lose himself. His voice was no more than a murmur in the pillow. His reddening hand was already asleep.

He was still talking: "I am thinking, and that hinders nothing. I am alone. How comfortable solitude is! Nothing soft is weighing on me.... The same reverie here as in the ship's cabin, or at the Café Lambert.... If a Bertha's arms become important, I am robbed—as by pain.... Any man who talks to me, if he has no proof, is an enemy. I prefer the brilliance of the least fact that happens. I am being and seeing myself; seeing me see myself, and so forth. Let's think very closely. Rubbish! Any subject at all will put you to sleep.... Sleep will prolong any idea at all...."

He was snoring softly. A little more softly, I took the candle and went out on tiptoe.

A Letter from Madame Émilie Teste

Kind Sir,

I send you thanks for your gift and for your letter to Monsieur Teste. I feel sure that the pineapple and the jam were not unwelcome, and I know that the cigarettes pleased him. As for the letter, anything I might say about it would be deceiving. I read it to my husband, but scarcely understood it. Yet I confess that it gave me a certain delight. Listening to things that are abstract or beyond my understanding does not bore me; I find an almost musical enchantment in them. A good part of the soul can enjoy without understanding, and in me it is a large part.

So I read your letter aloud to Monsieur Teste. He listened without showing what he thought of it, nor even that he was thinking about it. You know that he reads almost nothing with his eyes, but uses them in a strange and somehow *inner* way. I am mistaken—I mean a *particular* way. But that is not it at all. I don't know how to put it; let's say *inner, particular...*, and *universal*! ! ! His eyes are beautiful; I admire them for being somewhat larger than all that is visible. One never knows if anything at all escapes them, or, on the other hand, whether the world itself is not simply a detail in all that they see, a floating speck that can besiege you but does not exist. Sir, in all the time I have been married to your friend I have never been sure of what he sees. The object his eyes fix upon may be the very object that his mind means to reduce to nothing.

Our life is still just as you know it: mine, dull and useful; his, all habit and abstraction. Not that he doesn't wake and come back, when he wishes, terribly alive. I like him this way. He is fierce and tall suddenly. The mechanism of his monotonous acts explodes; his face sparkles; he says things that, often, I can barely make out, yet they remain un-diminished in my memory. But I don't wish to hide any-thing from you, or very little: *at times he is impenetrable.* I don't believe anyone can be so adamant as he is. He breaks your spirit with a word, and I feel like a flawed vase rejected by the potter. He is stern as an angel, Sir. He does not know his strength: he utters unexpected words that carry too much truth; they destroy people, waken them in the midst of their stupidity, face to face with themselves, trapped in what they are, and living so naturally on nonsense. We live at ease, each in his own absurdity like fish in water, and are never aware but by accident of all the folly contained in the life of a reasonable person. We never think that what we think conceals from us what we are. I do hope, Sir, that we are worth more than all our thoughts, and that our greatest merit before God will be in having tried to stand on some-thing more durable than our mind babbling to itself, how-ever beautifully.

Moreover, Monsieur Teste need not speak to reduce those around him to humility and an almost animal stupidity. His very existence seems to disqualify all others, and even his manias make one think.

But you must not imagine that he is always difficult or overwhelming. If you knew, Sir, how otherwise he can be!...Certainly he is stern on occasion; but at other times he takes on an exquisite and surprising gentleness that seems to come down from the heavens. His smile is a mysterious and irresistible gift, and his rare tenderness is a winter's rose. Yet neither his mildness nor his violence can be foreseen. It is vain to predict either his harshness or his kindness; all the ordinary calculations that people make about the character of their fellows are thrown off by his profound abstraction and the impenetrable order of his thoughts. My kindnesses, my willingness, my silly notions, my little feelings—I never know how they will affect Monsieur Teste. But I confess that nothing binds me to him more than the uncertainty of his moods. After all, I am quite happy not to understand him too well, not to foresee every day, every night, every next moment of my passage on earth. My soul longs to be surprised more than anything else. Expectation, risk, a bit of doubt, these exalt and vivify my spirit far more than certainty. I believe this is not good; but it is how I am, though I reproach myself for it. I have more than once made confession for thinking that I would rather believe in God than see Him in all His glory, and I was blamed for it. My confessor told me that it was nonsense rather than a sin.

Forgive me for writing to you about my poor self when you want only to have news of the man who interests you so much. But I am somewhat more than the witness of his life; I am a part, almost an organ of it, though nonessential. Husband and wife as we are, our actions are harmonized in marriage and our temporal necessities are well enough adjusted, despite the immense and indefinable difference of our minds. So I am obliged to tell you incidentally about her, who is now telling you about him. Perhaps you find it difficult to conceive my situation with Monsieur Teste, and how I manage to spend my days in the intimacy of such an original man, finding myself so near and so far from him?

The ladies of my age, my true or apparent friends, are

19

greatly surprised that I, who seem so well suited to a life like theirs, being an agreeable enough woman, not undeserving of a simple comprehensible life, should accept a role they cannot in the least imagine for themselves in the life of such a man, whose reputation for eccentricities must shock and scandalize them. They are unaware that the slightest show of affection from my dear husband is a thousand times more precious than all the caresses of theirs. What is their love, always repeating itself, always the same—love that long since lost all surprise, the unknown, the impossible, everything that charges the slightest touch with meaning, risk, and power, knowing that the substance of one voice is the only sustenance of the soul, and that in the end all things are more beautiful, more meaningful—more luminous or sinister, more remarkable or empty—according to a mere guess at what is going on inside a changing person who has become mysteriously essential to us?

You see then, Sir, one must not be a connoisseur of the pleasures if he wants them free of anxiety. However sheltered I may be, I can well imagine how much the voluptuous delights lose in being tamed and suited to domestic habits. Mutual abandon and possession gain infinitely, I believe, by beginning in ignorance of their approach. That supreme certainty must arise out of a supreme uncertainty, and show itself to be the climax of a kind of drama whose pace and development we should find it difficult to trace, from calm up to the extreme threat of the event. . . .

Fortunately—or ⸍not—I am never sure of Monsieur Teste's feelings toward me; and this matters less to me than you would believe. Though mine is a very strange marriage, I am fully aware that it is so. I knew very well that great souls set up a household only by accident; or perhaps to provide a warm room where, insofar as a woman can enter into the system of their lives, she will always be at hand and shut in. The soft glow of a rather smooth shoulder is not to be despised, seen dawning between two thoughts!...Men are like that, even the deep ones.

I do not say this about Monsieur Teste. He is so strange! In fact, nothing can be said about him that is not mistaken at the moment!...I believe he has too much sequence in his ideas. He misleads you at every step in a web that he alone knows how to weave, break off, take up again. He spins out in himself such fragile threads that they survive their delicacy only with the concerted help of all his vital powers. He stretches them over the unknown depths within him, and ventures no doubt far beyond ordinary time, into some abyss of the difficult. I wonder what becomes of him there? It is clear that one is no longer himself under those constraints. Our humanity cannot follow us toward such distant lights. His soul, no doubt, changes into some peculiar plant whose root, and not the foliage, would thrust against nature toward the light!

Is that not aiming beyond the world? Will he find life or death, at the extremity of his attentive will? Will it be God, or some frightful sense of encountering, at the deepest point of thought, nothing but the pale ray of his own miserable substance?

One would have to have seen him in those excesses of abstraction! At such times, his whole countenance is altered—obscured!...A bit more of such absorption, and I am sure that he would be invisible!...

But Sir, when he comes back to me from the depths! He seems to discover me like a new land! To him I seem unknown, new, necessary. He seizes me blindly in his arms, as if I were a living rock of real presence, on which his great and incommunicable genius might stumble, clutch, and suddenly take hold, after so much monstrous and inhuman silence! He falls back upon me as if I were the earth itself. He awakes in me, comes back to himself in me, what joy!

His head lies heavy on my face, and I am prey to all his nervous strength. He has a force and frightening presence in his hands. I feel myself in the grip of a stonecutter, a surgeon, a murderer, under their brutal and precise handling; and I imagine, in terror, that I have fallen under the claws of an intellectual eagle. Shall I give you the whole of my thought? I imagine that he is not fully aware of what he is doing, what he is molding.

His whole being, concentrated in a certain *place* on the frontiers of consciousness, has just lost its ideal object, that object which does and does not exist, since it is only a matter of slightly more or less tension. It required the whole energy of the whole of a great body to sustain in the mind that diamond instant, at once idea and Thing, both entrance and end. You see, Sir, when this extraordinary husband takes hold and masters me, as it were, putting the imprint of his strength upon me, I feel that I am a substitute for some object of his will that just then escaped him. I am like the plaything of a muscular thought—I express it as best I can. The truth he was awaiting took on my strength and my living resistance; and by a quite ineffable transposition, his inner urges subside, discharged through his hard and determined hands. These are very difficult moments. What can I do then! I take refuge in my heart, where I love him as I wish.

As to his feeling for me, what opinion of myself he may have, these are things I do not know, just as I know nothing more about him than is to be seen and heard. I told you a moment ago what I assume, but I do not really know what thoughts or plans occupy him for so many hours. As for myself, I keep to the surface of life; I drift with the passing days. I tell myself that I am the servant of that incomprehensible moment when my marriage was decided, as of itself. A wonderful moment, perhaps supernatural?

I cannot say that I am loved. You may be sure that the word love, so vague in its ordinary use and suggesting many different images, is entirely meaningless when it describes the relations between my husband's heart and my person. His head is a locked treasury, and I am not sure that he has a heart. Am I ever sure that he recognizes me; that he loves or observes me? Or does he observe through me? You will understand that I do not mean to make much of this. In short, I feel that I am in his hands and among his thoughts, like an object, at times the most familiar and again the strangest thing in the world to him, according to the nature of his sight, varying as it focuses.

If I dared tell you about a frequent impression of mine, just as I am aware of it myself, and as I have often confided it to Abbé Mosson, I would say, figuratively, that I feel as if I live and move in a cage, where a superior mind holds me captive—*by its very existence*. His mind contains my own, as a man's mind contains a child's or a dog's. Don't mistake me, Sir. At times I move about in our house, going and coming; the notion of singing comes over me, and rises as I skip and dance from room to room with improvised gaiety and a remainder of youth. But however sprightly my dance, I never cease to feel the sway of that powerful absent figure, somewhere in an armchair, musing, smoking, looking at his hand, slowly flexing all its joints. Never do I feel my spirit without its bounds. But surrounded, enclosed. Heavens!

How difficult it is to explain! I don't at all mean *captive*. I am free, but classified.

What we have that is most ours, most precious, is obscure to ourselves, as you well know. It seems to me that I should lose my being, if I knew myself completely. Well, for one man I am transparent, seen and foreseen just as I am, without mystery, or darkness, or any possible recourse to my unknown self—to my own ignorance of myself!

I am a fly, flitting through its meager life in the universe of an unflinching eye; seen at times, then unseen, but never out of sight. I know at every moment that I exist within a consciousness always vaster and more general than all my vigilance, always quicker than my promptest and quickest thoughts. The highest impulses of my soul are for him small and insignificant events. And yet I have an infinity of my own. . . .I feel it. I cannot but recognize that it is contained in his, and I cannot consent that it should be so. It is something inexpressible, Sir, that I should be capable of thinking and acting absolutely as I will, and yet can never, *never*, think nor will anything that is unforeseen, or important, or new to Monsieur Teste! . . .I can assure you that such a strange and constant feeling gives me ideas that go very deep. . . .I may say that my life seems to me at every moment a living model of man's existence in the divine mind. I have the personal experience of being within the sphere of a being, just as all souls are in Being.

But alas! This very sense of a presence one cannot escape, and of such deep insight, does not fail to lead me at times into vile thoughts. I am tempted. I tell myself that this man is perhaps damned, that in his company I am in great danger, and that I am living in the shade of an evil tree. . . .But then almost immediately I am aware that these specious reflections themselves conceal the peril which they warn me to beware of. I sense in their implications a very clever temptation to dream of another and more delightful life, of other men...and I am appalled at myself. I think back over my own life; I feel that it is as it must be; I tell myself that I *will* my lot, that I choose it anew at every instant; I hear within me the clear deep voice of Monsieur Teste calling me.... But if you knew by what names!

No woman in the world is called by such names as I am. You know what ridiculous epithets lovers use with each other: pet names of dogs and parrots are the natural fruits of carnal intimacy. The voices of the heart are childish. The voices of the flesh are elemental. In fact, Monsieur Teste thinks that love consists in the privilege of *being silly beasts together*—the complete licence of nonsense and bestiality. So he calls me whatever he will. He nearly always names me according to what he wants of me. The name alone that he gives me tells me in one word what I am to expect or what I must do. When he wants nothing in particular, he calls me "Being" or "Thing." And sometimes he calls me "Oasis," which pleases me.

But he never tells me that I am stupid—and this touches me very deeply.

Our priest, who has a great and charitable curiosity about my husband and a sort of compassionate sympathy for a mind so isolated, tells me frankly that Monsieur Teste inspires feelings in him very difficult to reconcile. He said to me the other day: *Your husband's faces are innumerable!*

He considers him "a monster of isolation and peculiar knowledge," and he explains him, though with regret, by his pride, one of those prides that cut us off from the living, and not only the now living but the eternally living; a pride that would be wholly abominable and almost Satanic, if, in a soul already too much exercised, such pride were not so bitterly turned against itself, and with so precise a knowledge of itself that the evil is somehow impaired at its source.

"He is frightfully cut off from the good," my confessor told me, "but fortunately he is also cut off from evil....He has in him a sort of frightening purity, a detachment, an undeniable strength and clarity. I have never observed such an absence of uncertainty and doubt in a mind so profoundly tormented. He is terribly tranquil! No uneasiness of spirit can be attributed to him, no inner darkness—and nothing, moreover, derived from the instincts of fear or desire.... Yet nothing that tends toward Charity.

"His heart is a desert island....The whole scope, the whole energy of his mind surround and protect him; his depths isolate him and guard him against the truth. He flatters himself that he is entirely alone there....Patience, dear lady. Perhaps, one day, he will discover some footprint on the sand....What holy and happy terror, what salutary fright, once he recognizes in that pure sign of grace that his island is mysteriously inhabited!..."

So I said to our priest that my husband often reminded me of a mystic without God....

"What an insight!" he said, "what insights women sometimes derive from the simplicity of their impressions and the vagueness of their language!..."

But immediately and to himself, he replied: "A mystic without God!...Brilliant nonsense!...It's too easy!... Spurious light....A Godless mystic, dear lady! But no movement is conceivable without direction and aim, with-

out going somewhere in the end!...A Godless mystic!...
Why not a Hippogryph, a Centaur!"

"Why not a Sphinx, Father?"

As a Christian, he is even grateful to Monsieur Teste for the
freedom allowed me to follow my faith and give myself to
my devotions. I am entirely free to love God and serve Him,
and I find it possible to share myself very happily between
Our Lord and my dear husband. Monsieur Teste sometimes
asks me to tell him about my prayers and explain to him as
exactly as I can how I go about them, how I concentrate and
sustain myself in them; and he wants to know if I lose myself in them as truly as I believe I do. But I have hardly begun
searching my memory for the words, when he is already
ahead of me, interrogating himself; then putting himself
miraculously in my place he tells me such things about my
own prayers, and in such precise detail that they are clarified,
penetrated somehow in their secret depths—and so he reveals
to me their tendency and desire!...His language has some
strange power to make us see and understand what is most
hidden in us....And yet his remarks are human, no more
than human; they are simply the deeper forms of faith re-
covered by artifice and marvelously articulated by a mind of
incomparable audacity and depth! He would seem to have
cooly explored the fervent soul....But what I find frightfully lacking in this restoration of my burning heart and its
faith, is its essence which is *hope*....There is not a grain of
hope in the whole substance of Monsieur Teste; and that is
why I feel a certain uneasiness in this exercise of his power.

I have very little more to tell you today. I shall not excuse
myself for writing at such length, since you asked me to do

so and since you say that you have an insatiable appetite for your friend's every act and gesture. But I must stop. It is time now for our daily walk. I am going to put on my hat. We shall walk slowly through the stony and tortuous little streets of this old city which you know somewhat. In the end, we go down where you would like to go if you were here, to that ancient garden where all those who think, or worry, or talk to themselves, go down towards evening as water goes to the river, and gather necessarily together. They are scholars, lovers, old men, priests, and the disillusioned; all *dreamers*, of every possible kind. They seem to be seeking their distances from each other. They must like to see but not know one another, and their separate sorts of bitterness are accustomed to encountering each other. One drags his illness, another is driven by his anguish; they are shadows fleeing from each other; but there is no other place to escape the others but this, where the same idea of solitude invincibly draws each of all those absorbed souls. In a few minutes we shall be in that place worthy of the dead. It is a botanical ruin. We shall be there a little before sunset. Imagine us walking slowly, exposed to the sun, the cypresses, the cries of birds. The wind is cool in the sun; the sky, too beautiful at times, grips my heart. The unseen cathedral tolls. Here and there are round basins, banked and standing waist-high. They are filled to the brim with dark impenetrable water, on which the enormous leaves of the Nymphea Nelumbo lie flat; and the drops that venture upon those leaves roll and glitter like mercury. Monsieur Teste absently gazes at those large living drops, or walks slowly among the rectangular flower beds with their green labels, where specimens of the vegetable kingdom are more or less cultivated. He is amused at this rather ridiculous order and takes delight in spelling out the baroque names

Antirrhinum Siculum
Solanum Warscewiezii! ! !

And that *Sisymbriifolium*, what jargon!...And the *Vulgare*, and the *Asper*, and the *Palustris*, and the *Sinuata*, and the *Flexuosum*, and the *Praealtum*! ! !

"This is a garden of epithets," he said the other day, "a dictionary and cemetery garden...."

And after a moment he said, "Learnedly to die.... *Transiit classificando.*"

Accept, Sir and Friend, all our thanks and our pleasant memories.

ÉMILIE TESTE

Various Essays

Introduction to the Method of
Leonardo da Vinci

[1894]

To Marcel Schwob

WHAT A MAN leaves after him are the dreams that his name inspires and the works that make his name a symbol of admiration, hate, or indifference. We think of how he thought, and we are able to find within his works a kind of thinking derived from ourselves that we attribute to him; we can refashion this thought in the image of our own. It is easy to picture to ourselves an ordinary man; his motives and elementary reactions can be supplied quite simply from our own memories. The commonplace acts that form the surface of his life and those that form the surface of ours are linked in the same fashion. We too can serve as the bond that holds the acts together, and the circle of activity suggested by his name is no wider than our own. If we choose an individual who excelled in some respect, we shall find it harder to picture the workings and the ways of

In the embarrassment of having to write on a great subject, I felt impelled to consider and state the problem before trying to solve it. That is not what usually happens with the literary mind, whose instinct is to leap across the crevasse, not to measure the depth of it.

Today I should write this first paragraph in a very different fashion, while preserving its essence and function.
For its purpose is to make us think about the possibility of any project of the sort— that is, about the situation of and the means available to a mind that sets out to imagine a mind.

his mind. In order to go beyond an indiscriminate admiration, we shall be forced to stretch in some particular way our conception of his dominating quality, which we doubtless possess only in the germ. But if all the faculties of the chosen mind were widely developed at the same time, or if considerable traces of its activity are to be found in all fields of endeavor, then the figure of our hero grows more and more difficult to conceive in its unity and tends to escape our strivings. From one boundary to another of this mental territory there are immense distances that we have never traveled. Our understanding fails to grasp the continuity of this whole—just as it fails to perceive those formless rags of space that separate known objects and fill in the random intervals between; just as it loses myriads of facts at every moment, beyond the small number of those evoked by speech. Nevertheless, we must linger over the task, become inured to it, and learn to surmount the difficulties imposed on our imagination by this combination of elements heterogeneous to it. In this process all our intelligence is applied to conceiving a unique order and a single motive force. We wish to place a being in our like-

34

ness at the heart of the system we impose on ourselves. We struggle to form a decisive image. And our mind, with a degree of violence depending on its lucidity and breadth, ends by winning back its own unity. As if produced by mechanism, a hypothesis takes shape and proves to be the individual who achieved all these things, the central vision where all this must have taken place, the monstrous brain or strange animal that wove a pure web connecting so many forms. These enigmatic and diverse constructions were the labors of this brain, its instinct making a home for itself. The production of such a hypothesis is a phenomenon that admits of variations but not of chance. It has the same value as the logical analysis of which it should be the object. It is the basis of the method that we will take up to serve our purpose.

I propose to imagine a man whose activities are so diverse that if I postulate a ruling idea behind them all, there could be none more universal. And I want this man to possess an infinitely keen perception of the difference of things, the adventures of which perception might well be called analysis. I see him as aiming at all things: he is

In reality man *and* Leonardo *were the names I gave to what then impressed me as being the power of the* mind.

Universe—*a better word would have been "universality." What I wished to designate was not so much the* fabulous totality *that the word "universe" generally tries to evoke, as the feeling that every object belongs to a system containing (by hypothesis) that which is necessary to define every object.*

always thinking in terms of the universe, and of rigor.* He is so formed as to overlook nothing that enters into the confusion of things; not the least shrub. He descends into the depths of that which exists for all men, but there he draws apart and studies himself. He penetrates to the habits and structures of nature, he works on them from every angle, and finally it is he alone who constructs, enumerates, sets in motion. He leaves behind him churches and fortresses; he fashions ornaments instinct with gentleness and grandeur, besides a thousand mechanical devices and the rigorous calculations of many a research. He leaves the abandoned relics and remnants of unimaginable games and fancies. In the midst of these pastimes, which are mingled with his science, which in turn cannot be distinguished from a passion, he has the charm of always seeming to think of something else....I shall follow him as he moves through the density and raw unity of the world, where he will become so familiar with nature that he will imitate it in order to use it, and will end by finding it difficult to

* *Hostinato rigore*, obstinate rigor—Leonardo's motto. [P.V., as all footnotes in this section.]

36

conceive of an object that nature does not contain.

This creation of our thoughts requires a name that will serve as a limit to the expansion of terms usually so far removed as to escape each other. I can find none more suitable than that of *Leonardo da Vinci*. Whoever pictures a tree must also picture a sky or background from which the tree stands forth; in this there is a sort of logic that is almost tangible and yet almost unknown. The figure I am presenting can be reduced to an inference from this type. Very little that I shall have to say of him should be applied to the man who made this name illustrious: I will not pursue a coincidence that I think would be impossible to define incorrectly. I am trying to give one view of the details of an intellectual life, one suggestion of the methods implied by every discovery, *one*, chosen among the multitude of imaginable things—a crude model, if you will, but preferable in every way to a collection of dubious anecdotes, or a commentary upon museum catalogues, or a list of dates. That kind of erudition would merely falsify the purely hypothetical intention of this essay. I am not ignorant of such

An author who composes a biography can try to live his subject or else to construct him, and there is a decided opposition between these two courses. To live him *is to transform oneself into what is necessarily incomplete, since life in this sense is composed of anecdotes, details, moments.* Construction, *on the other hand, implies the* a priori *conditions of an existence that could be* completely different.

This sort of logic is what leads by way of sensory impressions to the construction of what I have just called a universe. *Here it leads to a personage.*

In short, the problem is to use the full potential of one's thinking, under the control of the highest

possible degree of consciousness.

matters, but my task above all is to omit them, so that a conjecture based on very general terms may in no way be confused with the visible fragments of a personality completely vanished, leaving us equally convinced both of his thinking existence and of the impossibility of ever knowing it better.

I should express all this quite differently today, but I can recognize myself in the double effort I was making: to imagine the labor, and at the same time to picture the accidental circumstances that may have engendered the works.

The effects of a work are never a simple *consequence of the circumstances in which it was generated. On the contrary, we might say that the secret aim of a work is to make us imagine that it created itself, by a process as remote as possible from the real one.*

Many an error that distorts our judgment of human achievements is due to a strange disregard of their genesis. We seldom remember that they did not always exist. This has led to a sort of reciprocal coquetry which leads authors to suppress, to conceal all too well, the origins of a work. We fear the latter may be humble; we even suspect them of being natural. And although there are very few authors with the courage to say how their work took shape, I believe there are not many more who venture even to understand the process. Such an understanding can only begin with one's painfully relinquishing all laudatory epithets and notions of glory; it will not allow for any idea of personal superiority or delusion of grandeur. It leads to the discovery of the relativity that underlies the apparent perfection. And this research into origins is necessary if we are not to believe that minds are as radically different as their productions would make it seem. Certain scientific works, for example—and particularly those of the mathematicians—are so limpid in their structure that it is hard to believe they have an author. There is something *inhuman* about them, and this quality has not been without its effect. It has led to the belief that there is such a great distance between certain disciplines, notably the sciences and the arts, that the minds devoted to each have been set as widely apart, in the common view, as the results of their labors seem to be. And yet these labors differ only in their variations from a common basis: by the part of the basis that each preserves, and the part that each neglects, in forming their languages and symbols. We must therefore be a little suspicious of books and expositions that seem too pure. Whatever is fixed deceives us, and whatever is made to be looked at is likely to change its appearance, to seem nobler. The operations of the mind can best serve our purpose of analysis while they are moving, unresolved, still at the mercy of a moment—before they have been given the name of enter-

Is it possible to make anything except under the illusion that one is making something else?—The objective of the artist is not so much the work itself as what people will think about it, which never depends simply on what it is.

An outstanding difference between the sciences and the arts is that the former must aim at results that are either certain or immensely probable, whereas the latter can only hope for results of an unknown probability.

Between the mode of generation and the

fruit, *there is an enormous difference.*

Pascal's famous Pensées are not so much straightforward private thoughts as arguments, or weapons or stultifying poisons, for others.
Their form is sometimes so finely wrought and deeply studied that it reveals the will to falsify the true "thought" by making it more imposing and terrifying than any thought could be.

tainment or law, theorem or work of art, and, being perfected, have lost their mutual resemblance.

Within the mind a drama takes place. Drama, adventure, agitation, any words of the sort can be used provided that several of them are used together, so that one is corrected by another. Most of those dramas are lost, like the plays of Menander, but we do have Leonardo's manuscripts and Pascal's dazzling notes. These fragments insist that we examine them. They help us to realize by what starts and snatches of thought, by what strange suggestions from human events or the flow of sensations, and after what immense moments of lassitude, men are able to see the shadows of their future works, the ghosts that come before. But without having recourse to such great examples that they might be dismissed as exceptional cases, we need merely observe someone who thinks he is alone and left to himself: he *recoils* from an idea, *grasps* it, denies or smiles or stiffens, and mimes the strange predicament of his own diversity. Madmen often act like this in public.

By such examples, physical movements that can be measured and defined are shown to be closely related to the personal drama of which I was speaking. The actors in the drama are mental images, and it is easy to understand that, if we eliminate the particular features of the images and consider only their succession, frequency, periodicity, varying capacity for association, and finally their duration, we are soon tempted to find analogies in the so-called material world, to compare them with scientific analyses, to postulate an environment, to endow them first with continuity, velocities, properties of displacement, then with mass and energy. Thereupon we may realize that many such systems are possible, that any one in particular is worth no more than another, and that our use of them—which is rewarding, since it always casts light on something —must be continually watched over and restored to its purely verbal function. For, in precise terms, analogy is only our faculty of changing images, of combining them, of making part of one coexist with part of another, and of perceiving, voluntarily or involuntarily, the connections in their structure. And this makes it impossible to describe the mind, where images exist. In the mind words lose their force.

I should be inclined to say that what is most real in our thinking is not the part of it that consists in forming a simple image of perceptible reality. Rather it is the process of observation—precarious and often untrustworthy as it may be —of what takes place within us and induces us to believe that the variations in the two worlds are comparable. This process enables us, at least in a rough way, to express what is properly the psychic world in terms of metaphors taken from the perceptible world, and particularly from acts and operations that we can effectuate. Thus, note the relation of "thinking"

*and "weighing"
(penser and peser),
of "grasping" and
"comprehending,"
of "hypothesis"
and "synthesis,"
etc.
"Duration" comes
from the same root
as dur, "hard." All
this amounts to giving
certain visual, tactile,
and motor images—
or their combinations
—a double* value.

They are formed, there they leap forth, under its *eyes*; it is the mind that describes words to us.

And so man carries away *visions*, whose power becomes his power. He connects it with his history, of which his visions are the geometrical site. From this process arise those decisive acts that astound us; those perspectives, miraculous divinations, exact judgments; those illuminations, those incomprehensible anxieties, and stupid blunders as well. In certain extraordinary cases, invoking abstract gods —genius, inspiration, a thousand others —we ask with stupefaction how these marvels came to be. Once again we believe that something must have created itself, for we worship mystery and the marvelous as much as we love to ignore what goes on behind the scenes; we ascribe logic to miracle, although the inspired author had been preparing for a year. He was ripe. He had always thought of this work, perhaps unconsciously; and while others were still not ready to see, he had looked, combined, and now was merely reading what was written in his mind. The secret—whether of Leonardo, or of Bonaparte, or that of the highest intelligence at a given time—lies and can only lie in the relations they found—and were compelled to find—*among things of which we cannot grasp the law of continuity*. It is certain that, at the decisive moment, they had only to complete definite acts. Their supreme achievement, the one that the world admires, had become a simple matter—almost like comparing two lengths.

From this point of view we can perceive the unity of the method with which we are concerned. It is native and elemental to this environment, of which it is the very life and definition. And when thinkers as powerful as the man whom I am contemplating through these lines discover the implicit resources of the method, in a clearer and more conscious moment they have the right to exclaim: "*Facil cosa è farsi universale!*—It is easy to become universal!" They can, for the moment, admire the prodigious instrument they are—at the price of instantly denying the element of prodigy.

But this final clarity is attained only after long wanderings and inevitable idolatries. A consciousness of the operations of thought, which is the unrecognized logic I mentioned before, exists but rarely, even in the

The word " continuity" was not at all the right choice. I remember having written it in place of another word that could not be found. I meant to say: among things that we cannot transpose or translate into a system of the totality of our acts —that is, into the system of our powers.

43

keenest minds. The number of conceptions, the ability to prolong them,
and the abundance of discoveries are
something different, and are produced
without respect to one's judgment
of their nature. Yet the importance of
that judgment is easy to appreciate.
A flower, a proposition, and a sound
can be imagined almost simultaneously; the intervals between them
can be made as short as we choose; and
each of these objects of thought can
also change, be deformed, lose its
initial qualities one after another at the
will of the mind that conceived it, but
it is in one's consciousness of this
power that all its value resides. That
consciousness alone permits us to criti-
cize these *formations*, to interpret them,
to find in them nothing more than
they contain, and not to confuse their
states with those of reality. With it
begins the analysis of all intellectual
phases, of all the states that consciousness will have the power to define as
fallacy, madness, discovery—which at
first were only nuances impossible to
distinguish. Equivalent variations of a
common substance, they were comparable one to another, existed at indefinite and almost irresponsible levels,
could sometimes be named, and all

according to the same system. To be conscious of one's thoughts, as thoughts, is to recognize this sort of equality or homogeneity; to feel that all combinations of the sort are legitimate, natural, and that the method consists in arousing them, in seeing them precisely, in seeking for what they imply.

At some time in this process of observation, this double life of the mind that reduces ordinary thinking to something like the dream of a wakened sleeper, it appears that the sequence of the dream—with its mass of combinations, contrasts, and perceptions, either grouped around some project or moving forward indeterminately, at one's pleasure—is developing with *perceptible* regularity, with the obvious continuity of a machine. The idea then arises (or the wish) that this movement might be accelerated, that the terms of the sequence might be carried to their *limit*, to that of their imaginable expressions, *after which everything will be changed.* And if this mode of being conscious becomes habitual, it will enable us, for example, to consider beforehand all the possible results of an imagined act and all the relationships of a conceived object, and

This observation (about carrying psychic processes to their limit) is one over which the author might well have lingered. It would suggest a further investigation of time, of the mental process I have sometimes described as subjecting ideas to the pressure of time, *of the part played by external circumstances, and of the willed establishment of certain thresholds. Here we should be entering an area of extremely delicate psychic mechanics, in which particular durations play an important part, are included one in another, etc.*

then to proceed further to the faculty of putting them aside, of divining something ever more intense or exact than the given object, to the ability to rouse oneself from any thought that was lasting too long. Whatever its nature, a thought that becomes fixed assumes the characteristics of a hypnosis and is called, in the language of logic, an idol; in the domain of art and poetic construction, it becomes a sterile monotony. The faculty of which I speak—one that leads the mind to foresee itself and to picture as a whole whatever was going to be pictured in detail, together with the effect of the sequence thus presented in brief—is the basis of all generalization. In certain individuals it manifests itself with remarkable energy, becoming a veritable passion; in the arts it is the cause of each separate advance and explains the continually more frequent use of contraction, suggestion, and violent contrast; while the same faculty exists implicitly, in its rational form, at the base of all mathematical concepts. It

My opinion is that the secret of this reasoning process or mathematical induction resides in a sort

is very similar to the operation which, under the name of reasoning by recurrence,* extends the application of

* The philosophical importance of this form of reasoning was demonstrated for the

these analyses—and which, from the type of simple addition to infinitesimal summation, does more than save us from making an infinite number of useless experiments; it produces more complex structures, since the conscious imitation of my act is a new act that envelops all the possible adaptations of the first.

of consciousness that the act in itself is independent of its subject matter.

This tableau of drama, agitation, lucidity stands in opposition to other scenes and movements that we call "Nature" or "the World." But we can do nothing with this natural world except to distinguish ourselves from it, and then immediately replace ourselves within its frame.

Philosophers have generally concluded by implying our existence in the notion we hold of nature, and nature in the notion we hold of ourselves; but they seldom go beyond this point, for we know they are more inclined to dispute the ideas of their predecessors than to look into the problem for themselves. Scientists and artists have exploited nature in

first time by M. Poincaré in a recent article. When consulted by the author, the eminent scientist confirmed our statement of his priority.

Here we have the essential vice of philosophy. Philosophy is something personal, but does not wish to be personal.

It hopes to accumulate a steadily increasing capital of transmissible values, as science has done.

Hence all the philo-sophical systems that pretend to have no author.

their different fashions: in the end the former measured, and then constructed; the latter came to construct as though they had measured. Everything they have made finds a place of its own accord in the natural world, where it also plays a part, helping to extend it by giving new forms to its constituent materials. But before generalizing and building we observe. From among the mass of qualities that present themselves, our senses— each in its own fashion, with its own degree of docility—distinguish and choose the qualities that will be retained and developed by the individual. At first the process is undergone passively, almost unconsciously, as a vessel lets itself be filled: there is a feeling of slow and pleasurable circulation. Later, one's interest being awakened, one assigns new values to things that had seemed closed and irreducible; one adds to them, takes more pleasure in particular features, finds expression for these; and what happens is like the restitution of an energy that our senses had received. Soon the energy will alter the environment in its turn, employing to this end the conscious thought of a person.

The universal man also begins with

simple observation, and continually renews this self-fertilization from what he sees. He returns to the intoxication of ordinary instinct and to the emotion aroused by the least of real things, when one considers both thing and instinct, so self-contained in all their qualities, and concentrating in every way so many effects.

Most people see with their intellects much more often than with their eyes. Instead of colored spaces, they become aware of concepts. Something whitish, cubical, erect, its planes broken by the sparkle of glass, is immediately a house for them—the House!—a complex idea, a combination of abstract qualities. If they change position, the movement of the rows of windows, the translation of surfaces which continuously alters their sensuous perceptions, all this escapes them, for their concept remains the same. They perceive with a dictionary rather than with the retina; and they approach objects so blindly, they have such a vague notion of the difficulties and pleasures of vision, that they have invented *beautiful views*. Of the rest they are unaware. In this one instance, however, they feast on a concept that

Why artists are useful: they preserve the subtlety and instability of sensory impressions.
A modern artist has to exhaust two-thirds of his time trying to see what is visible—and above all, trying not to see what is invisible. Philosophers often pay a high price for striving to do the opposite.

49

swarms with words. (A general rule
that applies to the weakness existing in
all branches of knowledge is precisely
our choice of *obvious* standpoints, our
being content with definite systems
that facilitate, that make it easy to
grasp. In this sense one can say that the
work of art is always more or less

A work of art should   didactic.) Even these beautiful views
always teach us that   are more or less concealed from ordin-
we had not seen   ary observers; and all the modulations
what we see.   so delicately contrived by little movements, changing light, and tiring eyes

The deeper education   are lost to them, neither adding to nor
consists in unlearning   subtracting from their sensations. Since
one's first education.   they know that the level of still water
is horizontal, they fail to observe that
the sea is *upright* at the horizon. Should
the tip of a nose, the whiteness of a
shoulder, or two fingers happen to dig
into a pool of light that isolates them,
our observers never think of regarding
them as new jewels enriching their
vision. Those jewels are fragments of a
person, and the person alone exists,
is known to them. Moreover, since
they utterly reject anything that lacks
a name, the number of their impressions is strictly limited in advance!*

   * See proposition CCLXXI of Leonardo's
treatise *On Painting:* "*Impossibile che una
memoria possa riserbare tutti gli aspetti o muta-*

The exercise of the opposite gift leads to analyses in the true sense. One cannot say that the gift is exercised in *nature*. This word, although it seems general and apparently contains every possibility of experience, is altogether personal. It evokes particular images, determining the memory or history of one man. In most cases it calls forth the vision of a green, vague, and continuous eruption; of some great elemental work as opposed to everything human; of a monotonous quantity that will some day cover us; of

That is, the gift for seeing more than one knows.
These remarks are the naïve expression of a doubt long held by the author, as to the true value or function of words. The words of ordinary speech are not made for logic. The permanence and universality of their meanings are never assured.

zioni d'alcun membro di qualunque animal si sia. . . . È perchè ogni quantità continua è divisibile in infinito—It is impossible for any memory to retain all the aspects of any limb of any animal whatever. This is because any continuous quantity is infinitely divisible."

What I have said of sight also applies to the other senses, but I have chosen sight because it seems to me the most *intellectual* of them all. In the mind, visual images predominate. It is between these images that the analogical faculty is most often exercised. When we make analogies between any two objects, the inferior term of the comparison may even originate in an error of judgment caused by an indistinct sensation. The form and colors of an object are so evidently uppermost in our minds that they enter into our concepts of qualities relating to another sense. If we speak of the hardness of iron, for example, the visual image of iron will almost always be produced, and seldom an auditive image.

In short, errors and analogies result from the fact that an impression can be completed in two or three different fashions. Land, a cloud, or a ship are three different ways of completing a certain appearance on the horizon, at sea. Desire or expectation puts one of these words in our minds.

something stronger than we are, entangled in itself and tearing itself apart while sleeping on and working on; of something to which, personified, the poets accorded cruelty, kindness, and several other motives. Hence, our ideal observer must be placed not in nature, but in any corner whatever of that which exists.

An early attempt of mine to represent an individual universe. An "I" and its Universe—if we admit that these myths are useful— should have, in any system, the same relation that exists between a retina and a source of light.

The observer is confined in a sphere that is never broken. It has variations that will reveal themselves as movements or objects, but its surface remains closed, although every portion of the sphere is renewed and changes position. At first the observer is only the condition of this finite space; at every moment he *is* this finite space. He is troubled by none of his memories or powers so long as he equates himself with what he sees. And if I were able to conceive of his remaining in this state, I should conceive that his impressions differed hardly at all from those received in a dream. He is vaguely conscious of pain, pleasure, and a sense of tranquility,* all imparted

* Without touching on physiological questions, I might mention the case of a man suffering from a form of depressive psychosis. This patient, whom I once saw in a clinic, was in a state of retarded life; he

52

to him by these indefinite forms, among which is numbered his own body. And now, slowly, some of the forms begin to be forgotten, almost disappearing from sight, while others make themselves visible for the first time—in the place where they had always been. It must also be noted that changes in vision resulting from the mere duration of one's attention, and from tired eyes, are likely to be indistinguishably confused with those due to ordinary movements. Certain areas in one's field of vision become exaggerated, in the same way as an ailing limb seems larger and, because of the importance it acquires from pain, distorts our notion of the body. These exaggerated areas will be more amenable to observation and easier to remember. At this point the spectator begins rising from simple perception to reverie; henceforth he will be able to extend the particular characteristics derived from the first and most familiar objects to other objects in greater and greater number. Remembering a precedent, he perfects the

Inequalities are certain to appear. Consciousness is by essence unstable.

recognized objects only after an extraordinary delay. Sensations took a very long time to reach his mind. He felt no needs. This form of insanity is exceedingly rare.

There is a sort of liberty with regard to groupings, corres-pondences, and neutralizations that is exercised in the entire field of per-ception. If several persons are speaking at the same time, we can, if we choose, listen to only one of them.

These are intuitions *in the narrow and etymological sense of the word.*
An image can serve as the anticipation of another image.

The persistence of impressions has an essential role.
There is a sort of symmetry in these mutually inverse transformations.
Corresponding to the

given space. Then, at his pleasure, he can arrange or undo his successive impressions. He can appreciate the value of strange combinations: a group of flowers, or of men, a hand or a cheek seen by itself, a spot of sunlight on a wall, a gathering of animals brought together by chance—all these he regards as complete and solid beings. He feels a desire to picture the invisible wholes of which he has been given some visible parts. Thus, he infers the planes designed by a bird in its flight, the trajectory of a missile, the surfaces delimited by our gestures, and the extraordinary fissures, the fluid ara-besques, the formless chambers created in an all-penetrating medium by the grating and quivering of a swarm of insects, by trees that roll like ships, by wheels, the human smile, the tide. Traces of what he imagined can some-times be seen on water or on rippled sand; and sometimes his own retina, as the moments pass, can compare some object with the form of its movement.

From such forms, born of move-ment, there is a transition to the move-ments into which forms may be dissolved by means of a simple change in duration. If a drop of rain appears to be a line, a thousand vibrations to be a continuous sound, and the irregularities of this paper to be a polished plane, and if duration is taken to be the sole cause of these impressions, then a stable form may be replaced by a sufficient rapidity in the periodic registration of a thing (or element) chosen for the purpose. Geometricians will be able to introduce time and velocity into the study of forms, just as they can eliminate both from the study of movements. In common speech, by a similar process, a road will *climb*, a jetty will *stretch*, a statue *rise*. And the intoxication of analogy, as well as the logic of continuity, will carry these actions to the limit of their tendency, to the impossibility of their ever being halted. Everything moves by gradations, imaginarily. Here in this room, and because I concentrate on this one thought, the objects about me are as *active* as the flame of the lamp. The armchair decays in its place, the table asserts itself so fast that it is motionless, and the curtains flow endlessly away. The result is an infinite complexity. To regain control of ourselves in the midst of the moving bodies, the circulation of their contours, the jumble of knots, the paths, the falls, the whirlpools, the confusion of velocities, we

spatialization of linear movements is something I once described as the chronolysis of space.

Something like this might be seen from a certain level of observation, if light and the retina were continuous—but then we should no longer see the objects themselves. Hence the function of the "mind" here is to combine two incompatible orders of size or quality, two levels of vision that are mutually exclusive.

It is thanks to the hierarchy of the senses and the varying duration of our perceptions that we can oppose to this chaos of palpitations and substitutions a world of solid masses and identifiable objects. There are only two things we perceive directly: persistence and averages.

must have recourse to our grand capacity for deliberately forgetting—and without destroying the acquired idea, we introduce a generalized concept, that of the orders of magnitude.

And so, by the extension of the "given quantity," we lose our intoxication with these particular objects, of which there can be no science. When we look at them fixedly, they change if we think of them; and if we do not think of them, we fall into a lasting torpor, of somewhat the same nature as a tranquil dream; we stare as if hypnotized at the corner of a table or the shadow of a leaf, only to waken the moment they are *seen*. There are men who feel with special delicacy the pleasure that is derived from the *individuality* of objects. What they prefer and are delighted to find in a thing is the quality of being unique—which all things possess. Their form of curiosity finds its ultimate expression in fiction and the arts of the theater and is called, at this extreme, the *faculty of identification*.* Nothing seems more deliberately absurd when described than the temerity of a person who declares that he *is* a certain object and feels its

Always the motive force of inequality.

* Edgar Allan Poe, "On Shakespeare" (*Marginalia*).

56

impressions—especially if the object is inanimate.* Yet there is nothing more powerful in the imaginative life. The chosen object becomes as it were the center of that life, a center of ever multiplying associations, depending on whether the object is more or less complicated. Essentially this faculty must be a means of exciting the imaginative vitality, of setting potential energy to work. Carried too far it becomes a pathological symptom and gains a frightening ascendancy over the increasing feebleness of a decaying mind.

From a pure observation of things to these complex states, the mind has merely extended its functions, forming concepts in response to the problems offered by all sensation and solving the problems more or less easily, depending on whether a larger or smaller production of such concepts is demanded. It is evident that we are touching, at this point, on the very *springs* of thought. Thinking consists, during almost all the time we devote to it, in wandering among themes

* Whoever explains why identification with a material object *seems* more absurd than that with a living object will have taken a step toward explaining the problem.

*Inequality again.
The transition from the less to the more is spontaneous. The transition from the more to the less is deliberate and rare,*

since it has to go against the customary practice and appearance of comprehension.

about which we know, first of all, that we know them *more or less well.* Hence, things can be classified according to the ease or difficulty they afford to our comprehension, according to our degree of familiarity with them, and according to the various resistances offered by their parts or conditions when we try to imagine them together. The history of this graduated complexity remains to be conjectured.

If everything were irregular, or if everything were regular, there would be no thinking—for thinking is only an effort to pass from disorder to order. It requires the former as an occasion for being exercised, and the latter for models to imitate.

The isolated, the exceptional, the singular are inexplicable—that is, they have no expression but themselves.
The insurmountable difficulties presented by prime numbers.

The world is irregularly strewn with regular arrangements. Crystals are of this nature; so are flowers and leaves, many striped or spotted ornaments on the fur, wings, or shells of animals, the patterns made by the wind on water or sand, etc. Sometimes these effects depend on a sort of perspective and on temporary juxtapositions. Distance produces or disfigures them. Time reveals or hides them. Thus, the number of births, deaths, crimes, and accidents presents a regularity in its fluctuations, one that becomes more and more evident as we follow the record through the years. The most surprising events, and the most *asymmetrical* in relation to neighboring moments, return to a semblance of order when considered in relation to longer periods. One might mention other examples in the realm of instincts, habits, and customs, as well as the semblances of periodicity that have given rise to so many philosophies of history.

The knowledge of regular combinations is divided among the different sciences; or, where none can be established, it comes under the calculation of probabilities. For our purpose we need only the observation made on introducing this topic: that regular combinations, whether of time or space, are irregularly distributed in the field of investigation. Mentally they seem to be opposed to a vast number of formless things.

—which has overrun almost all of Physics since 1894.

I think they might be described as "first guides of the human mind," except that such a proposition is immediately reversible. In any case they represent continuity.* Any thought permits of a change or transfer (of attention, for example) among ele-

* Here the word is not employed in its mathematical sense. It is not a question of inserting a numerable infinity and an innumerable infinity of values into an interval; it is only a question of simple intuition, of objects that suggest laws, of laws that are evident to the eyes. The existence or possibility of such things is the first—and not the least surprising—fact of this order.

ments apparently fixed in their relation to the thought, which it selects from memory or immediate perception. If the elements are perfectly similar, or if their difference can be reduced to mere distance, to the elementary fact of their existing separately, then the *labor* to be performed is in turn reduced to this purely differential notion. Thus, a straight line will be the easiest of all lines to conceive, because there is no smaller effort for the mind than that exerted in passing from one point of a straight line to another, each of the points being similarly placed in relation to all the rest. In other words, all portions of the line are so homogeneous, however short we may conceive them to be, that they can all be reduced to one, always the same; and that is the reason why the dimensions of shapes are always expressed in terms of straight lines. At a higher degree of complexity, periodicity is employed to represent continuous properties; for this periodicity, whether it exists in space or time, is nothing else than the division of an object of thought into fragments, such that they can be replaced one by the other under certain conditions—or else it is the multiplication of an object under those same conditions.

The easiest to conceive, but extremely difficult to define. This whole passage is a youthful and not very successful attempt to describe the simplest intuitions—by means of which the world of sensory images and the system of concepts can sometimes be brought together.

Why is it that only a part of all that exists can be so reduced? There is a moment when the figure becomes so complicated, or the event seems so new, that we must abandon the attempt to consider them as a whole, or to proceed with their translation into continuous values. At what point did our Euclids halt in their apprehension of forms? What was the particular degree of interruption that set a limit to their notion of continuity? They had reached what appeared to be the furthest point of a research at which one cannot fail to be tempted by the doctrines of evolution. One is loath to admit to oneself that this limit could be final.

It is certain, in any case, that the basis and aim of every speculation is the extension of continuity with the help of metaphors, abstractions, and special languages. These are employed by the arts in a fashion to be discussed in a moment.

We have arrived at the conception that parts of the world let themselves be reduced, here and there, to intelligible elements. Sometimes our senses suffice for the task; sometimes the most ingenious methods must be employed; but always there are voids. The

We are now—1930 —at a stage in which those difficulties have become pressing. What I awkwardly tried to express in 1894 is the state we are in today. We have come to despair of finding any figurative—or even any intelligible— explanation.

Langevin is hopeful on this point; I, not at all. Discussed at the Société de Philosophie, 1929.

What takes place, in other words, is a sort of adaptation to the diversity, multiplicity, and instability of facts.

attempts remain lacunary. It is here that we find the kingdom of our hero. He has an extraordinary sense of symmetry that makes him regard everything as a problem. Wherever the understanding breaks off he introduces the productions of his mind. It is evident how extremely convenient he can be. He is like a scientific hypothesis. We should have to invent him, but he exists; the universal man can now be imagined. A Leonardo da Vinci can exist in our minds, without too much dazzling them, in the form of a concept; our dream of his power need not be quickly lost in a fog of big words and ponderous epithets conducive to inconsistent thinking. Could one believe that Leonardo himself would be satisfied with such mirages?

By now—after thirty-six years—this hypothesis has been curiously confirmed. Theoretical physics of the boldest and most difficult sort has been forced to abandon images *and the whole notion of visual and motor representation. In its effort to subjugate its vast domain—to unify its laws and make them independent of the place, time, and movement of the observer—it has no other guide than the* symmetry *of its formulas.*

This *symbolic* mind held an immense collection of forms, an ever lucid treasury of the dispositions of nature, a potentiality always ready to be translated into action and growing with the extension of its domain. A host of concepts, a throng of possible memories, the power to recognize an extraordinary number of distinct things in the world at large and arrange them in a thousand fashions: this constituted

Leonardo. He was the master of faces, anatomies, machines. He knew how a smile was made; he could put it on the façade of a house or into the mazes of a garden. He disordered and curled the filaments of water and the tongues of flames. If his hand traces the vicissitudes of the attacks which he has planned, he depicts in fearful bouquets the trajectories of balls from thousands of cannon; they raze the bastions of cities and strongholds which he has just constructed in all their details, and fortified. As though he found the metamorphoses of things too gradual when observed in a calm, he adores battles, tempests, the deluge. Regarding them from a height, he can see them as mechanical processes; and he can feel them in the apparent independence or life of their fragments; in a handful of sand driven by the wind; in the stray idea of any fighter distorted by passion and inner torment.* He is there in the "shy and blunt" little bodies of children, in the constricted gestures of old men and women, in the simplicity of

* See the description of a battle, of the deluge, etc., in his treatise *On Painting* and in the manuscripts at the Institut de France (ed. Ravaisson-Mollien). Drawings of tempests, bombardments, etc., can be seen in the Windsor manuscripts.

the corpse. He has the secret of composing fantastic beings and of making their existence seem probable; the logic that harmonizes their discordant parts is so rigorous that it suggests the life and the naturalness of the whole. He makes a Christ, an angel, a monster, by taking what is known, what exists everywhere, and arranging it in a new order. Here he profits by the illusion and abstraction of painting, an art that depicts only a single quality of things, but thereby evokes them all.

He passes from the headlong or seemingly retarded movement of the avalanche and landslide, from massive curves to multitudinous draperies; from smoke sprouting on roofs to distant tree-forms, to the vaporous beeches of the horizon; from fish to birds; from the sea glittering in the sun to birch leaves in their thousand slender mirrors; from scales and shells to the gleams that sail over gulfs; from ears and ringlets to the frozen whorls of the nautilus. From the shell he proceeds to the spiral tumescence of the waves; from the skin on the water of shallow pools to the veins that would warm it, and thence to the elemental movements of crawling, to the fluid serpent. He vivifies. He molds the

Sketches of this type are often to be found in Leonardo's manuscripts. His precise imagination

64

water round a swimmer* into clinging scarves, draperies that show the effort of the muscles in relief. As for the air, he transfixes it in the wake of soaring larks as ravelings of shadow; it is pictured in the frothy flights of bubbles which these aerial journeys and delicate breaths must disturb and leave trailing across the blue-tinted pages of space, the dense, vague crystal of space.

He reconstructs all buildings, tempted by every mode of combining the most diverse materials. He enjoys things distributed in the dimensions of space; vaults and beams and soaring domes; rows of galleries and loggias; masses held aloft by the weight in their arches; bridges flung from pier to pier; the depth of green in trees rising into the air from which it drinks; and the structures formed by migratory birds, those acute triangles pointing to the south, revealing a rational combination of living beings.

He makes sport of difficulties, and, growing bolder, he translates all his feelings with clarity into this universal language. The abundance of his metaphorical resources makes this possible.

creates the sort of effects that photography has since revealed as fact.

From this point of view his intellectual labors are part of the slow transformation by which the notion of space—at first that of a complete vacuum or an isotropic volume—has little by little developed into the notion of a system inseparable from the matter it contains, and from time.

* Sketch in the manuscripts of the Institut de France.

His desire to probe utterly the slightest fragment, the merest shard, of the world renews the force and cohesion of his being. His joy finds an outlet in his decorations for fêtes and in other charming inventions; when he dreams of constructing a *flying man*, he sees him soaring to the mountaintops for snow and coming back to scatter it over the streets of cities pulsing with the heat of summer. His emotion delights in pure faces touched by a frown of shadow and in the gesture of a silent god. His hate knows all weapons: all the artifices of the engineer, all the stratagems of the general. He establishes terrible engines of war and protects them with bastions, caponiers, salients, and moats which he provides with water-gates, so as suddenly to transform the aspects of a siege; and I recall—while savoring the fine Italian wariness of the *cinquecento*—that he built strongholds in which four flights of steps, independent round the same axis, separate the mercenaries from their leaders and the troops of hired soldiers one from the other.

He worships the human body, male and female, which measures and is measured by all things. He can feel its height; how a rose can grow up to its lips while a great plane tree leaps twenty times higher, in a jet whence the leaves hang down to its head. He knows that a radiant body will fill a possible room, or the concavity of a vault that is deduced from the human form, or a natural background that is measured by its steps. He studies the lightest footfall; spies on the skeleton silent in the flesh, the concurrent motions of the human walk, and all the superficial play of heat and cool-ness over naked flesh, perceiving these as a diffused whiteness or bronze welded over a mechanism. And the face, that enlightening and enlightened thing—of all visible things the most particular, the most magnetic, the most difficult to regard without study-ing it—the face haunts him. In each man's memory there remain in-distinctly a few hundred faces with their variations. In his, they were classi-fied and proceeded consecutively from one physiognomy to another, from one irony to another, from one wisdom to a lesser wisdom, from benignity to the divine—by way of symmetry. About the eyes—fixed points of vari-able brilliance—he adjusts the mask that hides a complex structure of bones and distinct muscles under a uniform skin; then drawing the mask tight, he makes it reveal all.

Among the multitude of minds, this mind impresses us as being one of the *regular combinations* already mentioned. In order to understand it, one does not feel that, like most of the others, it has to be attached to a nation, a tradition, or a group practicing the same art. Its acts, by virtue of their number and intercommunication, together form a symmetrical object, a sort of *system complete in itself*, or completing itself continually.

Perhaps this highest degree of self-possession deprives an individual of all particularities— except the very one of being master and center of himself? . . . In the "Note and Digression" this notion is developed at some length.

Leonardo is bound to be the despair of modern man who, from adolescence, is directed into a speciality, where it is hoped he may excel simply because he is confined to it. The variety of methods is offered as an excuse, and the quantity of details, and the constant accumulation of facts and theories, with the result that the patient observer, the meticulous accountant of existence, the individual who reduces himself—not without earning our gratitude, if the phrase has any meaning here—to the minute aptitudes of an instrument, is confounded with the man for whom this work is done, the poet of hypothesis, the architect of analytical materials. The first needs patience, monotonous direction, specialization, and time. The absence of thought is his virtue. But the other must circulate through barriers and partitions. His function is to disregard them. At this point I might suggest an analogy between specialization and the state of stupor due to a prolonged sensation that was mentioned above. But the best argument is that, nine times out of ten, every great improvement in a field of endeavor is obtained by the intrusion of methods and notions that were not foreseen within it. Having just attributed those advances to the formation of images, then of idioms, we cannot evade this consequence, that the number of such idioms possessed by any man has a singular bearing on his chance of finding new ones. It would be easy to demonstrate that all the minds that have served as substance to generations of seekers and quibblers, all those whose remains have nourished, for centuries on end, human opinion and the human mania for echoing, have been more or less universal. The names of Aristotle, Descartes, Leibniz, Kant, Diderot are sufficient confirmation.

Here we are verging on another topic, the joys of *construction*. I shall

What I should write today is that the number of ways an individual can employ a single word is more important than the number of words at his disposal.
Cf. Racine and Victor Hugo.

Diderot is unexpected here.
His one truly philosophic quality

was the lightness of touch that all philo- sophers should have— and so many of them lack.

try to justify the preceding remarks with a few examples and to show, in its application, the possibility and almost the necessity of a general inter- play of thought. I should like to point out that the particular results I shall mention in passing would be difficult to obtain without our employing a num- ber of apparently unrelated concepts.

He who has never been seized—were it in a dream!—by a project he is free to abandon, by the adventure of a con-

The arbitrary creating the necessary. . . .

struction already completed when others see it only beginning; who has never experienced either the fire of enthusiasm that utterly consumes a moment of himself, the poison of conception, the scruples, the chill of interior objections, as well as that struggle between alternative ideas in which the stronger and more universal must triumph, even over habit, even over novelty; the man who never, in the whiteness of his paper, has seen an image troubled by the possible and by regret for all the symbols that will not be chosen, any more than he has seen, in the limpid air, a building that does not exist; the man who has not been haunted by the intoxication of a distant aim, by anxiety as to means, by the foreknowledge of delays and despair, by the calculation of successive phases, or by the reasoning that is projected into the future to designate the very things that must not be reasoned about *even then*: that man, however great his knowledge, will never know the riches or the broad intellectual domains that are illuminated by the conscious act of *constructing*. And it was from the human mind that even the gods received their gift of *creation*, because that mind, being periodic and abstract, can expand any of its conceptions to the point at which they are no longer conceivable.

Constructing takes place between a project or a particular vision and the materials that one has chosen. For one order of things, which is initial, we substitute another order, whatever may be the objects rearranged: stones, colors, words, concepts, men, etc. Their specific nature does not change the general conditions of that sort of music in which, at this point, the chosen material serves only as the timbre, if we pursue the metaphor. The wonder is that we sometimes receive an impression of accuracy and consistency from human constructions made of an agglomeration of seeming-

This independence is essential to the pursuit of form. But the artist, in another phase, tries to restore the particularity, even the singularity, that he had begun by eliminating from his attention.

ly incompatible elements, as though the mind that arranged them had recognized their secret affinities. But the wonder passes all bounds when we perceive that the author, in the vast majority of cases, is himself unable to give an account of the paths he followed, and that he wields a power whose motive forces he does not know. He can never lay claim in advance to a success. By what process are the parts of an edifice, the elements of a drama, the factors in a victory, reconciled one with another? By what series of obscure analyses is anyone led to the production of a work?

In such cases it is customary to explain everything by instinct, but that leaves instinct itself to be explained.

Instinct is a mental force of which the cause and the purpose are both immeasurable—*if we admit that* cause *and* purpose *have any meaning in this connection.*

In the present case, moreover, we should be making our appeal to strictly personal and exceptional instincts, that is, to the contradictory notion of "hereditary habit," something that would be no more habitual than it was hereditary.

The act of constructing, as soon as it leads to some comprehensible result, would lead us to think that some common measure of terms has been applied, an element or principle already presupposed by the simple fact of our becoming conscious, and which can have only an abstract or imaginary existence. We cannot conceive of a whole composed of changes—a picture or an edifice of multiple qualities—except as the locus of the modalities of a single *matter* or *law*, of which we affirm the hidden continuity in the very same instant that we recognize the edifice as a unified whole, as the limited field of our investigation. Here again we encounter that psychological postulate of continuity which, in our faculty of knowing, resembles the principle of inertia in mechanics. Only such purely abstract, purely differential combinations as those of numbers can be constructed with the aid of fixed units; and it is to be noted that the relation of these to other possible constructions is the same as that of the regular portions of the world to the irregular portions.

The word differential *is not used here in its technical sense. What I meant was that the combinations would consist of identical elements.*

In art there is a word that can be applied to all its modes and fantasies, while suppressing, at a stroke, all the supposed difficulties involved in the opposition or resemblance between art and the nature that is never defined, and for good reason: that word is *ornament.* Let us only recall in succes-

Ornament, that answer to emptiness,

73

that compensation of the possible, in a sense completes and is also the annulment of a liberty.

sion the groups of curved lines and balancing sections that cover the oldest known objects, the profiles of vases or temples; then the lozenges, volutes, ova, and striae of the ancients; the crystallized forms and voluptuous wall-surfaces of the Arabs; the skeletal Gothic symmetries; the waves, the flames, the flowers on Japanese lacquer or bronze; and in each of these eras the introduction of the likenesses of plants, animals, and men, the perfecting of those resemblances: painting, sculpture. Or think of speech and its primitive melody, the separation of words from music and the branching development of each; on the one hand, the invention of verbs, of writing, the *figurative* complexity of language that becomes possible, and the occurrence —so peculiar—of abstract words; on the other hand, the system of tones rendered more flexible, extending from the voice to the resonance of materials, enriched by harmony, then varied by the use of different timbres. And finally let us observe a similar progression in the structures of thought, first through a sort of primitive psychic onomatopoeia, then through elementary symmetries and contrasts, till it reaches the ideas of substances, meta-

74

phors, a faltering sort of logic, formalism, entities, metaphysical concepts. . . .

All this multiform vitality can be regarded from the standpoint of ornament. The manifestations we have listed can be considered as finished portions of space or time containing different variations. Some of these are known and characterized objects, but their meaning and ordinary use are ignored so that only their order and mutual reactions may subsist. On this order depends the effect. The effect is the aim of ornament, and thus the work of art takes on the character of a machine to impress a public; to arouse emotions and their corresponding images.

From this point of view the conception bears the same relation to the particular arts that mathematics bears to the other sciences. Just as the physical notions of time, length, density, mass, etc., exist in mathematical calculations merely as homogeneous quantities and do not recover their individuality until the results are interpreted, so the objects chosen and arranged to obtain an effect are, as it were, detached from most of their attributes, which they only reassume

Here is another word —homogeneous— that is not being used in its technical sense. I simply wished to say that quantitative symbols are assigned to widely different

qualities, and that the qualities do not exist for and during a mathematical calculation except as numbers.
Likewise a painter, when planning a picture, regards objects as colors and colors as the elements with which he operates.

in the effect—that is, in the open mind of the spectator. Hence it is by a process of abstraction that works of art are constructed; and the process is more or less powerful, more or less easy to define, depending on whether the elements taken from reality are more or less complex. Inversely, it is by a sort of induction, by the production of mental images, that works of art are appreciated; and this process likewise demands more or less energy, causes more or less *fatigue*, depending on whether it is set in motion by a simple pattern on a vase or by one of Pascal's broken phrases.

The painter disposes pigments on a plane surface and expresses himself by means of their lines of separation, their varying thicknesses, their fusions and clashes. What the spectator sees is only a more or less faithful representation of bodies, gestures, and landscapes, as though he were looking out through a window of the museum. The picture is judged in the same spirit as reality. Some complain that the face is ugly, others fall in love with it, still others are psychological and verbose; a few look only at the hands, which they always say are unfinished. The fact is that the picture, in accordance with unconscious demands, is supposed to represent the physical and natural conditions of our own environment. Light radiates and weight makes itself felt, just as they do here; and anatomy and perspective gradually assumed a foremost rank among pictorial studies. I believe, on the contrary, that the surest method of judging a picture is to identify nothing at first, but, step by step, to make the series of inductions demanded by the simultaneous presence of colored masses in a definite area; then one can rise from metaphor to metaphor, from supposition to supposition, and so attain, in the end, to knowledge of the subject— or sometimes to sheer consciousness of pleasure, which we did not always feel in the beginning.

No example I could give of the general attitude toward painting would be more amusing than the celebrated "smile of Mona Lisa," to which the epithet "mysterious" seems irrevocably fixed. That dimpled face has evoked the sort of phraseology justified in all literatures, under the title of "Sensations" or "Impressions" of art. It is buried beneath a mass of words and disappears among the

I have made a similar suggestion for poetry: that one should approach it as pure sonority, reading and rereading it as a sort of music, and should not introduce meanings or intentions into the diction before clearly grasping the system of sounds that every poem must offer on pain of nonexistence.

many paragraphs that start by calling it *disturbing* and end with a generally vague description of a state of *soul*. It might deserve less intoxicating studies. Leonardo had no use for inexact observations or arbitrary symbols, or Mona Lisa would never have been painted. He was guided by a perpetual sagacity.

In the background of *The Last Supper* there are three windows. The one in the middle, which opens behind Jesus, is distinguished from the others by a cornice that forms the arc of a circle. If we prolong the arc, we obtain a circumference with Christ as its center. All the great lines of the fresco converge at this point; the symmetry of the whole is relative to this center and to the long line of the table of the agape. The mystery, if one exists, is to know how we come to regard such combinations as mysterious, and that, I fear, can be explained.

It is not from painting, however, that we shall choose the striking example we need of the communication between the different activities of thought. The host of suggestions rising from the painter's need to diversify and people a surface; the resemblance between the first attempts of this order and certain dispositions in the natural world; the evolution of visual sensibility—all these will be disregarded at this point, for fear of conducting the reader into all too arid speculations. A vaster art that is the ancestor, as it were, of painting will serve our purpose better.

The word *construction*—which I purposely employed so as to indicate more forcibly the problem of human intervention in natural things and so as to direct the mind of the reader toward the logic of the subject by a material suggestion—now resumes its more limited meaning. Architecture becomes our example.

The monument (which composes the City, which in turn is almost the whole of civilization) is such a complex entity that our understanding of it passes through several successive phases. First we grasp a changeable background that merges with the sky, then a rich texture of motifs in height, breadth, and depth, infinitely varied by perspective, then something solid, bold, resistant, with certain animal characteristics—organs, members— then finally a machine having gravity for its motive force, one that carries us

*What physics dis-
covers in matter
today is no longer an
edifice of any sort,
but rather the in-
describable in* essence
—and the unfore-
seen! 1930.

in thought from geometry to dynamics
and thence to the most tenuous speculations of molecular physics, suggesting as it does not only the theories of
that science but the models used to
represent molecular structures. It is
through the monument or, one might
rather say, among such imaginary
scaffoldings as might be conceived to
harmonize its conditions one with
another—its purpose with its stability,
its proportions with its site, its form
with its matter, and harmonizing each
of these conditions with itself, its
millions of aspects among themselves,
its types of balance among themselves,
its three dimensions with one another
—that we are best able to reconstitute
the clear intelligence of a Leonardo.
Such a mind can play at imagining
the future sensations of the man who
will make a circuit of the edifice, draw
near, appear at a window, and by
picturing what the man will see; or
by following the weight of the roof as
it is carried down walls and buttresses
to the foundations; or by feeling the
balanced stress of the beams and the
vibration of the wind that will torment them; or by foreseeing the forms
of light playing freely over tiles and
cornices, then diffused, encaged in

rooms where the sun touches the floors. It will test and judge the pressure of the lintel on its supports, the expediency of the arch, the difficulties of the vaulting, the cascades of steps gushing from their landings, and all the power of invention that terminates in a durable mass, embellished, defended, and made liquid with windows, built for our lives, to contain our words, and out of it our smoke will rise.

Architecture is commonly misunderstood. Our notion of it varies from stage setting to that of an investment in housing. I suggest we refer to the idea of the City in order to appreciate its universality, and that we should come to know its complex charm by recalling the multiplicity of its aspects. For a building to be motionless is the exception; our pleasure comes from moving about it so as to make the building move in turn, while we enjoy all the combinations of its parts, as they vary: the column turns, depths recede, galleries glide; a thousand visions escape from the monument, a thousand harmonies.

(Many a project for a church, never realized, is to be found among Leonardo's manuscripts. Generally we may guess it to be a St. Peter's in

The most difficult problem for architecture as an art is to provide in advance for these endlessly varied aspects. It is the test of a monument—and a fatal test for any building designed as if it were a stage setting.

Rome; the St. Peter's of Michelangelo makes us wish it had been. At the end of the Gothic period, during a time when ancient temples were being unearthed, Leonardo found, between these two styles, the great design of the Byzantines: a cupola rising above cupolas; domes topped with swelling domes that cluster round the highest dome of all. His plans, however, show a boldness and pure ornamentation that Justinian's architects never mastered.)

The monument, that creature of stone, exists in space. What we call space is relative to the existence of whatever structures we may choose to conceive. The architectural structure interprets space, and leads to hypotheses on the nature of space, in a quite special manner; for it is an equilibrium of materials with respect to gravity, a visible static whole, and at the same time, within each of its materials, another equilibrium—molecular, in this case, and imperfectly understood. He who designs a monument speculates on the nature of gravity and then immediately penetrates into the obscure atomic realm. He is faced with the problem of structure, that is, to know what combinations must be imagined in order to satisfy the conditions of resistance, resilience, etc., obtaining in a given space. We can see the logical extension of the problem and how one passes from the architectural domain, usually handed over to the specialists, into the most abstruse theories of general physics and mechanics.

Thanks to the docility of the imagination, the properties of an edifice and those inherent in a given substance help to explain each other. Space, as soon as we try to represent it in our minds, at once ceases to be a void and is filled with a host of arbitrary constructions; and in all cases it can be replaced by a juxta-position of forms, which we know can be rendered as required. However complicated we may suppose an edifice to be, it will represent, when multiplied and proportionally dimin-ished in size, the basic unit of a forma-tion of space, and the qualities of the formation will depend on those of the unit. Thus, we can find ourselves sur-rounded by and moving among a multitude of structures. Let us note, for example, in how many different fashions the space around us is occu-pied—in other words, is formed, is conceivable—and let us try to grasp

This might be the place for a few remarks on space, a word that changes its meaning with one's angle of vision or manner of speaking. The space of ordinary

practice is not quite the same as that of the physicists, which is not quite the same as that of geometri- cians—since none of these is defined by all *the same exper- iences and operations. It follows that the cardinal properties of* identity *do not apply equally in the dif- ferent fields. In chem- istry, for example, there is no* infinitely small. *Today, in physics, one is privileged to doubt whether a* length *is infinitely divisible. This means that the idea of division and the idea of the thing to be divided are no longer independent. The operation itself is no longer conceivable beyond a certain point.*

the conditions implied in our being able to perceive the variety of things with their particular qualities: a fabric, a mineral, a liquid, a cloud of smoke. We can form a clear idea of any of these textures only by enlarging a single particle and by inserting into it a structure so organized that, by simple multiplication, it will form a substance having the same qualities as the substance under consideration. . . . With the aid of concepts like these we can move continuously through the apparently quite separate domains of the artist and the scientist, proceeding from the most poetic, even the most fantastic, construction to one that is tangible and ponderable. The problems of composition and those of analysis are reciprocal; and when our age abandoned oversimplified concepts with regard to the constitution of matter, it gained a triumph no less *psychological* than that of abandoning similar concepts with regard to the formation of ideas. Dogmatic explana- tions of matter and substantialist reveries are disappearing at the same time; and the science of forming hypotheses, names, models, is being liberated from preconceived theories and the idol of simplicity.

I have just indicated, with a brevity for which the reader who differs will either thank or excuse me, an evolution I believe to be important. I could give no better example of it than to quote, from the writings of Leonardo himself, a sentence of which one might say that each of its terms has been so purified and elaborated as to become a concept fundamental to our modern understanding of the world. "The air," he says, "is full of infinite lines, straight and radiating, intercrossing and interweaving without ever coinciding one with another; and they *represent* for every object the true FORM of their reason (or their explanation)." *L'aria e piena d'infinite linie rette e radiose insieme intersegate e intessute sanza ochupatione luna dellaltra rapresantano aqualunche obieto lauera forma della lor chagione.* (Manuscript A, folio 2.) The sentence seems to contain the first germ of the theory of light waves, especially when it is compared with other remarks that Leonardo made on the same subject.* It

* See Manuscript A, *Siccome la pietra gittata nell'acqua...*, *etc.*; also the curious and lively *Histoire des sciences mathématiques*, by G. Libri, and the *Essai sur les ouvrages mathématiques de Léonard*, by J.-B. Venturi, Paris, An. v (1797).

gives the skeleton, as it were, of a system of waves all the lines of which are directions of propagation. But I do not set much store by scientific prophecies of this sort, which are always suspect; too many people think that the ancients discovered everything. Besides, a theory acquires value only through its logical and experimental developments. In this instance all we have is a few *assertions* based intuitively on the observation of rays, as found in waves of sound or water. The interest of the quotation resides in its form, which gives authentic light on a method, the very one I have been discussing throughout this essay. Leonardo's explanation does not *as yet* assume the character of a measurement. It consists merely in the emission of an image, a concrete mental relation between phenomena— or, let us say to be exact, between the images of phenomena. He seems to have engaged consciously in this form of psychic experimentation, and I believe that nobody else clearly recognized the method during the three centuries after his death, although everyone made use of it—necessarily. I also believe—though perhaps it is going too far—that the famous and

As I said above, the phenomena of mental imagery have received far too little attention. I remain firmly convinced of their importance. I hold that certain laws proper to the field are essential and have an extra-ordinary range of application. If we investigated such phenomena as the variations of images, the restrictions

age-old question of whether there is such a thing as empty space can be related to one's awareness or unawareness of this *imaginative logic*. An action at a distance is something that cannot be imagined. We can explain it only by using an abstraction. In our minds only an abstraction can make a leap, *potest facere saltus*. Even Newton, who gave their analytic form to "actions at a distance," realized that his explanations were inadequate. It was Faraday who rediscovered Leonardo's method as applied to the physical sciences. After the glorious mathematical researches of Lagrange, d'Alembert, Laplace, Ampère, and many others, he came forward with admirably bold concepts that were literally only the projection, in his imagination, of observed phenomena; and his imagination was so remarkably lucid "that his ideas were capable of being expressed in the ordinary mathematical forms, and thus compared with those of the professed mathematicians."* The *regular combinations* formed by iron filings round the poles of a magnet were, in his mind, models of the transmission of the former "actions at a distance."

imposed on those variations, and the spontaneous production of reflex images or their complements, we would be able to reunite worlds *as distinct from one another as the worlds of dream, of the mystical state, and of deduction by analogy.*

* Preface to the treatise on *Electricity and Magnetism*, by J. Clerk Maxwell.

Like Leonardo he *saw* systems of lines uniting all bodies, filling the whole of space, and in this way *explained* electrical phenomena and even gravity; such lines of force can be regarded, for the purpose of this essay, as those of least resistance to the understanding. Faraday was not a mathematician, but he differed from mathematicians only in the expression of his thoughts and by the absence of analytical symbols. "Faraday, in his mind's eye, saw lines of force traversing all space, where mathematicians saw centers of force attracting at a distance; Faraday saw a medium where they saw nothing but distance."* Beginning with Faraday a new era opened for physical science; and when J. Clerk Maxwell translated his master's ideas into the language of mathematics, scientific imaginations were filled with dominating visions of much the same type. The study of the medium that he discovered, a scene of electrical activity and intermolecular reactions, remains the principal occupation of modern physics. Inspired partly by the demand for more and more precision in representing the modes of energy, partly by the will to *see*, and partly by something that

Today there are still lines of force traversing all space, but one can no longer see them.
Might they perhaps be heard? It is only the mental flights suggested by melodies that can give us some idea or intuition of trajectories in space-time. A sustained note represents a point.

* J. Clerk Maxwell.

88

might be called the kinetic mania, hypothetical constructions have appeared that are of the greatest logical and psychological interest. Lord Kelvin, for example, feels such a pressing need to express even the subtlest of natural processes by mental images, and to carry these to a point at which they can be reproduced in tangible form, that he believes every explanation should lead to a mechanical model. Such a mind rejects the inert atom, the mere point imagined by Boscovich and the physicists of the early nineteenth century, and replaces it with an already extremely complex mechanism caught in a web of ether, which itself becomes a rather elaborate construction as a result of the many different conditions it is asked to fulfill. It is no effort for a mind like his to pass from the architecture of crystals to that of stone and iron; in our viaducts, in the symmetries of beams and girders, he finds the symmetries of resistance that quartz and gypsum offer to compression and cleavage—or, in a different fashion, to the passage of light waves.

We no longer think of the atom as a mechanism. Today it is another world.

Such men seem to have had an intuitive grasp of the methods discussed in this essay. We might even permit ourselves to extend those methods beyond the physical sciences; and we believe that it would be neither absurd nor entirely impossible to create a model of the continuity of the intellectual operations of a Leonardo da Vinci, or of any other mind, determined by the analysis of the conditions to be fulfilled. . . .

The artists and art-lovers who have turned these pages in the hope of renewing some of the impressions to be obtained at the Louvre, or in Florence and Milan, must excuse me for disappointing them. Nevertheless, I doubt if I have strayed too far from their favorite occupation, in spite of appearances. I believe, on the contrary, that I have touched on their central problem, that of composition. Some of them will doubtless be astonished to hear me saying that questions concerning the effect of a work of art are usually discussed and answered with the help of words and notions that not only are obscure but involve a thousand difficulties. More than one critic has spent a lifetime changing his definition of *the beautiful*, or *life*, or *mystery*. Ten minutes of simply considering one's own mind should suffice to destroy those idols of the cave and make one realize the inconsistency of attaching an abstract noun, always empty, to an always personal and strictly personal vision. In the same way, most of the disappointments that artists suffer are based on the difficulty or impossibility of *rendering*, through the medium of their art, an image that seems to lose its color and wither as soon as they try to capture it in words, on a canvas, or in a certain key. A few additional moments of *consciousness* might be spent in ascertaining that we merely delude ourselves when we wish to reproduce the fantasies of our own minds in those of others. It might even be said that the attempt is nearly incomprehensible. What is called in art a *realization*, is in fact a problem of rendering—one in which the private meaning, the key attributed by every author to his materials, plays no part, and in which the principal factors are the nature of those materials and the mentality of the public. Edgar Poe, who in this century of literary perturbation was the very lightning of the confusion, of the poetic storm, and whose analysis sometimes ends, like Leonardo's, in mysterious smiles, has clearly established his reader's approach

Nothing seems harder for the public—and even for critics—to admit than this incompetence of the author with regard to his own work, once he has completed it.

on the basis of psychology and probable effects. From that point of view,
every combination of elements made
to be perceived and judged depends
on a few general laws and on a particular adaptation, defined in advance
for a foreseen category of minds to
which the whole is specially addressed;
and the work of art becomes a machine
designed to arouse and assemble the
individual formations of those minds.
This suggestion is quite opposite to the
ordinary notion of the sublime, and I
can guess the indignation it might
arouse; but that very indignation
would help to confirm what I am
saying—without this essay's being in
any respect a work of art.

I can see Leonardo da Vinci exploring
the depths of this mechanism, which
he called the paradise of the sciences,
with the same natural power with
which he dedicated himself to the
invention of pure and misty faces.
And that same luminous territory,
with its docile throng of possible
beings, was the field of those activities
which slowed down and solidified into
distinct works of art. Leonardo himself did not feel that these expressed
different passions. On the last page of

that slender notebook, deeply scored with his secret script and those risky calculations in which he gropes toward his favorite research, aviation, he exclaims—in a flash that strikes at his imperfect labors, and illuminates his patience and its obstacles with the vision of a supreme spiritual aim, an obstinate certainty: "The great bird will take his first flight mounted on the back of his great swan, and filling the universe with stupor, filling all writings with his renown, and eternal glory to the nest where he was born! —*Piglierà il primo volo il grande uccello sopra del dosso del suo magno cecero e empiendo l'universo di stupore, empiendo di sua fama tutte le scritture e gloria eterna al nido dove nacque.*"

Here is an astonishing prophecy, though one that would be easy to dismiss if it were merely a view of the possible. All its sublimity is due to its being proffered by the first man who really studied the problem of flight, and the first to imagine its technical solution— at the beginning of the sixteenth century!

The Crisis of the Mind

[1919]

First Letter

WE LATER civilizations . . . we too now know that we are mortal.

We had long heard tell of whole worlds that had vanished, of empires sunk without a trace, gone down with all their men and all their machines into the unexplorable depths of the centuries, with their gods and their laws, their academies and their sciences pure and applied, their grammars and their dictionaries, their Classics, their Romantics, and their Symbolists, their critics and the critics of their critics. . . . We were aware that the visible earth is made of ashes, and that ashes signify something. Through the obscure depths of history we could make out the phantoms of great ships laden with riches and intellect; we could not count them. But the disasters that had sent them down were, after all, none of our affair.

Elam, Nineveh, Babylon were but beautiful vague names, and the total ruin of those worlds had as little significance for us as their very existence. But France, England, Russia . . . these too would be beautiful names. *Lusitania*, too, is a beautiful name. And we see now that the abyss of history is deep enough to hold us all. We are aware that a civilization has the same fragility as a life. The circumstances that could send the works of Keats and Baudelaire to join the works of Menander are no longer inconceivable; they are in the newspapers.

That is not all. The searing lesson is more complete still. It was not enough for our generation to learn from its own experience how the most beautiful things and the most ancient, the most formidable and the best ordered, can perish *by accident*; in the realm of thought, feeling, and common sense, we witnessed extraordinary phenomena: paradox suddenly become fact, and obvious fact brutally belied.

I shall cite but one example: the great virtues of the German peoples have begotten more evils, than idleness ever bred vices. With our own eyes, we have seen conscientious labor, the most solid learning, the most serious discipline and application adapted to appalling ends.

So many horrors could not have been possible without so many virtues. Doubtless, much science was needed to kill so many, to waste so much property, annihilate so many cities in so short a time; but *moral qualities* in like number were also needed. Are Knowledge and Duty, then, suspect?

So the Persepolis of the spirit is no less ravaged than the Susa of material fact. Everything has not been lost, but everything has sensed that it might perish.

An extraordinary shudder ran through the marrow of Europe. She felt in every nucleus of her mind that she was no longer the same, that she was no longer herself, that she was about to lose consciousness, a consciousness acquired through centuries of bearable calamities, by thousands of men of the first rank, from innumerable geographical, ethnic, and historical coincidences.

So—as though in desperate defense of her own physiological being and resources—all her memory confusedly returned. Her great men and her great books came back pell-mell. Never has so much been read, nor with such passion, as during the war: ask the booksellers. . . . Never have people prayed so much and so deeply: ask the priests. All the saviors, founders, protectors, martyrs, heroes, all the fathers of their country, the sacred heroines, the national poets were invoked. . . .

And in the same disorder of mind, at the summons of the same anguish, all cultivated Europe underwent the rapid revival of her innumerable ways of thought: dogmas, philosophies, heterogeneous ideals; the three hundred ways of explaining the World, the thousand and one versions of Christianity, the two dozen kinds of positivism; the whole spectrum of intellectual light spread out its incompatible colors, illuminating with a strange and contradictory glow the death agony of the European soul. While inventors were feverishly searching their imaginations and the annals of former wars for the means of doing away with barbed wire, of outwitting submarines or paralyzing the flight of airplanes, her soul was intoning at the same time all the incantations it ever knew, and giving serious consideration to the most bizarre prophecies; she sought refuge, guidance, consolation throughout the whole register of her memories, past acts, and ancestral attitudes. Such are the known effects of anxiety, the disordered behavior of a mind fleeing from reality to nightmare and from nightmare back to reality, terrified, like a rat caught in a trap. . . .

The military crisis may be over. The economic crisis is still with us in all its force. But the intellectual crisis, being more subtle and, by its nature, assuming the most deceptive appearances (since it takes place in the very realm of dissimulation) . . . this crisis will hardly allow us to grasp its true extent, its *phase*.

No one can say what will be dead or alive tomorrow, in

literature, philosophy, aesthetics; no one yet knows what ideas and modes of expression will be inscribed on the casualty list, what novelties will be proclaimed.

Hope, of course, remains—singing in an undertone:

Et cum vorandi vicerit libidinem
Late triumphet imperator spiritus.

But hope is only man's mistrust of the clear foresight of his mind. Hope suggests that any conclusion unfavorable to us *must be* an error of the mind. And yet the facts are clear and pitiless: thousands of young writers and young artists have died; the illusion of a European culture has been lost, and knowledge has been proved impotent to save anything whatever; science is mortally wounded in its moral ambitions and, as it were, put to shame by the cruelty of its applications; idealism is barely surviving, deeply stricken, and called to account for its dreams; realism is hopeless, beaten, routed by its own crimes and errors; greed and abstinence are equally flouted; faiths are confused in their aim—cross against cross, crescent against crescent; and even the skeptics, confounded by the sudden, violent, and moving events that play with our minds as a cat with a mouse . . . even the skeptics lose their doubts, recover, and lose them again, no longer master of the motions of their thought.

The swaying of the ship has been so violent that the best-hung lamps have finally overturned. . . .

What gives this critical condition of the mind its depth and gravity is the patient's condition when she was overcome.

I have neither the time nor the ability to define the intellectual situation in Europe in 1914. And who could pretend to picture that situation? The subject is immense, requiring every order of knowledge and endless information. Besides, when such a complex whole is in question, the difficulty of reconstructing the past, even the recent past, is altogether comparable to that of constructing the future, even the near future; or rather, they are the same difficulty. The prophet is in the same boat as the historian. Let us leave them there.

For all I need is a vague general recollection of what was being thought just before the war, the kinds of intellectual pursuit then in progress, the works being published.

So if I disregard all detail and confine myself to a quick impression, to that *natural whole* given by a moment's perception, I see . . . *nothing*! Nothing . . . and yet an infinitely potential nothing.

The physicists tell us that if the eye could survive in an oven fired to the point of incandescence, it would see . . . nothing. There would be no unequal intensities of light left to mark off points in space. That formidable contained energy would produce invisibility, indistinct equality. Now, equality of that kind is nothing else than a perfect state of *disorder*.

And what made that disorder in the mind of Europe? The free coexistence, in all her cultivated minds, of the most dissimilar ideas, the most contradictory principles of life and learning. That is characteristic of a *modern* epoch.

I am not averse to generalizing the notion of "modern" to designate a certain way of life, rather than making it purely a synonym of *contemporary*. There are moments and places in history to which *we moderns* could return without too greatly disturbing the harmony of those times, without seeming objects infinitely curious and conspicuous . . . creatures shocking, dissonant, and unassimilable. Wherever our entrance would create the least possible sensation, that is where we should feel almost at home. It is clear that Rome in the time of Trajan, or Alexandria under the Ptolemies, would take us in more easily than many places less remote in time but more specialized in a single type of manners and entirely given over to a single race, a single culture, and a single system of life.

Well then! Europe in 1914 had perhaps reached the limit of modernism in this sense. Every mind of any scope was a crossroads for all shades of opinion; every thinker was an international exposition of thought. There were works of the mind in which the wealth of contrasts and contradictory tendencies was like the insane displays of light in the capitals of those days: eyes were fatigued, scorched. . . . How much material wealth, how much labor and planning it took, how many centuries were ransacked, how many heterogeneous lives were combined, to make possible such a carnival, and to set it up as the supreme wisdom and the triumph of humanity?

In a book of that era—and not one of the most mediocre—we should have no trouble in finding: the influence of the Russian ballet, a touch of Pascal's gloom, numerous impressions of the Goncourt type, something of Nietzsche, something of Rimbaud, certain effects due to a familiarity with painters, and sometimes the tone of a scientific publication . . . the whole flavored with an indefinably British quality difficult to assess! . . . Let us notice, by the way, that within each of the components of this mixture other *bodies* could well be found. It would be useless to point them out: it would be merely to repeat what I have just said about modernism, and to give the whole history of the European mind.

Standing, now, on an immense sort of terrace of Elsinore that stretches from Basel to Cologne, bordered by the sands of

Nieuport, the marshes of the Somme, the limestone of Champagne, the granites of Alsace . . . our Hamlet of Europe is watching millions of ghosts.

But he is an intellectual Hamlet, meditating on the life and death of truths; for ghosts, he has all the subjects of our controversies; for remorse, all the titles of our fame. He is bowed under the weight of all the discoveries and varieties of knowledge, incapable of resuming this endless activity; he broods on the tedium of rehearsing the past and the folly of always trying to innovate. He staggers between two abysses— for two dangers never cease threatening the world: order and disorder.

Every skull he picks up is an illustrious skull. *Whose was it?** This one was *Lionardo*. He invented the flying man, but the flying man has not exactly served his inventor's purposes. We know that, mounted on his great swan (*il grande uccello sopra del dosso del suo magnio cecero*) he has other tasks in our day than fetching snow from the mountain peaks during the hot season to scatter it on the streets of towns. And that other skull was *Leibnitz*, who dreamed of universal peace. And this one was *Kant* . . . *and Kant begat Hegel, and Hegel begat Marx, and Marx begat.* . . .

Hamlet hardly knows what to make of so many skulls. But suppose he forgets them! Will he still be himself? . . . His terribly lucid mind contemplates the passage from war to peace: darker, more dangerous than the passage from peace to war; all peoples are troubled by it. . . . "What about Me," he says, "what is to become of Me, the European intellect?. . . And what is peace? . . . *Peace is perhaps that state of things in which the natural hostility between men is manifested in creation, rather than destruction as in war.* Peace is a time of creative

*Hamlet's words are in English in the French text.—J.M.

rivalry and the battle of production; but am I not tired of producing? . . . Have I not exhausted my desire for radical experiment, indulged too much in cunning compounds? . . . Should I not perhaps lay aside my hard duties and transcendent ambitions? . . . Perhaps follow the trend and do like Polonius who is now director of a great newspaper; like Laertes, who is something in aviation; like Rosencrantz, who is doing God knows what under a Russian name?

"Farewell, ghosts! The world no longer needs you—or me. By giving the name of progress to its own tendency to a fatal precision, the world is seeking to add to the benefits of life the advantages of death. A certain confusion still reigns; but in a little while all will be made clear, and we shall witness at last the miracle of an animal society, the perfect and ultimate anthill."

Second Letter

I was saying the other day that peace is the kind of war that allows acts of love and creation in its course; it is, then, a more complex and obscure process than war properly so-called, as life is more obscure and more profound than death.

But the origin and early stages of peace are more obscure than peace itself, as the fecundation and beginnings of life are more mysterious than the functioning of a body once it is made and adapted.

Everyone today feels the presence of this mystery as an actual sensation; a few men must doubtless feel that their own inner being is positively a part of the mystery; and perhaps there is someone with a sensibility so clear, subtle, and rich that he senses in himself certain aspects of our destiny more advanced than our destiny itself.

I have not that ambition. The things of the world interest

me only as they relate to the intellect; for me, everything relates to the intellect. Bacon would say that this notion of the intellect is an *idol*. I agree, but I have not found a better idol.

I am thinking then of the establishment of peace insofar as it involves the intellect and things of the intellect. This point of view is *false*, since it separates the mind from all other activities; but such abstract operations and falsifications are inevitable: every point of view is false.

A first thought dawns. The idea of culture, of intelligence, of great works, has for us a very ancient connection with the idea of Europe—so ancient that we rarely go back so far.

Other parts of the world have had admirable civilizations, poets of the first order, builders, and even scientists. But no part of the world has possessed this singular *physical* property: the most intense power of radiation combined with an equally intense power of assimilation.

Everything came to Europe, and everything came from it. Or almost everything.

Now, the present day brings with it this important question: can Europe hold its pre-eminence in all fields?

Will Europe become *what it is in reality*—that is, a little promontory on the continent of Asia?

Or will it remain *what it seems*—that is, the elect portion of the terrestrial globe, the pearl of the sphere, the brain of a vast body?

In order to make clear the strict necessity of this alternative, let me develop here a kind of basic theorem.

Consider a map of the world. On this planisphere are all the habitable lands. The whole is divided into regions, and in each of these regions there is a certain density of population, a certain quality of men. In each of these regions, also, there are corresponding natural resources—a more or less fertile soil, a more or less rich substratum, a more or less watered terrain, which may be more or less easily developed for transport, etc.

All these characteristics make it possible, at any period, to classify the regions we are speaking of, so that at any given time *the situation on the earth may be defined by a formula showing the inequalities between the inhabited regions of its surface.*

At each moment, the *history* of the next moment will depend on this given inequality.

Let us now examine, not our theoretical classification, but the one that actually prevailed in the world until recently. We notice a striking fact, which we take too much for granted:

Small though it be, Europe has for centuries figured at the head of the list. In spite of her limited extent—and although the richness of her soil is not out of the ordinary—she dominates the picture. By what miracle? Certainly the miracle must lie in the high quality of her population. That quality must compensate for the smaller number of men, of square miles, of tons of ore, found in Europe. In one scale put the empire of India and in the other the United Kingdom: the scale with the smaller weight tilts down!

That is an extraordinary upset in equilibrium. But its consequences are still more so: *they will shortly allow us to foresee a gradual change in the opposite direction.*

We suggested just now that the quality of her men must be the determining factor in Europe's superiority. I cannot analyze this quality in detail; but from a summary examination I would say that a driving thirst, an ardent and disinterested curiosity, a happy mixture of imagination and rigorous logic, a certain unpessimistic skepticism, an unresigned mysticism . . . are the most specifically active characteristics of the European psyche.

A single example of that spirit, an example of the highest order and of the very first importance, is Greece—since the whole Mediterranean littoral must be counted in Europe. Smyrna and Alexandria are as much a part of Europe as Athens and Marseilles. Greece founded geometry. It was a mad undertaking: we are still arguing about the *possibility* of such a folly.

What did it take to bring about that fantastic creation? Consider that neither the Egyptians nor the Chinese nor the Chaldeans nor the Hindus managed it. Consider what a fascinating adventure it was, a conquest a thousand times richer and actually far more poetic than that of the Golden Fleece. No sheepskin is worth the golden thigh of Pythagoras.

This was an enterprise requiring gifts that, when found together, are usually the most incompatible. It required argonauts of the mind, tough pilots who refused to be either lost in their thoughts or distracted by their impressions. Neither the frailty of the premises that supported them, nor the infinite number and subtlety of the inferences they explored could dismay them. They were as though equidistant from the inconsistent Negro and the indefinite fakir. They accomplished the extremely delicate and improbable feat of adapting common speech to precise reasoning; they analyzed the most complex combinations of motor and visual functions, and found that these corresponded to certain linguistic and grammatical properties; they trusted in words to lead them through space like far-seeing blind men. And space itself became, from century to century, a richer and more surprising creation, as thought gained possession of itself and had more

confidence in the marvelous system of reason and in the original intuition which had endowed it with such incomparable
instruments as definitions, axioms, lemmas, theorems, problems, porisms, etc.

I should need a whole book to treat the subject properly.
I wanted merely to indicate in a few words one of the characteristic inventions of the European genius. This example
brings me straight back to my thesis.

I have claimed that the imbalance maintained for so long in
Europe's favor was, *by its own reaction*, bound to change by
degrees into an imbalance in the opposite direction. That is
what I called by the ambitious name of basic theorem.

How is this proposition to be proved? I take the same
example, that of the geometry of the Greeks; and I ask the
reader to consider the consequences of this discipline through
the ages. We see it gradually, very slowly but very surely,
assuming such authority that all research, all the ways of
acquiring knowledge tend inevitably to borrow its rigorous
procedure, its scrupulous economy of "matter," its automatic
generalizations, its subtle methods, and that infinite discretion
which authorizes the wildest audacity. Modern science was
born of this education in the grand style.

But once born, once tested and proved by its practical applications, our science became a means of power, a means of
physical domination, a creator of material wealth, an apparatus
for exploiting the resources of the whole planet—ceasing to
be an "end in itself" and an artistic activity. Knowledge, which
was a consumer value, became an exchange value. The utility
of knowledge made knowledge a *commodity*, no longer desired
by a few distinguished amateurs but by Everybody.

This commodity, then, was to be turned out in more and

more manageable or consumable forms; it was to be distributed to a more and more numerous clientele; it was to become an article of commerce, an article, in short, that can be imitated and produced almost anywhere.

Result: the inequality that once existed between the regions of the world as regards the mechanical arts, the applied sciences, the scientific instruments of war or peace—an inequality on which Europe's predominance was based—is tending gradually to disappear.

So, the classification of the habitable regions of the world is becoming one in which gross material size, mere statistics and figures (e.g., population, area, raw materials) finally and alone determine the rating of the various sections of the globe.

And so the scales that used to tip in our favor, although we *appeared* the lighter, are beginning to lift us gently, as though we had stupidly shifted to the other side the mysterious excess that was ours. *We have foolishly made force proportional to mass!*

This coming phenomenon, moreover, may be connected with another to be found in every nation: I mean the diffusion of culture, and its acquisition by ever larger categories of individuals.

An attempt to predict the consequences of such diffusion, or to find whether it will or not inevitably bring on *decadence*, would be a delightfully complicated problem in intellectual physics.

The charm of the problem for the speculative mind proceeds, first, from its *resemblance* to the physical fact of diffusion and, next, from a sudden transformation into a profound *difference* when the thinker remembers that his primary object is *men* not *molecules*.

A drop of wine falling into water barely colors it, and tends to disappear after showing as a pink cloud. That is the physical fact. But suppose now that some time after it has vanished, gone back to limpidity, we should see, here and there in our glass—which seemed once more to hold *pure* water—drops of wine forming, dark and *pure*—what a surprise! . . .

This phenomenon of Cana is not impossible in intellectual and social physics. We then speak of *genius*, and contrast it with diffusion.

Just now we were considering a curious balance that worked in inverse ratio to weight. Then we saw a liquid system pass as though spontaneously from homogeneous to hetero-geneous, from intimate mingling to clear separation. . . . These paradoxical images give the simplest and most practical notion of the role played in the World by what—for five or ten thousand years—has been called Mind.

But can the European Mind—or at least its most precious content—be totally diffused? Must such phenomena as de-mocracy, the exploitation of the globe, and the general spread of technology, all of which presage a *deminutio capitis* for Europe . . . must these be taken as absolute decisions of fate? Or have we some freedom *against* this threatening con-spiracy of things?

Perhaps in seeking that freedom we may create it. But in order to seek it, we must for a time give up considering groups, and study the thinking individual in his struggle for a per-sonal life against his life in society.

Man and the Sea Shell

SINCE *the strangely delicate drawings, woven rather than traced by the fine and sensitive point of Henri Mondor's pencil, have provided an occasion to reprint this little work, I should like to say a few words more on the subject, as though, having taken leave of a friend, I should go back to add a detail or two to our conversation.*

It was chance that made me write about sea shells, very much as though bidding me, by the seashore, to take notice of one of these delightful objects. In taking this marvel as my theme, I did the same as a passer-by who has just picked up a small, curiously formed, calcareous shell in the sand; who examines it and handles it, admiring its mineral convolutions and the arrangement of spots, streaks, spines suggesting the past movement in which they were engendered. I meditated my unexpected theme and raised it closer to the eyes of my mind; I turned it over and over in my thoughts. . . . I knew next to nothing about mollusks, and I took pleasure in illumining, one by one, the facets of my ignorance.

Ignorance is a treasure of infinite price that most men squander, when they should cherish its least fragments; some ruin it by educating themselves, others, unable so much as to conceive of making use of it, let it waste away. Quite on the contrary, we should search for it assiduously in what we think we know best. Leaf through a dictionary or try to make one, and you will find that every word covers and masks a well so bottomless that the questions you toss into it arouse no more than an echo.

In the matter of shells, then, I did my best to define my ignorance, to organize it, and above all to preserve it.

Among the many objects that confront man's mind with questions, some more legitimate than others, he is particularly fascinated by those which, by their form or properties, lead him to reflect on his own powers or tendencies. He is amazed to find objects which, though it is inconceivable to him that they should have been made, he can compare to those he is able to make. In such objects he seems to recognize his own familiar modes of thought, his own types of conscious action: his incorrigible "causality" and "finality"; his geometry; his ingenuity; his need for order and his bursts of inventiveness. As soon as he glimpses an adaptation, a regular functioning, definable forms, an order, in a product of "nature," he cannot help trying to "understand"; that is, the object becomes a problem for him and he begins to consider it as the effect or result of some sort of making, which remains to be defined.

Complete human action, with its own possibility and necessity, its means, its material, its aim, is the inevitable and unique type on which every "explanation" is modeled. What we know of ourselves, our acts, our impulses, of what satisfies our instincts and fits in with our structure, in other words the "forces," the "time," the "space" that suit us, these are the instruments by which we reduce all things to our measure. When we are perplexed, that is, when we have carried our familiar questionnaire too far, an appropriately vague language comes to our aid, masks our helplessness, and enables us (what an admirable thing) to go on arguing indefinitely.

We talk about creation, evolution, chance, *and we endow these terms with precisely everything required in the way of power, disorder, time, and large numbers, to stimulate our minds and, by an odd contradiction, to satisfy them. It is a great mystery to me how opinions on subjects of this kind can differ as much as we know they do.*

But I see that I am gradually slipping from one problem to another, from the formation of shells to the formation of hypotheses, which is perhaps less disheartening to meditate upon. Our intellect is not so rich as it supposes in tenable hypotheses. A man is always at a loss when experience shows him that one phenomenon must be connected with another which seemed unrelated to it. He must own that the connection would never have occurred to him.

Yet mysterious as the genesis of shells may be to the metaphysical eye, an artist, at all events, can examine them as long as he pleases without wasting his time.

Run off by the billions, each different from the rest (though the difference is sometimes imperceptible), they offer an infinite number of solutions to the most delicate problems of art, and of absolutely perfect answers to the questions they suggest to us.

I have indicated in the text of my essay that it was child's play for what we call "living nature" to obtain the relation between form and matter that we take so much pains to attempt or to make some show of achieving. Our hands busy themselves in various acts, all distinct and determinate; with our eyes and our intention we order and supervise this superficial maneuver; but our activity is composite and must always be so; and thus we can never, in our object, arrive at the happy union of substance and shape that is achieved by the inarticulate creature which makes nothing, *but whose work, little by little, is differentiated from its flesh, progressively moving away from the living state as though passing from one state of balance to another.*

In this invincible and one might say flawless progression of form, which involves and develops its whole setting according to the con-tinuous fatality of its convolutions and seems to create its own time, we admire the combination of rhythm, *marked by the regular spots or spines, and of* indivisible movement. *It is like seeing music. The correspondence of ornaments on successive spirals suggests a counterpoint, while the continuity sustains the main theme of the rotation of the surface.*

But suddenly an end must come. This strange torsion must cease, the nacre on the inside and the coarser covering must join, and the distinction between the two substances of the shell must vanish or explain itself, while at the same time its form must be completed by some decision that remains to be arrived at.

The problem is very general in kind. Living nature must solve it in all the types it displays, all of which involve extremities to be modeled and cavities or tubes that must be made to reach the outside world. The mind staggers at the mere thought of analyzing the in-numerable solutions it has found. We yearn for a profound geometry, a very exact knowledge of what is revealed by dissection and micro-scopic examination, and an exquisite artistic feeling which, taken together, might enable us to isolate some simple basic principle of natural morphology.

This is a mystery that has always teased my mind, for I can find nothing in the arts that captivates me more than forms or phases of transition, *the refinements of* modulation. *For me, perfect modula-tion is the crown of art. But in our time little importance is attached to this ideal of mine. The architect knows only his rule and square. The musician does pretty much as he pleases. The poet proceeds by leaps and bounds. But nature has preserved her cautious methods, the inflection in which she envelops her changes of pace, direction, or physiological function. She knows how to finish a plant, how to open nostrils, a mouth, a vulva, how to create a setting for an eyeball; she thinks suddenly of the sea shell when she has to unfold the pavilion of an ear, which she seems to fashion the more intricately as the species is more alert.*

IF THERE were a poetry of the marvels and emotions of the intellect (something I have dreamed of all my life), it could find no subject more delightful and stimulating than the portrayal of a mind responding to the appeal of one of those remarkable natural formations which we observe (or rather which make us observe them) here and there, among the innumerable things of indifferent and accidental form that surround us.

Like a pure sound or a melodic system of pure sounds in the midst of noises, so a *crystal*, a *flower*, a *sea shell* stand out from the common disorder of perceptible things. For us they are privileged objects, more intelligible to the view, although more mysterious upon reflection, than all those which we see indiscriminately. They present us with a strange union of ideas: order and fantasy, invention and necessity, law and exception. In their appearance we find a kind of *intention* and *action* that seem to have fashioned them rather as man might have done, but at the same time we find evidence of methods forbidden and inaccessible to us. We can imitate these singular forms; our hands can cut a prism, fashion an imitation flower, turn or model a shell; we are even able to express their characteristics of symmetry in a formula, or represent them quite accurately in a geometric construction. Up to this point we can share with "nature": we can endow her with designs, a sort of mathematics, a certain taste and imagination that are not infinitely different from ours; but then, after we have endowed her with all the human qualities she needs to make herself understood by human beings, she displays all the inhuman qualities needed to disconcert us. . . . We can conceive of the *structure* of these objects, and this is what interests us and holds our attention; but we do not understand their gradual *formation*, and that is what intrigues us. Although we ourselves were formed by imperceptible growth, we do not know how to create anything in that way.

The shell which I hold and turn between my fingers, and which offers me a combined development of the simple themes of the helix and the spiral, involves me in a degree of astonishment and concentration that leads where it may: to superficial remarks and observations, naïve questions, "poetic" comparisons, beginnings of reckless "theories." . . . And my mind vaguely anticipates the entire innate treasure of responses that rise within me in the presence of a thing that arrests and questions me. . . .

First I try to describe this thing to my own satisfaction. It suggests to me the movement we make when we roll a sheet of paper into a cone. One edge of the paper forms an inclined plane that rises toward the tip and ends after a few turns. The mineral cone, however, is formed by a tube and not by a flat sheet. With a tube closed at one end and assumed to be flexible, I not only can reproduce quite well the essential form of a shell, but can also fashion a number of others, some of which, like this one I am examining, might be inscribed in a cone; while the others, obtained by reducing the *pitch* of the conic helix, will end by coiling like the spring of a watch.

Thus the idea of a *tube* and the concept of *torsion* suffice for a first approximation of the form under consideration.

But this simplicity applies only in principle. If I examine a whole collection of shells, I find a marvelous variety. The cone lengthens or flattens, narrows or broadens; the spirals become more pronounced or merge with one another; the surface is incrusted with knobs or spines, sometimes strikingly long, radiating from a center; or it may swell, puffing out into bulbs separated by strangulations or concave gorges where the curved lines meet. Engraved in hard matter, furrows, wrinkles, or ribs follow and accentuate one another, while, aligned on the generatrix, the protuberances, the spines, the little bumps rise in tiers, corresponding from row to row and breaking up the regular intervals of the planes. The alternation of these "ornaments" illustrates, more than it interrupts, the continuity of the general *convolution* of the form. It enriches but does not modify the basic motif of the helical spiral.

Without modifying it, without ceasing to follow and confirm its own unique law, this *idea* of periodic progression exploits all the abstract fecundity of the helix and develops its full capacity for sensuous charm. It beguiles the eye, drawing it into a kind of controlled vertigo. A mathematician, no doubt, would easily read this system of "skew" lines and surfaces and would sum it up in a few signs, a numerical relation, for it is in the nature of the intelligence to do away with the infinite and to abolish repetition. But common language is ill suited to describing forms, and I despair of expressing their whirling grace. Actually, even the mathematician is baffled when in the end the tube suddenly broadens, breaks, curls back, and overflows into uneven lips, often bordered, waved, or fluted, which part as though made of flesh, disclosing in a fold of the softest mother-of-pearl the smoothly inclined starting point of an internal whorl that recedes into darkness.

Helices, spirals, spatial developments of angular relations— the observer who considers them and endeavors to translate them into his own modes of expression and understanding, cannot fail to perceive one essential characteristic of forms of this type. Like a hand, like an ear, one shell cannot be mistaken for another that is its symmetrical counterpart. If we draw two spirals, one the mirror image of the other, no manner of moving these twin curves will enable us to superimpose one on the other. It is the same with two stairways, similar but turning in opposite directions. All shells whose form derives from the rolling of a tube necessarily manifest this *dissymmetry*, to which Pasteur attached so profound an importance, and from which he derived the main idea for the investigations that led him from the study of certain crystals to that of ferments and their living agents.

But despite the dissymmetry of all shells we might, among a thousand specimens, expect the number of those whose spirals turn "clockwise" to be approximately equal to those turning in the opposite direction. This is not the case. Just as there are few left-handed men, there are few shells which viewed from the tip disclose a spiral receding from right to left. Here we have another, quite remarkable sort of statistical dissymmetry. To say that this difference in bias is *accidental* is only to say that it exists. . . .

Thus the mathematician I mentioned a moment ago has been able to make three simple observations in his study of shells.

He first noted that he could describe their general form with the help of very simple notions drawn from his arsenal of definitions and operations. Next, he saw that quite sudden —one might say unforeseen—changes occurred in the forms he was contemplating: the curves and surfaces that made it possible to represent their construction suddenly broke off or degenerated: whereas the cone, the helix, the spiral can well go on "indefinitely," the shell suddenly wearies of following them. *But why not one turn more?*

Lastly, he finds that the statistics of right-handed and left-handed shells marks a strong preference for the former.

We have given a superficial and very general description of a shell chosen at random; and now, if we have time and the inclination to follow the development of our immediate impressions, we might ask ourselves a very naïve question, one of those questions that arise in us before we remember that we are not newborn, but already know something. First of all, we must allow for this; and remember that our knowledge consists largely in "thinking that we know" and in thinking that others know.

We are always refusing to listen to the simple soul within us. We ignore the inner child who always wants to see things for the first time. If he questions, we discourage his curiosity, calling it childish because it is boundless, on the pretext that we have been to school and learned that there is a science of all things, which we might consult if we wished, and that it would be a waste of time to think in our own way and no other about an object that suddenly arrests us and calls for an answer. Perhaps we are too well aware that an enormous stock of facts and theories has been amassed, and that in thumbing through the encyclopedias we may find hundreds of names and words that represent this potential wealth; and we are too sure that we can always find someone somewhere who, if only to impress us, will be glad to enlighten us on any subject whatsoever. And we promptly withdraw our attention from most of the things that begin to arouse it, thinking of the learned men who must have explored or disposed of the event that has just stirred our intelligence. But such caution is sometimes laziness; and moreover, there is no proof that everything has really been examined, and in all its aspects.

So I shall ask my very naïve question. I can easily imagine that I know nothing about shells except what I see on picking this one up; and that I know nothing about this shell's origin, its function, its relations with what I am not considering at this particular moment. I am following the example of the man who one day made *tabula rasa*.

I look *for the first time* at this thing I have found. I note what I have said about its form, and I am perplexed. Then I ask myself the question: *Who made this?*

Who made this? asks the naïve moment.

My first stir of thought has been to think of *making*.

The idea of *making* is the first and most human of ideas. "To explain" is never anything more than to describe a way of *making*: it is merely to remake in thought. The *why* and the *how*, which are only ways of expressing the implications of this idea, inject themselves into every statement, demanding satisfaction at all costs. Metaphysics and science are merely an *unlimited* development of this demand. They may even lead us to pretend not to know what we know, when what we know refuses to be reduced to a clear knowledge of how to make something. . . . This is what we mean by going back to the beginnings of knowledge.

Here then I will introduce the artifice of a doubt: considering this shell, in whose shape I think I can discern a certain "construction" and as it were the work of some hand not acting "at random," I ask myself: *Who made it?*

But soon my question undergoes a transformation. It takes a short step forward along the path of my naïveté, and I begin to inquire by what sign we recognize that a given object is or is not *made by a man?*

It may seem somewhat absurd to pretend not to know that a wheel, a vase, a piece of cloth, or a table has been produced by someone's industry, since we know perfectly well that it has. But what I say is that we do not know this *just by examining these things*. If no one had ever told us, then by what marks, by what signs should we know? What is it that indicates the presence or absence of a human operation? When an anthropologist finds a piece of flint, does he not often hesitate as to whether man or chance fashioned it?

The problem after all is no more futile nor any more naïve than speculation about *who made* a certain fine work in music or poetry; whether it was born of the Muse, or sent by Fortune, or whether it was the fruit of long labor. To say that someone composed it, that his name was Mozart or Virgil, is not to say much; a statement of this sort is lifeless, for the creative spirit in us bears no name; such a remark merely eliminates from our concern all men *but one*, within whose inner mystery the enigma lies hidden, intact. . . .

On the contrary I look at the object and nothing else: nothing could be more deliberately planned, or speak more harmoniously to our feeling for plastic shapes, to the instinct that makes us model with our fingers something we should delight to touch, than this calcareous jewel I am caressing, whose origin and purpose I wish for a time to disregard.

As we say a "sonnet," an "ode," a "sonata," or a "fugue," to designate well-defined forms, so we say a "conch," a "helmet," a "cameo," a "haliotis," a "porcelain"—all of them names of shells; and each one of these words suggests an action that aims to make something beautiful and succeeds.

What can prevent me from concluding that *someone* has made this curiously conceived, curiously turned and ornamented shell that troubles my imagination—and made it perhaps *for someone?*

I found this one in the sand. It attracted me because it was not a formless thing but one whose parts and aspects manifested an interrelation, a sequence and harmony as it were, that enabled me, after a single look, to conceive and foresee the aspects I had not yet examined. Its parts are joined by something more than the cohesion and solidity of matter. If I compare this thing to a stone, I find that the shell has an identity which the stone lacks. If I break them both, the fragments of the shell are not shells; but the fragments of the stone remain stones, just as the stone itself was once no doubt part of a still larger one. Yet even now certain fragments of the shell suggest the fragments that were joined to them; in a measure they engage my imagination and incite me to think further; they call for a *whole.* . . .

My observations thus far concur to make me think it would be *possible* to construct a shell; and that the process would be quite the same as that of making any of the objects I can produce with my hands by choosing some appropriate material, forming the design in my mind, and proceeding, part by part, to carry it out. The unity, the wholeness of the shell's form, force me to conclude that a directing idea presides over the execution; a pre-existing idea, quite separate from the work itself, an idea that maintains itself, supervises and governs, while on the other hand and in *another area* it is put into execution by means of my energies successively applied. I divide myself in order to create.

Then someone made this object. But *of what*? And *why*?

However, if I now attempt to model or chisel out a similar object, I am first of all compelled to seek a suitable way of molding or cutting it; and it turns out that there are only too many possibilities. I am in a quandary. I can think of bronze, clay, stone: in respect to form, the final result of my operation will be independent of the material chosen. Of this material I demand only "sufficient," not strictly "necessary," conditions. According to the material employed, my acts will vary, no doubt; but different as they, and it, may be, I obtain in the end the same desired figure: I have several ways of passing from my idea to its effigy by way of the material.

In any case I am unable to imagine or define a *material* with such precision that the consideration of form will wholly determine my choice.

Moreover, just as I may hesitate in regard to the material, I may hesitate about the dimensions I shall give to my work. I see no necessary dependence between form and size; I can conceive of no form that might not be larger or smaller— it is *as though the idea of a certain figure called forth in my mind an endless number of similar figures*.

Thus I have been able to separate form from matter and both of these from size; and merely by thinking in some detail of my projected action, I have been able to see how it breaks down into stages. The least reflection, the slightest meditation on *how I should go about fashioning a shell*, tells me at once that

I should have to act in several different ways, in several different capacities as it were, for I am not able to carry on all at once the numerous operations required to form the desired object. I shall have to connect them as though intervening from outside; and indeed, it is by a judgment independent of my action that I shall recognize that my work is "finished," that the object is "made," since the object in itself is only one possible stage, among others, in a series of transformations that might continue beyond their goal—*indefinitely*.

In reality I do not *make* this object; I only substitute certain attributes for certain others, and a certain relation that interests me for a certain diversity of forces and properties that I can only consider and utilize one by one.

I feel, finally, that if I have undertaken to produce one particular form, it is because I could have chosen to create entirely different ones. This is an absolute condition: if one can only make a single thing and in a single way, it means that the thing almost makes itself; therefore, such an action is not truly human (since thought is not necessary to it), and *we do not understand it*. What we make in this way really makes *us* more than we make it. What are we, if not a momentary balance between a multitude of hidden actions that are not specifically human? Our life is a tissue of such local acts in which choice plays no part, and which in some incomprehensible way perform themselves. Man walks, breathes, remembers—but in all this he is in no way different from animals. He knows neither how he moves, nor how he remembers; and he has no need to know in order to move or remember, nor does he need to know *before* doing so. But if he builds a house or a ship, if he forges a tool or a weapon, a design must first act upon him and make him into a specialized instrument; an *idea* must co-ordinate what he desires, what he can do, what he knows, what he sees, what he touches and manipulates, and must organize all this expressly toward a particular and exclusive action, starting from a state in which he was entirely open and free from all intention. Once he is called upon to act, his freedom diminishes, relinquishes its rights, and for a time he accepts a constraint that is the price he must pay if he wishes to impress upon a certain "reality" the configured desire that he carries in his mind.

To sum up: all specifically human production is effected in successive, distinct, limited, enumerable acts. But up to this point certain animals, the builders of hives or nests, are quite like us. Man's specific work becomes unique when the separate, independent acts involved require his deliberate thinking presence to provoke them and adjust their diversity to an aim. Man consciously sustains his mental image and his will. We know only too well how precarious and costly this "presence of mind" is; how quickly the effort wanes, how our attention disintegrates, and that what arouses, assembles, corrects, and revives the efforts of our separate functions is of a nature quite different from them; and this is why our *considered* projects, our *intentional* constructions or fabrications *seem very alien to our underlying organic activity*.

Thus I can make a shell rather like this one I have examined; and I can make it only by means of a composite, sustained action such as I have just described. I can choose the material and the moment; I can take my time, interrupt the work, and return to it; there is no hurry, for my life in no way depends on the outcome but participates only in a revocable, one might say incidental, way; and though my life may spend itself on an object so far removed from its needs, it can equally well refrain from doing so. My life is indispensable to my work, but my work is not indispensable to my life.

All in all, within the limits stated, *I have understood this object.* I have *explained* it to myself by a system of acts that are eminently mine, and I have thereby exhausted my problem: any attempt to go farther would modify it essentially and would lead me to slip from an explanation of the shell into an explanation of myself.

Up to this point, consequently, I can imagine that this shell is a work of man.

Still, one element of a human work is lacking. I do not see the *utility* of this thing; it calls to mind no need which it satisfies. It has intrigued me; it delights my eyes and fingers; I stop to look at it as I would stop to listen to a melody; and unconsciously I consign it to oblivion, for we unthinkingly withhold the future from whatever is of no use to us. . . . And I find but one answer to the question that comes to my mind: *Why was this object made?* But what, I ask myself, is the use of the things that artists produce? What they make is of a strange kind: there is no vital need for it. *It does not result from any necessity,* which as a matter of fact would determine its whole character; *still less can it be attributed to "chance."*

So far I have purposely ignored the true origin of sea shells, and attempted in my reasoning—or raving—to stick as close as possible to this feigned ignorance.

In this I have been imitating the philosopher, who makes every effort to know *just as little* about the well-known origin of well-defined things as is known about the origin of the "world" and the beginnings of "life."

Doesn't philosophy after all consist in pretending not to know what one does know, and to know what one does not? It doubts existence, but speaks seriously of the "Universe." . . .

If I have dwelt at some length on the act of a man who might apply himself to making a sea shell, it is because in my opinion one should never lose an opportunity to compare, in some detail, our way of making things with the work performed by what we call *nature*. Nature: that is to say, the genetrix, the *producer*. Whenever we run across something we do not know how to *make* but that appears to be *made*, we say that nature produced it. Yet there are certain special cases where we can compete with nature, and attain by our own methods what it accomplishes in its way. We are able to make heavy bodies swim or fly and to construct certain "organic" molecules. . . .

All the rest—everything that we can assign neither to thinking man nor to nature's power of generation—we attribute to "chance." The word is an excellent invention. It is very convenient to have a word which enables us to say that a *remarkable* thing (remarkable in itself or in its immediate effects) is brought about *in exactly the same way as something else* that is not remarkable. But to say that a thing is *remarkable* is to bring in a *man*—a person who is particularly sensitive to it, and it is this person who supplies everything that is remarkable about it. What difference does it make to me, if I have no lottery ticket, whether one number or another is picked out of the urn? I have not been "sensitized" to the event. For me there is no "chance" in the drawing, no contrast between the uniform way in which these numbers are drawn and the inequality of the consequences. Take away man and his expectation, and everything comes out the same, sea shell or stone; but chance *makes* nothing in this world, apart from making us take notice of it. . . .

But now it is time for me to stop pretending and come back to the area of certainty, to the surface of common experience.

A sea shell emanates from a mollusk. To *emanate* strikes

me as the only term close enough to the truth since its proper meaning is: to *exude*. A grotto emanates stalactites; a mollusk emanates its shell. As to the elementary process of this emanation scientists tell us many things that they have seen under the microscope. They add a number of other things which I think they have not seen: some are inconceivable, though that scarcely precludes discoursing about them; others would require observation over hundreds of millions of years, for that much time is needed to change anything into anything. Others insist that some extremely favorable accident occurred at one point or another. . . .

Such an accident, according to science, is what enabled the mollusk to spin out so skillfully the charming object that holds our attention.

Beginning in the germ, we are told, this mollusk, the maker of our shell, suffered a strange limitation of its growth, an atrophy of no less than half its organism. In most mollusks the right (and in the others the left) half has been sacrificed, while, on the other side, the visceral mass bent itself into a semicircle and then twisted. We are told that the nervous system, whose first intention it was to form two parallel networks, crisscrossed strangely and inverted its central ganglia. On the outside, the shell was exuded, and solidified. . . .

More than one hypothesis has been suggested to explain why certain mollusks (and not certain others that are very much like them) develop this strange predilection for one side of their organism; and—as is inevitable in the realm of supposition—what one supposes is deduced from what one needs to suppose: the question is human, the answer too human. This is the whole basis of our famous Principle of Causality. It leads us to *imagine*, that is, to substitute our own machinations for the gaps in our knowledge. But in general the greatest and most precious discoveries are quite unexpected. They demolish, more often than they confirm, the products of our preferences: they consist in facts that are not yet *humanized*, that no imagination could have foreseen.

As for me, I am perfectly willing to admit that I do not know certain things, and that all genuine knowledge reduces itself to what one sees and what one has power over. If the hypothesis is seductive and the theory is attractive, I take pleasure in them without worrying about whether they are true. . . .

If then we disregard our intellectual inventions, sometimes naïve and often wholly verbal, we are obliged to recognize that our knowledge of living things is insignificant beside our knowledge of the inorganic world. This is tantamount to saying that we possess incomparably greater power over inorganic than over organic things, for I see no way to measure knowledge except by the real power it confers. *I know only what I know how to handle.* For it is strange, and deserving of some attention, that despite so much effort, despite our marvelously subtle tools and methods, we should have so little power over this living nature, *which is ours.* On closer scrutiny we should find, no doubt, that our mind is baffled by everything that is born, reproduces, and dies on our planet, because the mind is strictly limited, in its representation of things, to its awareness of its means of *external action* and of the form this action—*of whose mechanics it need know nothing*—will take.

This type of action, it seems to me, is the only model we can follow in trying to resolve a phenomenon into imaginary and voluntary operations that will at last enable us either to reproduce at will or to foresee a development with some degree of accuracy. Everything that diverges too much from this type defies our intellect (as may be seen in the most recent physics). If we attempt to force this barrier, we are faced at once with all sorts of contradictions, linguistic illusions, sentimental falsifications; and it sometimes happens that these mythical products occupy and even delight the minds of men for many years to come.

The little problem of the sea shell suffices to illustrate this quite well, and to throw light on our limitations. Since man is not the maker of this object and chance is not responsible for it, we are reduced to inventing something we have called *living nature*. There seems to be no other way of defining it except by the difference between its work and ours; and that is why I have been impelled to say something about our way of doing things. I have said that we undertake our works on the basis of several kinds of *freedom*: freedom with respect to *material*, with respect to *size and shape*, with respect to *time*; the mollusk seems deprived of all these—a creature that can only recite its lesson, which is hardly distinguishable from its very existence. Full of fancy as it may seem (so much so that we borrow certain of our ornamental motifs from it), the mollusk's work, never retouched, unmarred by changes or reservations, is a fancy that repeats itself indefinitely; we cannot even see why certain eccentrics among the gastropods should work leftward where others work to the right. Still less do we understand the oddly shaped complexities that some shells disclose; or those spines and spots of color, to which we vaguely ascribe some utility that escapes us, without even stopping to think that, *outside of man's little intellectual sphere, our idea of the useful has no meaning*. These oddities add to our perplexity, for a *machine* produces no such deviations; a *mind* would have chosen them with some intention; *chance* would have equalized the possibilities. Neither machine, nor intention, nor chance. . . . All our methods have been rejected. Machine and chance, these are the two methods of our physics; as for intention, it can intervene only if man himself is involved, explicitly or in disguise.

But the making of the shell is lived, not calculated: nothing could be more contrary to our organized action preceded by an aim and operating as a cause.

Nevertheless, let us try to gain an idea of this mysterious act of formation. Let us leaf through some learned works, with no intention of getting to the bottom of them, and without in the least forgoing the advantages of ignorance or of the caprices of error.

I observe first of all that living nature is unable to work directly with solids. In the solid state neither stone nor metal is of any use to it. When nature wishes to turn out a hard article of set shape, a support, a lever, a brace, an armor plate; or when it aims to produce a tree trunk, a femur, a tooth or a tusk, a skull or a sea shell, it works in the same indirect way: it takes the liquids or fluids from which all organic matter is made, and slowly separates out the solid substances it needs. Everything that lives or has lived results from the properties and modifications of a few liquids. And every present solid has passed through the liquid phase, molten or in solution. But living nature does not tolerate the high temperatures that enable us to work with the "elements," to shape molten glass, bronze, or iron into the forms we desire, which will set in cooling. In molding solid organs life has only solutions, suspensions, or emulsions.

I have read that the animal we are examining draws food containing calcium salts from its environment, and that the calcium is extracted and digested by the liver, whence it passes into the blood stream. This is the raw material for the mineral part of the shell—it will feed the activity of a strange organ specialized in the craft of secreting the elements of the solid body to be constructed and of putting them in place.

This organ, a muscular mass that encloses the animal's viscera and extends to the foot on which it stands and moves, is called the *mantle*, and performs a dual function. Through its *epithelium*, the edge exudes the outer coating of the shell, which covers a layer of very curiously and subtly shaped calcareous prisms.

This gives us the outside of the shell. But it grows in thickness, and this growth involves very different material, structure, tools. Protected by the solid rampart that the edge of the mantle has built, the rest of this admirable organ fashions the refinements of the inner wall, the water-smooth lining of the animal's home. There is nothing too precious or delicate for the meditations of a life so much of which is spent at home; successive layers of mucus spread a coating as thin as a soap bubble over the deep, twisted cavity into which the solitary creature withdraws in concentration. But never will it become aware of the beauty of this retreat it has made. After its death the exquisite substance it has formed by depositing alternately the organic product of its mucus cells and the calcite from its nacre cells will see the light; it will break the sun's rays into their wave lengths, and will enchant our eyes with the tender richness of its iridescent bands.

This, we are told, is how nature builds the dwelling and mobile refuge of this strange animal clothed in a muscle cloaked in a shell. But I must own that my curiosity is not satisfied. Microscopic analysis is a fine thing. But while I am occupied with cells, making the acquaintance of blastomeres and chromosomes, I lose sight of my mollusk. And if I concern myself with all this detail in the hope that it will ultimately enlighten me about the formation of the whole, a certain disappointment is in store for me. . . . But this perhaps is an essential difficulty—that is, a difficulty arising from the very nature of our senses and of our mind.

In order to imagine this formative process, we must first dispose of an obstacle, and in so doing we automatically sacrifice the inner consistency of our image. For actually *we*—who cannot even perceive our own growth—*are unable to visualize a movement so slow that a perceptible result springs from an imperceptible change.* We can imagine the living process only by lending it a rhythm which is specifically ours and has no connection with *what happens in the creature we are observing.* . . .

Indeed, it seems quite probable that in the growth of the mollusk and its shell according to the ineluctable theme of the spiral, all the components which the no less ineluctable form of the human act has taught us to consider and define *separately*, are *indistinct and indivisible*: the *energy*, the *time*, the *material*, the *connections*, and the different "orders of magnitude" between which our senses compel us to distinguish. Life passes continuously from the molecule to the micelle, from the micelle to the perceptible mass, without concern for the compartments of our sciences, that is to say, for our means of action.

Without the slightest effort life creates a very "generalized" relativity.

It does not separate its geometry from its physics but endows each species with all the axioms and more or less "differential" *invariants* it needs to maintain a satisfactory harmony between the individual and the world around it. . . .

Clearly the rather secretive individual, addicted to asymmetry and torsion, who fashions a shell, has long abandoned the postulates that were Euclid's idols. Euclid believed that a stick keeps its length under any circumstances; that one can toss it up to the moon or twirl it about, and that neither distance, movement, nor change of orientation will detract from its clear conscience as an infallible unit of measurement. Euclid worked on a sheet of papyrus and traced figures that *to him seemed similar*; he saw no other obstacle to the growth of his triangles than the size of his papyrus. He was very far—two thousand light-years—from imagining that one day a certain Mr. Einstein would develop an octopus capable of ensnaring and devouring all geometry; and not only geometry, but time, matter, and gravitation, and a good many other things unsuspected by the Greeks, which, ground up and digested together, provide a dainty dish for the all-powerful *Mollusk of Reference*. This monstrous cephalopod need only count its tentacles and the suckers on each tentacle to feel that it is "master of itself and of the Universe."

But millions of years before Euclid and the illustrious Einstein, our hero, who is only a simple gastropod and has no tentacles, was himself obliged to solve some rather knotty problems. He had his shell to make—and his living. These are very different activities. Spinoza made spectacles. More than one poet has been an excellent civil servant. And possibly two trades practiced by one and the same individual can be kept reasonably separate. After all, what do we mean by *the same*? But we are speaking of a mollusk and we know nothing of his inner unity.

What are our findings? The internal construction is organized in a mysterious way. The secretory cells of the mantle and its edge operate in *rhythm*: the turns of the spiral progress; the walls are built; the nacre is deposited on them. But the microscope does not show what creates the harmony between the different points and different moments in this simultaneous progress of the whole periphery. The pattern of the colored furrows or bands that curve round the shell, and of the bands that intersect them, reminds us of "geodesic lines" and suggests the existence of some sort of "field of force" which we are unable to discern, but whose action would give the growth of the shell the irresistible torsion and rhythmic progress we observe in the finished product. Nothing we know of our own actions enables us to imagine what it may be that so gracefully modulates these surfaces, element by element, row by row, without other tools than those contained in the thing that is being fashioned; what it may be that so miraculously harmonizes and adjusts the curves, and finishes the work with a boldness, an ease, a precision which the most graceful creations of the potter or bronze founder are far from equaling. Our artists do not derive the material of their works from their own substance, and the form for which they strive springs from a specialized application of their mind, which can be *completely* disengaged from their being. Perhaps what we call *perfection* in art (which all do not strive for and some disdain) is only a sense of desiring or finding in a human work the sureness of execution, the inner necessity, the indissoluble bond between form and material that are revealed to us by the humblest of shells.

But our mollusk has other things to do besides this rhythmic distillation of his marvelous covering. He must supply the mantle which constructs the durable shell with energy and mineral salts; from the resources of his environment he must gather what perhaps, some day in the future, will be a frag-

ment of the foundations of a continent. Thus he must sometimes forsake his secret, subtle work of emanation and venture
out into the world, bearing his dwelling, his den, his fortress,
his masterpiece, like a wondrous tiara or turban. At once he is
involved in an entirely new set of circumstances. Here we
are tempted to credit him with a genius of the first order, for
he must confront two utterly different realities accordingly
as he closets himself in laborious, concentrated aloofness to
co-ordinate the efforts of his mantle, or as he ventures out
into the vast world and explores it, his eyes groping, his
feelers questioning, his firm *foot* with its broad viscous sole
supporting the majestic traveler and his sanctuary, rocking
them to and fro. How is he to combine, under a single set
of principles and laws, the two kinds of consciousness, the
two forms of space and time, the two geometries, and the
two systems of mechanics with which these two modes of
existence and experience alternately confront him? Perhaps
when he is all inside, he takes his spiral arc for his "straight
line," just as we take for ours a little arc of a meridian, or,
unaware that its trajectory is relative, a ray of light. And
perhaps he measures his private "time" by the sensation of
secreting a little prism of calcite and putting it in place. But
once he leaves his shelter and takes up his outside life, heaven
only knows what hypotheses or conventional rule of thumb
he lives by! . . . The mobility of the feelers; the touch, sight,
and movement associated with the exquisite elasticity of the
wonderfully sensitive shafts by which they are oriented, the
perfect retractility of the body of which the whole shell is an
appendage, the binding obligation to skip over nothing, to
adhere strictly to his path—all this is bound to move a gifted
mollusk, when he withdraws from the world and buttons up
once more in his case of nacre, to profound meditations and

radical synthetic abstractions. He will need what Laplace rather pompously called "the resources of the most sublime analysis" if he is to adjust the experience of his worldly life to that of his private life. He will have to reason profoundly if he is to discover "the unity of nature" underlying the two so different aspects between which his organization compels him to alternate.

But do we not, ourselves, fluctuate between "the world of bodies" and that of the "mind"; and all our philosophy, is it not an eternal quest for the formula that will efface the difference between them and reconcile two divergent orders, two systems of time, two modes of transformation, two types of "forces," in short, two frames of reference which thus far have seemed, the more closely we examine them, to become more and more distinct, though concomitantly more interwoven?

In a more immediate order of things, far from all metaphysics, do we not make ourselves at home amid the most irreconcilable disparity of sensory experience; do we not, for example, accustom ourselves to a visual and an auditory world which resemble each other in no way and which, if we thought about it, would give us a perpetual impression of perfect incoherence? Of course we say that such an impression is effaced, fused as it were, by custom and habit, and that the parts join to form a single "reality." . . . But with this we are not saying very much.

I shall throw away this thing that I have found as one throws away a cigarette stub. This sea shell has *served* me, suggesting by turns what I am, what I know, and what I do not know. . . . Just as Hamlet, picking up a skull in the rich earth and bring-

ing it close to his living face, finds a gruesome image of himself, and enters upon a meditation without issue, bounded on
all sides by a circle of consternation, so beneath the human
eye, this little, hollow, spiral-shaped calcareous body summons up a number of thoughts, all inconclusive. . . .

Poetry and Abstract Thought

THE IDEA of Poetry is often contrasted with that of Thought, and particularly "Abstract Thought." People say "Poetry and Abstract Thought" as they say Good and Evil, Vice and Virtue, Hot and Cold. Most people, without thinking any further, believe that the analytical work of the intellect, the efforts of will and precision in which it implicates the mind, are incompatible with that freshness of inspiration, that flow of expression, that grace and fancy which are the signs of poetry and which reveal it at its very first words. If a poet's work is judged profound, its profundity seems to be of a quite different order from that of a philosopher or a scientist. Some people go so far as to think that even meditation on his art, the kind of exact reasoning applied to the cultivation of roses, can only harm a poet, since the principal and most charming object of his desire must be to communicate the impression of a newly and happily born state of creative emotion which, through surprise and pleasure, has the power to remove the poem once and for all from any further criticism.

This opinion may possibly contain a grain of truth, though its simplicity makes me suspect it to be of scholarly origin. I feel we have learned and adopted this antithesis without reflection, and that we now find it firmly fixed in our mind, as a verbal contrast, as though it represented a clear and real relationship between two well-defined notions. It must be admitted that that character always in a hurry to have done, whom we call *our mind*, has a weakness for this kind of simplification, which freely enables him to form all kinds of combinations and judgments, to display his logic, and to develop his rhetorical resources—in short, to carry out as brilliantly as possible his business of being a mind.

At all events, this classic contrast, crystallized, as it were, by language, has always seemed to me too abrupt, and at the same time too facile, not to provoke me to examine the things themselves more closely.

Poetry, Abstract Thought. That is soon said, and we immediately assume that we have said something sufficiently clear and sufficiently precise for us to proceed, without having to go back over our experiences; and to build a theory or begin a discussion using this contrast (so attractive in its simplicity) as pretext, argument, and substance. One could even fashion a whole metaphysics—or at the least a "psychology"—on this basis, and evolve for oneself a system of mental life, of knowledge, and of the invention and production of works of the mind, whose consequence would inevitably be the same terminological dissonance that had served as its starting point. . . .

For my part I have the strange and dangerous habit, in every subject, of wanting to begin at the beginning (that is, at my *own* beginning), which entails beginning again, going back over the whole road, just as though many others had not already mapped and traveled it. . . .

This is the road offered to us, or imposed on us, by *language*.

With every question, before making any deep examination of the content, I take a look at the language; I generally proceed like a surgeon who sterilizes his hands and prepares the area to be operated on. This is what I call *cleaning up the verbal situation*. You must excuse this expression equating the words and forms of speech with the hands and instruments of a surgeon.

I maintain that we must be careful of a problem's first contact with our minds. We should be careful of the first words a question utters in our mind. A new question arising in us is in a state of infancy; it stammers; it finds only strange terms, loaded with adventitious values and associations; it is forced to borrow these. But it thereby insensibly deflects our true need. Without realizing it we desert our original problem, and in the end we shall come to believe that we have chosen an opinion wholly our own, forgetting that our choice was exercised only on a mass of opinions that are the more or less blind work of other men and of chance. This is what happens with the programs of political parties, no one of which is (or can be) the one that would exactly match our temperament and our interests. If we choose one among them, we gradually become the man suited to that party and to that program.

Philosophical and aesthetic questions are so richly obscured by the quantity, diversity, and antiquity of researches, arguments, and solutions, all produced within the orbit of a very restricted vocabulary, of which each author uses the words according to his own inclinations, that taken as a whole such works give me the impression of a district in the classical Underworld especially reserved for deep thinkers. Here, are the Danaïdes, Ixions, and Sisyphuses, eternally laboring to fill bottomless casks and to push back the falling rock, that is, to redefine the same dozen words whose combinations form the treasure of Speculative Knowledge.

Allow me to add to these preliminary considerations one last remark and one illustration. Here is the remark: you have surely noticed the curious fact that a certain *word*, which is perfectly clear when you hear or use it in *everyday* speech, and which presents no difficulty when caught up in the rapidity of an ordinary sentence, becomes mysteriously cumbersome, offers a strange resistance, defeats all efforts at definition, the moment you withdraw it from circulation for separate study and try to find its meaning after taking away its temporary function. It is almost comic to inquire the exact meaning of a term that one uses constantly with complete satisfaction. For example: I stop the word *Time* in its flight. This word was utterly limpid, precise, honest, and faithful in its service as long as it was part of a remark and was uttered by someone who wished to say something. But here it is, isolated, caught on the wing. It takes its revenge. It makes us believe that it has more meanings than uses. It was only a *means*, and it has become an *end*, the object of a terrible philosophical desire. It turns into an enigma, an abyss, a torment of thought. . . .

It is the same with the word *Life* and all the rest.

This readily observed phenomenon has taken on great critical value for me. Moreover, I have drawn from it an illustration that, for me, nicely conveys this strange property of our verbal material.

Each and every word that enables us to leap so rapidly across the chasm of thought, and to follow the prompting of an idea that constructs its own expression, appears to me like one of those light planks which one throws across a ditch or a mountain crevasse and which will bear a man crossing it rapidly. But he must pass without weighing on it, without stopping—above all, he must not take it into his head to dance on the slender plank to test its resistance! . . . Otherwise the fragile bridge tips or breaks immediately, and all is hurled into the depths. Consult your own experience; and you will find that we understand each other, and ourselves, only thanks to our *rapid passage over words*. We must not lay stress upon them, or we shall see the clearest discourse dissolve into enigmas and more or less learned illusions.

But how are we to think—I should say *rethink*, study deeply whatever seems to merit deep study—if we hold language to be something essentially provisional, as a banknote or a check is provisional, what we call its "value" requiring us to forget its true nature, which is that of a piece of paper, generally dirty? The paper has passed through so many hands. . . . But words have passed through so many mouths, so many phrases, so many uses and abuses, that the most delicate precautions must be taken to avoid too much confusion in our minds between what we think and are trying to think, and what dictionaries, authors, and, for that matter, the whole human race since the beginning of language, want us to think. . . .

I shall therefore take care not to accept what the words *Poetry* and *Abstract Thought* suggest to me the moment they are pronounced. But I shall look into myself. There I shall seek my real difficulties and my actual observations of my real states; there I shall find my own sense of the rational and the irrational; I shall see whether the alleged antithesis exists and how it exists in a living condition. I confess that it is my habit, when dealing with problems of the mind, to distinguish between those which I might have invented and which represent a need truly felt by my mind, and the rest, which are other people's problems. Of the latter, more than one (say forty per cent) seem to me to be nonexistent, to be no more than apparent problems: *I do not feel them*. And as for the rest, more than one seem to me to be badly stated. . . . I do not say I am right. I say that I observe what occurs within myself when I attempt to replace the verbal formulas by values and meanings that are nonverbal, that are independent of the language used. I discover naïve impulses and images, raw products of my needs and of my personal experiences. *It is my life itself that is surprised,* and my life must, if it can, provide my answers, for it is only in the reactions of our life that the full force, and as it were the necessity, of our truth can reside. The thought proceeding from that life never uses for its own account certain words which seem to it fit only for external consumption; nor certain others whose depths are obscure and which may only deceive thought as to its real strength and value.

I have, then, noticed in myself certain states which I may well call *poetic,* since some of them were finally realized in poems. They came about from no apparent cause, arising from some accident or other; they developed according to their own nature, and consequently I found myself for a time jolted out of my habitual state of mind. Then, the cycle completed, I returned to the rule of ordinary exchanges between my life and my thought. But meanwhile *a poem had been made,* and in completing itself the cycle left something behind. This closed cycle is the cycle of an act which has, as it were, aroused and given external form to a poetic power. . . .

On other occasions I have noticed that some no less insignificant incident caused—or seemed to cause—a quite different excursion, a digression of another nature and with another result. For example, a sudden concatenation of ideas, an analogy, would strike me in much the way the sound of a horn in the heart of a forest makes one prick up one's ears, and virtually directs the co-ordinated attention of all one's muscles toward some point in the distance, among the leafy depths. But this time, instead of a poem, it was an analysis of the sudden intellectual sensation that was taking hold of me. It was not verses that were being formed more or less easily during this phase, but some proposition or other that was destined to be incorporated among my habits of thought, some formula that would henceforward serve as an instrument for further researches. . . .

I apologize for thus revealing myself to you; but in my opinion it is more useful to speak of what one has experienced than to pretend to a knowledge that is entirely impersonal, an observation with no observer. In fact there is no theory that is not a fragment, carefully prepared, of some autobiography.

I do not pretend to be teaching you anything at all. I will say nothing you do not already know; but I will, perhaps, say it in a different order. You do not need to be told that a poet is not always incapable of solving a *rule of three;* or that a logician is not always incapable of seeing in words something other than concepts, categories, and mere pretexts for syllogisms.

On this point I would add this paradoxical remark: if the logician could never be other than a logician, he would not, and could not, be a logician; and if the poet were never anything but a poet, without the slightest hope of being able to reason abstractly, he would leave no poetic traces behind him. I believe in all sincerity that if each man were not able to live a number of other lives besides his own, he would not be able to live his own life.

My experience has thus shown me that the same *self* can take very different forms, can become an abstract thinker or a poet, by successive specializations, each of which is a deviation from that entirely unattached state which is superficially in accord with exterior surroundings and which is the average state of our existence, the state of undifferentiated exchanges.

Let us first see in what may consist that initial and *invariably accidental* shock which will construct the poetic instrument within us, and above all, what are its effects. The problem can be put in this way: Poetry is an art of Language; certain combinations of words can produce an emotion that others do not produce, and which we shall call *poetic*. What kind of emotion is this?

I recognize it in myself by this: that all possible objects of the ordinary world, external or internal, beings, events, feelings, and actions, while keeping their usual appearance, are suddenly placed in an indefinable but wonderfully fitting relationship with the modes of our general sensibility. That is to say that these well-known things and beings—or rather the ideas that represent them—somehow change in value. They attract one another, they are connected in ways quite different from the ordinary; they become (if you will permit the expression) *musicalized*, resonant, and, as it were, harmonically related. The poetic universe, thus defined, offers extensive analogies with what we can postulate of the dream world.

Since the word *dream* has found its way into this talk, I shall say in passing that in modern times, beginning with Romanticism, there has arisen a fairly understandable confusion between the notion of the dream and that of poetry. Neither the dream nor the daydream is necessarily poetic; it may be so: but figures formed *by chance* are only *by chance* harmonious figures.

In any case, our memories of dreams teach us, by frequent and common experience, that our consciousness can be invaded, filled, entirely absorbed by the production of an *existence* in which objects and beings seem the same as those in the waking state; but their meanings, relationships, modes of variation and of substitution are quite different and doubt-less represent, like symbols or allegories, the immediate fluctuations of our *general* sensibility uncontrolled by the sensitivities of our *specialized* senses. In very much the same way the *poetic state* takes hold of us, develops, and finally disintegrates.

This is to say that the *state of poetry* is completely irregular, inconstant, involuntary, and fragile, and that we lose it, as we find it, *by accident*. But this state is not enough to make a poet, any more than it is enough to see a treasure in a dream to find it, on waking, sparkling at the foot of one's bed.

A poet's function—do not be startled by this remark—is not to experience the poetic state: that is a private affair. His function is to create it in others. The poet is recognized—or at least everyone recognizes his own poet—by the simple fact that he causes his reader to become "inspired." Positively speaking, inspiration is a graceful attribute with which the reader endows his poet: the reader sees in us the transcendent merits of virtues and graces that develop in him. He seeks and finds in us the wondrous cause of his own wonder.

But poetic feeling and the artificial synthesis of this state in some work are two quite distinct things, as different as sensation and action. A sustained action is much more complex than any spontaneous production, particularly when it has to be carried out in a sphere as conventional as that of language. Here you see emerging through my explanations the famous ABSTRACT THOUGHT which custom opposes to POETRY. We shall come back to that in a moment. Meanwhile I should like to tell you a true story, so that you may feel as

I felt, and in a curiously clear way, the whole difference that exists between the poetic state or emotion, even creative and original, and the production of a work. It is a rather remarkable observation of myself that I made about a year ago.

I had left my house to relax from some tedious piece of work by walking and by a consequent change of scene. As I went along the street where I live, I was suddenly *gripped* by a rhythm which took possession of me and soon gave me the impression of some force outside myself. It was as though someone else were making use of my *living-machine*. Then another rhythm overtook and combined with the first, and certain strange *transverse* relations were set up between these two principles (I am explaining myself as best I can). They combined the movement of my walking legs and some kind of song I was murmuring, or rather which was being murmured *through me*. This composition became more and more complicated and soon in its complexity went far beyond anything I could reasonably produce with my ordinary, usable rhythmic faculties. The sense of strangeness that I mentioned became almost painful, almost disquieting. I am no musician; I am completely ignorant of musical technique; yet here I was, prey to a development in several parts more complicated than any poet could dream. I argued that there had been an error of person, that this grace had descended on the wrong head, since I could make no use of a gift which for a musician would doubtless have assumed value, form, and duration, while these parts that mingled and separated offered me in vain a composition whose cunningly organized sequence amazed my ignorance and reduced it to despair.

After about twenty minutes the magic suddenly vanished, leaving me on the bank of the Seine, as perplexed as the duck in the fable, that saw a swan emerge from the egg she had hatched. As the swan flew away, my surprise changed to reflection. I knew that walking often induces in me a quickened flow of ideas and that there is a certain reciprocity between my pace and my thoughts—my thoughts modify my pace; my pace provokes my thoughts—which after all is remarkable enough, but is fairly understandable. Our various "reaction periods" are doubtless synchronized, and it is interesting to have to admit that a reciprocal modification is possible between a form of action which is purely muscular and a varied production of images, judgments, and reasonings.

But in the case I am speaking of, my movement in walking became in my consciousness a very subtle system of rhythms, instead of instigating those images, interior words, and potential actions which one calls *ideas*. As for ideas, they are things of a species familiar to me; they are things that I can note, provoke, and handle. . . . *But I cannot say the same of my unexpected rhythms.*

What was I to think? I supposed that mental activity while walking must correspond with a general excitement exerting itself in the region of my brain; this excitement satisfied and relieved itself as best it could, and so long as its energy was expended, it mattered little whether this was on ideas, memories, or rhythms unconsciously hummed. On that day, the energy was expended in a rhythmical intuition that developed before the awakening in my consciousness of *the person who knows that he does not know music.* I imagine it is the same as when *the person who knows he cannot fly* has not yet become active in the man who dreams he is flying.

I apologize for this long and true story—as true, that is, as a story of this kind can be. Notice that everything I have said, or tried to say, happened in relation to what we call the *External World,* what we call *Our Body,* and what we call *Our*

Mind, and requires a kind of vague collaboration between these three great powers.

Why have I told you this? In order to bring out the profound difference existing between spontaneous production by the mind—or rather by our *sensibility as a whole*—and the fabrication of works. In my story, the substance of a musical composition was freely given to me, but the organization which would have seized, fixed, and reshaped it was lacking. The great painter Degas often repeated to me a very true and simple remark by Mallarmé. Degas occasionally wrote verses, and some of those he left were delightful. But he often found great difficulty in this work accessory to his painting. (He was, by the way, the kind of man who would bring all possible difficulty to any art whatever.) One day he said to Mallarmé: "Yours is a hellish craft. I can't manage to say what I want, and yet I'm full of ideas. . . ." And Mallarmé answered: "My dear Degas, one does not make poetry with ideas, but with *words*."

Mallarmé was right. But when Degas spoke of ideas, he was, after all, thinking of inner speech or of images, which might have been expressed in *words*. But these words, these secret phrases which he called ideas, all these intentions and perceptions of the mind, do not make verses. There is something else, then, a modification, or a transformation, sudden or not, spontaneous or not, laborious or not, which must necessarily intervene between the thought that produces ideas—that activity and multiplicity of inner questions and solutions—and, on the other hand, that discourse, so different from ordinary speech, which is verse, which is so curiously ordered, which answers no need *unless it be the need it must itself create*, which never speaks but of absent things or of things profoundly and secretly felt: strange discourse, as

though made by someone *other* than the speaker and addressed to someone *other* than the listener. In short, it is a
language within a language.

Let us look into these mysteries.

Poetry is an art of language. But language is a practical
creation. It may be observed that in all communication between men, certainty comes only from practical acts and from
the verification which practical acts give us. *I ask you for a light.
You give me a light:* you have understood me.

But in asking me for a light, you were able to speak those
few unimportant words with a certain intonation, a certain
tone of voice, a certain inflection, a certain languor or brisk-
ness perceptible to me. I have understood your words, since
without even thinking I handed you what you asked for—a
light. But the matter does not end there. The strange thing:
the sound and as it were the features of your little sentence
come back to me, echo within me, as though they were
pleased to be there; I, too, like to hear myself repeat this little
phrase, which has almost lost its meaning, which has stopped
being of use, and which can yet go on living, though with
quite another life. It has acquired a value; and has acquired it
at the expense of its finite significance. It has created the need to
be heard again. . . . Here we are on the very threshold of the
poetic state. This tiny experience will help us to the discovery
of more than one truth.

It has shown us that language can produce effects of two
quite different kinds. One of them tends to bring about the
complete negation of language itself. I speak to you, and if
you have understood my words, those very words are abolished. If you have understood, it means that the words have
vanished from your minds and are replaced by their counterpart, by images, relationships, impulses; so that you have

within you the means to retransmit these ideas and images in a language that may be very different from the one you received. *Understanding* consists in the more or less rapid replacement of a system of sounds, intervals, and signs by something quite different, which is, in short, a modification or interior reorganization of the person to whom one is speaking. And here is the counterproof of this proposition: the person who does not understand *repeats* the words, or *has them repeated* to him.

Consequently, the perfection of a discourse whose sole aim is comprehension obviously consists in the ease with which the words forming it are transformed into something quite different: the *language* is transformed first into *non-language* and then, if we wish, into a form of language differing from the original form.

In other terms, in practical or abstract uses of language, the form—that is the physical, the concrete part, the very act of speech—does not last; it does not outlive understanding; it dissolves in the light; it has acted; it has done its work; it has brought about understanding; it has lived.

But on the other hand, the moment this concrete form takes on, by an effect of its own, such importance that it asserts itself and makes itself, as it were, respected; and not only remarked and respected, but desired and therefore repeated—then something new happens: we are insensibly transformed and ready to live, breathe, and think in accordance with a rule and under laws which are no longer of the practical order—that is, nothing that may occur in this state will be resolved, finished, or abolished by a specific act. We are entering the poetic universe.

Permit me to support this notion of a *poetic universe* by referring to a similar notion that, being much simpler, is easier to explain: the notion of a *musical universe*. I would ask you to make a small sacrifice: limit yourselves for a moment to your faculty of hearing. One simple sense, like that of hearing, will offer us all we need for our definition and will absolve us from entering into all the difficulties and subtleties to which the conventional structure and historical complex-ities of ordinary language would lead us. We live by ear in the world of noises. Taken as a whole, it is generally incohe-rent and irregularly supplied by all the mechanical incidents which the ear may interpret as it can. But the same ear isolates from this chaos a group of noises particularly remarkable and simple—that is, easily recognizable by our sense of hearing and furnishing it with points of reference. These elements have relations with one another which we sense as we do the elements themselves. The interval between two of these privileged noises is as clear to us as each of them. These are the *sounds*, and these units of sonority tend to form clear combinations, successive or simultaneous implications, series, and intersections which one may term *intelligible:* this is why abstract possibilities exist in music. But I must return to my subject.

I will confine myself to saying that the contrast between noise and sound is the contrast between pure and impure, order and disorder; that this differentiation between pure sensations and others has permitted the constitution of music; that it has been possible to control, unify, and codify this constitution, thanks to the intervention of physical science, which knows how to adjust measure to sensation so as to obtain the important result of teaching us to produce this sonorous sensation consistently, and in a continuous and identical fashion, by instruments that are, in reality, *measuring instruments*.

The musician is thus in possession of a perfect system of

well-defined means which exactly match sensations with acts. From this it results that music has formed a domain absolutely its own. The world of the art of music, a world of sounds, is distinct from the world of noises. Whereas a *noise* merely rouses in us some isolated event—a dog, a door, a motor car —*a sound evokes, of itself, the musical universe.* If, in this hall where I am speaking to you and where you hear the noise of my voice, a tuning fork or a well-tempered instrument began to vibrate, you would at once, as soon as you were affected by this pure and exceptional noise that cannot be confused with others, have the feeling of a beginning, the beginning of a world; a quite different atmosphere would immediately be created, a new order would arise, and you yourselves would unconsciously *organize* yourselves to receive it. The musical universe, therefore, was within you, with all its associations and proportions—as in a saturated salt solution a crystalline universe awaits the molecular shock of a minute crystal in order *to declare itself.* I dare not say: the crystalline idea of such a system awaits. . . .

And here is the counter proof of our little experiment: if, in a concert hall dominated by a resounding symphony, a chair happens to fall, someone coughs, or a door shuts, we immediately have the impression of a kind of rupture. Something indefinable, something like a spell or a Venetian glass, has been broken or cracked. . . .

The poetic universe is not created so powerfully or so easily. It exists, but the poet is deprived of the immense advantages possessed by the musician. He does not have before him, ready for the uses of beauty, a body of resources expressly made for his art. He has to borrow *language*—the voice of the public, that collection of traditional and irrational terms and rules, oddly created and transformed, oddly codified, and very variedly understood and pronounced. Here there is no physicist who has determined the relations between these elements; no tuning forks, no metronomes, no inventors of scales or theoreticians of harmony. Rather, on the contrary, the phonetic and semantic fluctuations of vocabulary. Nothing pure; but a mixture of completely incoherent auditive and psychic stimuli. Each word is an instantaneous coupling of a *sound* and a *sense* that have no connection with each other. Each sentence is an act so complex that I doubt whether anyone has yet been able to provide a tolerable definition of it. As for the use of the resources of language and the modes of this action, you know what diversity there is, and what confusion sometimes results. A discourse can be logical, packed with sense, but devoid of rhythm and measure. It can be pleasing to the ear, yet completely absurd or insignificant; it can be clear, yet useless; vague, yet delightful. But to grasp its strange multiplicity, which is no more than the multiplicity of life itself, it suffices to name all the sciences which have been created to deal with this diversity, each to study one of its aspects. One can analyze a text in many different ways, for it falls successively under the jurisdiction of phonetics, semantics, syntax, logic, rhetoric, philology, not to mention metrics, prosody, and etymology. . . .

So the poet is at grips with this verbal matter, obliged to speculate on sound and sense at once, and to satisfy not only harmony and musical timing but all the various intellectual and aesthetic conditions, not to mention the conventional rules. . . .

You can see what an effort the poet's undertaking would require if he had *consciously* to solve all these problems. . . .

It is always interesting to try to reconstruct one of our complex activities, one of those complete actions which demand a specialization at once mental, sensuous, and motor, supposing that in order to accomplish this act we were obliged to understand and organize all the functions that we know play their part in it. Even if this attempt, at once imaginative and analytical, is clumsy, it will always teach us something. As for myself, who am, I admit, much more attentive to the formation or fabrication of works than to the works themselves, I have a habit, or obsession, of appreciating works only as actions. In my eyes a poet is a man who, as a result of a certain incident, undergoes a hidden transformation. He leaves his ordinary condition of general disposability, and I see taking shape in him an agent, a living system for producing verses. As among animals one suddenly sees emerging a capable hunter, a nest maker, a bridge builder, a digger of tunnels and galleries, so in a man one sees a composite organization declare itself, bending its functions to a specific piece of work. Think of a very small child: the child we have all been bore many possibilities within him. After a few months of life he has learned, at the same or almost the same time, to speak and to walk. He has acquired two types of action. That is to say that he now possesses two kinds of potentiality from which the accidental circumstances of each moment will draw what they can, in answer to his varying needs and imaginings.

Having learned to use his legs, he will discover that he can not only walk, but run; and not only walk and run, but dance. This is a great event. He has at that moment both invented and discovered a kind of *secondary use* for his limbs, a generalization of his formula of movement. In fact, whereas walking is after all a rather dull and not easily perfectible action, this new form of action, the Dance, admits of an infinite number of creations and variations or *figures*.

But will he not find an analogous development in speech?

He will explore the possibilities of his faculty of speech; he will discover that more can be done with it than to ask for jam and deny his little sins. He will grasp the power of reasoning; he will invent stories to amuse himself when he is alone; he will repeat to himself words that he loves for their strangeness and mystery.

So, parallel with *Walking* and *Dancing*, he will acquire and distinguish the divergent types, *Prose and Poetry*.

This parallel has long struck and attracted me; but someone saw it before I did. According to Racan, Malherbe made use of it. In my opinion it is more than a simple comparison. I see in it an analogy as substantial and pregnant as those found in physics when one observes the identity of formulas that represent the measurement of seemingly very different phenomena. Here is how our comparison develops.

Walking, like prose, has a definite aim. It is an act directed at something we wish to reach. Actual circumstances, such as the need for some object, the impulse of my desire, the state of my body, my sight, the terrain, etc., which order the manner of walking, prescribe its direction and its speed, and give it a *definite end*. All the characteristics of walking derive from these instantaneous conditions, which combine *in a novel way* each time. There are no movements in walking that are not special adaptations, but, each time, they are abolished and, as it were, absorbed by the accomplishment of the act, by the attainment of the goal.

The dance is quite another matter. It is, of course, a system of actions; but of actions whose end is in themselves. It goes nowhere. If it pursues an object, it is only an ideal object, a state, an enchantment, the phantom of a flower, an extreme of life, a smile—which forms at last on the face of the one who summoned it from empty space.

It is therefore not a question of carrying out a limited

operation whose end is situated somewhere in our surround-ings, but rather of creating, maintaining, and exalting a certain *state*, by a periodic movement that can be executed on the spot; a movement which is almost entirely dissociated from sight, but which is stimulated and regulated by auditive rhythms.

But please note this very simple observation, that however different the dance may be from walking and utilitarian movements, it uses the same organs, the same bones, the same muscles, only differently co-ordinated and aroused.

Here we come again to the contrast between prose and poetry. Prose and poetry use the same words, the same syntax, the same forms, and the same sounds or tones, but differently co-ordinated and differently aroused. Prose and poetry are therefore distinguished by the difference between certain links and associations which form and dissolve in our psychic and nervous organism, whereas the components of these modes of functioning are identical. This is why one should guard against reasoning about poetry as one does about prose. What is true of one very often has no meaning when it is sought in the other. But here is the great and decisive difference. When the man who is walking has reached his goal—as I said—when he has reached the place, book, fruit, the object of his desire (which desire drew him from his repose), this possession at once entirely annuls his whole act; the effect swallows up the cause, the end absorbs the means; and, whatever the act, only the result remains. It is the same with utilitarian language: the language I use to express my design, my desire, my command, my opinion; this language, when it has served its purpose, evaporates almost as it is heard. I have given it forth to perish, to be radically transformed into something else in your mind; and I shall know that I was *understood* by the remarkable fact that my speech no longer exists: it has been completely replaced by its *meaning*—that is, by images, impulses, reactions, or acts that belong to you: in short, by an interior modification in you.

As a result the perfection of this kind of language, whose sole end is to be understood, obviously consists in the ease with which it is transformed into something altogether different.

The poem, on the other hand, does not die for having lived: it is expressly designed to be born again from its ashes and to become endlessly what it has just been. Poetry can be recognized by this property, that it tends to get itself reproduced in its own form: it stimulates us to reconstruct it identically.

That is an admirable and uniquely characteristic property.

I should like to give you a simple illustration. Think of a pendulum oscillating between two symmetrical points. Suppose that one of these extremes represents *form:* the concrete characteristics of the language, sound, rhythm, accent, tone, movement—in a word, the *Voice* in action. Then associate with the other point, the acnode of the first, all significant values, images and ideas, stimuli of feeling and memory, virtual impulses and structures of understanding—in short, everything that makes the *content*, the meaning of a discourse. Now observe the effect of poetry on yourselves. You will find that at each line the meaning produced within you, far from destroying the musical form communicated to you, recalls it. The living pendulum that has swung from *sound* to *sense* swings back to its felt point of departure, as though the very sense which is present to your mind can find no other outlet or expression, no other answer, than the very music which gave it birth.

So between the form and the content, between the sound

and the sense, between the poem and the state of poetry, a symmetry is revealed, an equality between importance, value, and power, which does not exist in prose; which is contrary to the law of prose—the law which ordains the inequality of the two constituents of language. The essential principle of the mechanics of poetry—that is, of the conditions for producing the poetic state by words—seems to me to be this harmonious exchange between expression and impression.

I introduce here a slight observation which I shall call "philosophical," meaning simply that we could do without it.

Our poetic pendulum travels from our sensation toward some idea or some sentiment, and returns toward some memory of the sensation and toward the potential act which could reproduce the sensation. Now, whatever is sensation is essentially *present*. There is no other definition of the present except sensation itself, which includes, perhaps, the impulse to action that would modify that sensation. On the other hand, whatever is properly thought, image, sentiment, is always, in some way, *a production of absent things*. Memory is the substance of all thought. Anticipation and its gropings, desire, planning, the projection of our hopes, of our fears, are the main interior activity of our being.

Thought is, in short, the activity which causes what does not exist to come alive in us, lending to it, whether we will or no, our present powers, making us take the part for the whole, the image for reality, and giving us the illusion of seeing, acting, suffering, and possessing independently of our dear old body, which we leave with its cigarette in an armchair until we suddenly retrieve it when the telephone rings or, no less strangely, when our stomach demands provender. . . .

Between Voice and Thought, between Thought and

Voice, between Presence and Absence, oscillates the poetic pendulum.

The result of this analysis is to show that the value of a poem resides in the indissolubility of sound and sense. Now this is a condition that seems to demand the impossible. There is no relation between the sound and the meaning of a word. The same thing is called HORSE in English, HIPPOS in Greek, EQUUS in Latin, and CHEVAL in French; but no manipulation of any of these terms will give me an idea of the animal in question; and no manipulation of the idea will yield me any of these words—otherwise, we should easily know all languages, beginning with our own.

Yet it is the poet's business to give us the feeling of an intimate union between the word and the mind.

This must be considered, strictly speaking, a marvelous result. I say *marvelous*, although it is not exceptionally rare. I use *marvelous* in the sense we give that word when we think of the miracles and prodigies of ancient magic. It must not be forgotten that for centuries poetry was used for purposes of enchantment. Those who took part in these strange operations had to believe in the power of the word, and far more in the efficacy of its sound than in its significance. Magic formulas are often without meaning; but it was never thought that their power depended on their intellectual content.

Let us listen to lines like these:

Mère des souvenirs, maîtresse des maîtresses...

or

Sois sage, ô ma Douleur, et tiens-toi plus tranquille. ...

These words work on us (or at least on some of us) without telling us very much. They tell us, perhaps, that they have

158

nothing to tell us; that, by the very means which usually tell us something, they are exercising a quite different function. They act on us like a chord of music. The impression produced depends largely on resonance, rhythm, and the number of syllables; but it is also the result of the simple bringing together of meanings. In the second of these lines the accord between the vague ideas of Wisdom and Grief, and the tender solemnity of the tone produce the inestimable value of a spell: the *momentary being* who made that line could not have done so had he been in a state where the form and the content occurred separately to his mind. On the contrary, he was in a special phase in the domain of his psychic existence, a phase in which the sound and the meaning of the word acquire or keep an equal importance—which is excluded from the habits of practical language, as from the needs of abstract language. The state in which the inseparability of sound and sense, in which the desire, the expectation, the possibility of their intimate and indissoluble fusion are required and sought or given, and sometimes anxiously awaited, is a comparatively rare state. It is rare, firstly because all the exigencies of life are against it; secondly because it is opposed to the crude simplifying and specializing of verbal notations.

But this state of inner modification, in which all the properties of our language are indistinctly but harmoniously summoned, is not enough to produce that complete object, that compound of beauties, that collection of happy chances for the mind which a noble poem offers us.

From this state we obtain only fragments. All the precious things that are found in the earth, gold, diamonds, uncut stones, are there scattered, strewn, grudgingly hidden in a quantity of rock or sand, where chance may sometimes uncover them. These riches would be nothing without the human labor that draws them from the massive night where they were sleeping, assembles them, alters and organizes them into ornaments. These fragments of metal embedded in formless matter, these oddly shaped crystals, must owe all their luster to intelligent labor. It is a labor of this kind that the true poet accomplishes. Faced with a beautiful poem, one can indeed feel that it is most unlikely that any man, however gifted, could have improvised without a backward glance, with no other effort than that of writing or dictating, such a simultaneous and complete system of lucky finds. Since the traces of effort, the second thoughts, the changes, the amount of time, the bad days, and the distaste have now vanished, effaced by the supreme return of a mind over its work, some people, seeing only the perfection of the result, will look on it as due to a sort of magic that they call INSPIRATION. They thus make of the poet a kind of temporary *medium*. If one were strictly to develop this doctrine of pure inspiration, one would arrive at some very strange results. For example, one would conclude that the poet, since he merely transmits what he receives, merely delivers to unknown people what he has taken from the unknown, has no need to understand what he writes, which is dictated by a mysterious voice. He could write poems in a language he did not know. . . .

In fact, the poet has indeed a kind of spiritual energy of a special nature: it is manifested in him and reveals him to himself in certain moments of infinite worth. Infinite for him. . . . I say, *infinite for him*, for, alas, experience shows us that these moments which seem to us to have a universal value are sometimes without a future, and in the end make us ponder on this maxim: *what is of value for one person only has no value*. This is the iron law of Literature.

But every true poet is necessarily a first-rate critic. If one doubts this, one can have no idea of what the work of the mind is: that struggle with the inequality of moments, with chance associations, lapses of attention, external distractions. The mind is terribly variable, deceptive and self-deceiving, fertile in insoluble problems and illusory solutions. How could a remarkable work emerge from this chaos if this chaos that contains everything did not also contain some serious chances to know oneself and to choose within oneself whatever is worth taking from each moment and using carefully?

That is not all. Every true poet is much more capable than is generally known of right reasoning and abstract thought.

But one must not look for his real philosophy in his more or less philosophical utterances. In my opinion, the most authentic philosophy lies not so much in the objects of our reflection as in the very act of thought and in its handling. Take from metaphysics all its pet or special terms, all its traditional vocabulary, and you may realize that you have not impoverished the thought. Indeed, you may perhaps have eased and freshened it, and you will have got rid of other people's problems, so as to deal only with your own difficulties, your surprises that owe nothing to anyone, and whose intellectual spur you feel actually and directly.

It has often happened, however, as literary history tells us, that poetry has been made to enunciate theses or hypotheses and that the *complete* language which is its own—the language whose *form*, that is to say the action and sensation of the *Voice*, is of the same power as the *content*, that is to say the eventual modification of a *mind*—has been used to communicate "abstract" ideas, which are on the contrary independent of their form, or so we believe. Some very great poets have occasionally attempted this. But whatever may be the talent which exerts itself in this very noble undertaking, it cannot prevent the attention given to following the ideas from competing with the attention that follows the song. The DE RERUM NATURA is here in conflict with the nature of things. The state of mind of the reader of poems is not the state of mind of the reader of pure thought. The state of mind of a man dancing is not that of a man advancing through difficult country of which he is making a topographical survey or a geological prospectus.

I have said, nevertheless, that the poet has his abstract thought and, if you like, his philosophy; and I have said that it is at work in his very activity as a poet. I said this because I have observed it, in myself and in several others. Here, as elsewhere, I have no other reference, no other claim or excuse, than recourse to my own experience or to the most common observation.

Well, every time I have worked as a poet, I have noticed that my work exacted of me not only that presence of the poetic universe I have spoken of, but many reflections, decisions, choices, and combinations, without which all possible gifts of the Muses, or of Chance, would have remained like precious materials in a workshop without an architect. Now an architect is not himself necessarily built of precious materials. In so far as he is an architect of poems, a poet is quite different from what he is as a producer of those precious elements of which all poetry should be composed, but whose composition is separate and requires an entirely different mental effort.

One day someone told me that lyricism is enthusiasm, and that the odes of the great lyricists were written at a single stroke, at the speed of the voice of delirium, and with the wind of inspiration blowing a gale. . . .

I replied that he was quite right; but that this was not a

privilege of poetry alone, and that everyone knew that in building a locomotive it is indispensable for the builder to work at eighty miles an hour in order to do his job.

A poem is really a kind of machine for producing the poetic state of mind by means of words. The effect of this machine is uncertain, for nothing is certain about action on other minds. But whatever may be the result, in its uncertainty, the construction of the machine demands the solution of many problems. If the term *machine* shocks you, if my mechanical comparison seems crude, please notice that while the composition of even a very short poem may absorb years, the action of the poem on the reader will take only a few minutes. In a few minutes the reader will receive his shock from discoveries, connections, glimmers of expression that have been accumulated during months of research, waiting, patience, and impatience. He may attribute much more to inspiration than it can give. He will imagine the kind of person it would take to create, without pause, hesitation, or revision, this powerful and perfect work which transports him into a world where things and people, passions and thoughts, sonorities and meanings proceed from the same energy, are transformed one into another, and correspond according to exceptional laws of harmony, for it can only be an exceptional form of stimulus that simultaneously produces the exaltation of our sensibility, our intellect, our memory, and our powers of verbal action, so rarely granted to us in the ordinary course of life.

Perhaps I should remark here that the execution of a poetic work—if one considers it as the engineer just mentioned would consider the conception and construction of his locomotive, that is, making explicit the problems to be solved—would appear impossible. In no other art is the number of conditions and independent functions to be co-ordinated so large. I will not inflict on you a detailed demonstration of this proposition. It is enough for me to remind you of what I said regarding sound and sense, which are linked only by pure convention, but which must be made to collaborate as effectively as possible. From their double nature words often make me think of those complex quantities which geometricians take such pleasure in manipulating.

Fortunately, some strange virtue resides in certain moments in certain people's lives which simplifies things and reduces the insurmountable difficulties I spoke of to the scale of human energies.

The poet awakes within man at an unexpected event, an outward or inward incident: a tree, a face, a "subject," an emotion, a word. Sometimes it is the will to expression that starts the game, a need to translate what one feels; another time, on the contrary, it is an element of form, the outline of an expression which seeks its origin, seeks a meaning within the space of my mind. . . . Note this possible duality in ways of getting started: either something wants to express itself, or some means of expression wants to be used.

My poem Le Cimetière marin began in me by a rhythm, that of a French line . . . of ten syllables, divided into four and six. I had as yet no idea with which to fill out this form. Gradually a few hovering words settled in it, little by little determining the subject, and my labor (a very long labor) was before me. Another poem, La Pythie, first appeared as an eight-syllable line whose sound came of its own accord. But this line implied a sentence, of which it was part, and this sentence, if it existed, implied many other sentences. A problem of this kind has an infinite number of solutions. But with poetry the musical and metrical conditions greatly restrict the indefiniteness. Here is what happened: my fragment acted like a living fragment, since, plunged in the (no doubt nourishing) surroundings of my desire and waiting thought, it proliferated, and engendered all that was lacking: several lines before and a great many lines after.

I apologize for having chosen my examples from my own little story: but I could hardly have taken them elsewhere.

Perhaps you think my conception of the poet and the poem rather singular. Try to imagine, however, what the least of our acts implies. Think of everything that must go on inside a man who utters the smallest intelligible sentence, and then calculate all that is needed for a poem by Keats or Baudelaire to be formed on an empty page in front of the poet.

Think, too, that of all the arts, ours is perhaps that which co-ordinates the greatest number of independent parts or factors: sound, sense, the real and the imaginary, logic, syntax, and the double invention of content and form . . . and all this by means of a medium essentially practical, perpetually changing, soiled, a maid of all work, *everyday language*, from which we must draw a pure, ideal Voice, capable of communicating without weakness, without apparent effort, without offense to the ear, and without breaking the ephemeral sphere of the poetic universe, an idea of some *self* miraculously superior to Myself.

Mallarmé

OF NECESSITY the most exalted project must also be the most difficult to conceive with precision, to undertake, and above all constantly to pursue.

The most difficult project to conceive, to undertake, and above all constantly to pursue in the arts, and especially poetry, is to *submit the production of a work to the conscious will* without this strict condition, deliberately adopted, being allowed to harm the essential qualities, the charms and the grace, which must be effectively carried by any work of art that aims to lead men's minds to the delights of the mind.

Stéphane Mallarmé was the first artist (and as yet doubtless the only one) who conceived and continued throughout his life to hold to the project of doing *what he wanted* in a domain of the mind wherein, by universal and time-honored consent, the action of the will is almost powerless, success being achieved by the favors of some fatality, or else of fickle gods who are unswayed by prayers and untouched by toil and the sacrifices of time and thought. There was, and there still remains, the mystery of *inspiration*, which is the name given to the spontaneous way speech or ideas are formed in a man and appear to him to be marvels that, of and by himself, he feels incapable of forming. He has, then, been *aided*.

From his twentieth year Mallarmé seems to have felt acutely that the poet's precarious condition was a degradation of the intelligence. He strove moreover to attain the highest purity, which implies accepting only the rarest offering of inspiration. When people speak of *sterility* in Mallarmé (and in some others), they forget that this indigence may be merely the effect of excessive scrupulousness and self-discipline. To obtain a particle of active substance tons of pitchblende have to be treated. At my own risk I shall say that Mallarmé brought the use of the will in art to a supreme degree of application and, going beyond the desire for inspiration which dictates a poetic moment, he came to desire the illumination which reveals the essence of poetry itself.

From 1865 no line he wrote fails to make us feel that its author had thought through language as if, on his own, he were reliving its multifarious invention; and, placing himself from that time on a summit where no one before him had even thought of settling, he remained until the day he died, intimately contemplating a truth whose proof he wished only to communicate by marvelous examples.

This revealed truth was destined, I believe, to initiate an unheard-of insight into poetry that would endow this creation by the human creature, this art of the mind, with a value quite different from the one accepted by naïve tradition and welcomed by the general sloth of the intellect. It was no longer a question of amusement, however sublime. Over and above what is Literature, Metaphysics, Religion, he had perceived the new duty that consisted in exercising and exalting the most spiritual of all the functions of the Word, which neither demonstrates, nor describes, nor represents anything at all; which therefore does not require, nor even allow, any confusion between reality and the verbal power of combining for some supreme end *the ideas that are born of words*.

In the poetry written up to his time he perceived the

fragments of a universal work that had been magnificently adumbrated but not rendered explicit, since none of the great men of the past had been able to conceive its whole or its guiding principle. He saw in the work he felt it to be his duty to write the essential undertaking of mankind, which he stated in familiar terms when he said that "everything would finally be expressed," that "the world had been created so as to end in a beautiful book," that "if there was a mystery of the world it could be contained in a *Figaro* editorial." These assertions proceeded from the substance of his thought, offering mere conversational glimpses of it. The conception was marvelously simple.

I want to picture a most rigorous state of meditation, fraught with anxiety, as though a life-or-death matter, yet inspired by that insignificant object insofar as life is concerned: poetry. To what could this passion of the intellect correspond— tormenting so deeply the man who has it, taking away his ability and, so to say, his right to sleep, making him blind to the most pressing demands of self-interest—if it were not to some Sovereign Good which he perhaps feels existing in himself and which a little more constancy, tension, and keen hope can at any moment allow him to grasp?

His singular consuming mysticism was destined to reach precision in a conception of language—I would almost say, a conception of the Word. In support of this sublimation of language, one may invoke all the uses of speech which do not satisfy needs of a practical nature and have no meaning except in relation to a wholly spiritual universe, deeply similar to the universe of poetry: prayer, invocation, incantation create the beings to whom they speak. Language thus becomes an instrument of "spirituality," that is to say, of the direct transmutation of desires and emotions into presences and powers that become "realities" in themselves, without the intervention of physically adequate means of action.

But neither poetic emotion nor creation is separate from the forms that engender them. Beauty is sovereign appearance. It results from some activity of ours which we bring to bear on a material we find around us. The artist in the material of language is generally happy to develop his talents from one work to the next, according as opportunity or chance gives them a certain subject or theme. Sometimes one fragment comes to his mind as if in sport, inciting him with the temptation or challenge to pursue and equal its perfection by way of his reflective powers. But, as soon as Mallarmé was in possession of his own firm conviction and poetic principle, that is to say, as soon as his *Truth* had *changed into his own true self*, he devoted himself without respite or reservation, without let or halt, to the extraordinary task of grasping in all its generality the nature of his art and, by a Cartesian analysis of the possibilities of language, of distinguishing all its means and classifying all its potential. On one occasion I compared this search to that which led from arithmetic, with its isolated processes, to the invention of algebra.

Language, when once we separate it from its practical uses, can receive certain sumptuary values that we call *philosophy*, or *poetry*, or otherwise. From this point the only question is to stimulate the need for these purposes. This is essential, as these new developments, these sophisticated formations, can be so aberrant that they produce amazement, and resistance on the part of the reader. But the more the need is created, and even aggravated, the more energy the reader finds to solve the problems of the text: from this he will often draw justifiable pride.

Mallarmé's transcendent view of the positive principles of poetry compelled him to undertake a labor of increasing precision which could have no end. Ordinary syntax appeared to him to exploit only a part of the combinations that are compatible with its rules: combinations whose simplicity allows the reader to skim over lines and to know the sense without becoming aware of language itself, just as one is not aware of the quality of a voice that speaks to us of business. Mallarmé sought entirely new arrangements with a daring and ingeniousness that made some exclaim in horror and others in admiration. He demonstrated, by astonishing proofs, that poetry must convey values that are equivalent to the meanings, sounds, the very appearance of words which, when brought unexpectedly together or fused with art, compose lines of poetry possessing a brilliance, fullness and resonance that are unprecedented. Here rhymes and alliteration on one hand, images, tropes, metaphors on the other, are no longer details and rhetorical ornaments that can be eliminated: they are substantial properties of the work. The subject is no longer the *cause* of the form: it is one of its effects. Each line becomes an entity having physical reasons for existence. It is a discovery, a sort of "intrinsic truth" that has been wrenched from the domain of chance. As for the world, all reality has no other excuse for existence except to offer the poet the chance to play a sublime match against it—a match that is lost in advance.

From *Poems in the Rough*

A B C

T THE BEGINNING there will be Sleep.
Animal locked deep in slumber; warm easy
mass mysteriously alone; shut Ark of life
bearing toward day my histories and
futures—you do not know me, you pre-
serve me, you are my ineffable continuance; your treasure is
my secret. Silence, my silence! Absence, my absence, O my
closed form, all other thought I abandon, to contemplate you
with full heart. You have made yourself an island of time,
you are a time that has become detached from that vast Time
in which your indefinite duration has the subsistence and
eternity of a smoke-ring. No deliberation has more of
strangeness or of piety; there is no more intimate marvel.
My love toward you is without limit. I lean over you, who
are I, and there is no communion between us. You await
me without knowing me and I am what you lack that you
may desire me. You are without defense. What ill you do
me with the noise of your breathing! I am too straitly
bound to your suspended sigh. Through this castoff mask
you exhale the murmur of stationary existence. I listen to my
frailty, and my stupidity stares me in the face. Man lost in
your own roads, a stranger in your own mansion, furnished
with alien hands that fetter your actions, cumbered with

arms and legs that shackle your movements, you do not even know the number of your members and ramble astray in their remoteness. Your very eyes have arranged their own darknesses, reflecting nothing at nothing, and their night sees but their night. Alas, how you yield to your matter, con-forming, dear thing of life, to the weight of what you are! Lying in such lassitude, with what simplicity do you offer me my shape of least resistance! But I am hazard, rupture, sign. I am your emanation and your angel. We are nothing without one another and yet between us is pure abyss. My vigor, in you thinly dispersed, in me is the hope of hope. A series of insensible modulations will draw my presence out of your absence; my energy, from your inertia; my will, from your fullness of equilibrium and prostration. I shall burst upon my members as a prodigy, I shall drive impotence out of my lands, I shall occupy my empire to its very toe-nails, your furthest outliers shall obey me and boldly we shall enter into the kingdom of our eyes. . . . But do not be reborn just yet. O rest still, rest *me*. . . . I am afraid of finding un-happy thoughts again. Let us wait separately until the simple monotonous churning of the machines of life has worn or swallowed every grain of the yet dividing hour. I was, you are, I shall be. . . . What will be is a gentle inference from what was. Therefore my anxious tenderness. . . . And now this Thing stirs, this form changes its form, the lips it seems to offer itself sketch out an act of discourse—a speech de-claimed by no one to no one, an appeal, a declaration of love, a begging, a mumble, all isolated in the universe, without connections, with no one and no other. . . . Tentative flashes, clumsy groanings toward self-resurrection. And now! here it is, *my* weariness, the miracle, solid objects; my cares, my projects, and the Day!

BOWLING over the shadows and the bed, tense, relaxed; parting, repelling, the billows of the uncertain sheet, the creature at last gets clear of their soothing chaos. The virtue of being Himself invades him. To be Himself seizes him like a surprise—sometimes happy, sometimes exceedingly not. How many wakings had better have been dreams!... But promptly unity claims the limbs, and from nape to heel an event becomes a man. *Up!* cries all my body, *you must break with the impossible!*...Up! The miracle of rising is achieved. What more simple, what less explicable, than this marvel, Balance? Get up now, walk, catch up with your attempts on space; follow your gaze that has taken flight into the visible; advance, step by countable step, into the sphere of lights and deeds; measure your strength against resisting bodies.... And you, a while I abandon you, Sweetness of un-being! I shall forget sleep till night. Good-bye till evening, mysterious games, monsters, murky scenes, and you, vain loves!... Now I divest myself of incognito. Ah, who can tell me how my self has been ferried, complete, across nonexistence or what vessel has carried me, lifeless, yet with all my life and mind, from one shore to the other of Nothing? How dares one sleep? Such trust in the loyalty of my body, in the still night, such faith in the order and constancy of the universe!... Tonight, Absence, you will return! Once again you will resume your few hours' throne, mysterious frightening impotence, quintessential weakness, unbreakable spell that chains the closed eyes to their images. . . . One cannot turn round, held fast in the soft ore of sleep, to catch him in the act—*the Monkey that shows the slides of Dream.* . . .

ALM, how calm the hour, how softly tinted the young end of night! Pushing back the shutters, to left, to right, with the quick breast-stroke of a swimmer, I launch into the ecstasies of space. It is pure, it is virgin, sweet, divine. I hail you, grandeur proffered to every act of gaze, beginning of perfect transparency! So vast a space, what an omen for the mind! I would bless you, O everything, if I knew the words.... Upon the balcony outlined above the leaves, upon the threshold of the prime hour and of all that is possible, I am sleeping and waking, I am night and day, protractedly I offer my unwearying love, my immeasurable timidity. The soul slakes its thirst at the cold spring of time, sips on shadows, swallows a mouthful of dawn, imagines herself a sleeping woman or an angel of light, falls into a study, is sad, flies in the shape of a bird up to that half-naked summit whose deep night-blue is pierced by a crag, all flesh and gold. Some orange tree breathes from the shade. Very high up a few exquisitely sharp but small stars linger. The moon is that chip of melting ice. Suddenly I am painfully aware that a gray-haired child is seeing old sorrows (half ghosts, half gods) in that celestial object of gleaming wasting matter, frail and cold in insensible dissolution. I look at it as though I were out of my heart. Long ago my youth pined, sensing the ascent of tears, at this same hour and under the same enchantment of the evaporating moon. My youth has seen this same morning, and I and my youth stand side by side. . . . Divided, how may I pray? How pray when another self is overhearing the prayer?—Therefore one must pray only in an unknown tongue. Render riddle for riddle, riddle to riddle. Lift up the mystery in you toward the mystery in itself. There is in you something equal to what is beyond you.

The Angel

A kind of angel was seated upon the rim of a well. He looked for his reflection and found that he was a Man, and in tears, and he was dumbfounded at the appearance in the naked water of this prey to an infinite sorrow.

(Or, if one wishes, it was a Sorrow in Man's shape that lacked a cause in crystal heaven.)

This face that was his, the grief that racked it, both seemed alien to him. So wretched an apparition aroused the interest of the fabulously pure spiritual matter of which he was composed; exercising it, asking questions that found no answers.

"O my Evil," *he said,* "what are you to me?"

He tried to smile: and wept. This infidelity of his features confounded his perfect intelligence; they had assumed an air of the particular and accidental, and their expression had become so unequal to the universality of his limpid knowing that he was mysteriously wounded in his unity.

"I have nothing to beweep," *he said;* "nor could that be possible to me."

The Movement of his Reason within the light of his eternal
expectancy found itself halted by a nameless query; for what would
create pain in our own imperfect natures does no more than arouse
questionings in essences that are absolute;—while indeed for us
every question too is or will be a sorrow.

"Then who is this," *he said,* "who loves himself to the point
of self-torment? I am all-knowing; and yet I see that I suffer.
This face is certainly my own, these tears are my tears. . . .
And yet am I not that power of clarity of which this face,
these tears, their cause and what might eliminate that cause,
are but the merest particles of its extent?"

But, in vain did these thoughts grow and multiply in all the
amplitude of the sphere of thought, in vain did the similes chime,
the contradictions announce themselves only to be resolved, in vain
was the miracle of clarity incessantly achieved, with each Idea
sparkling in the glitter thrown off by every other, jewels as they are
of the circlet of undivided knowing: nothing at all resembling a
harm offered itself to his faultless gaze, nothing by which to explain
this visage of sorrow, these tears that he saw through his tears.

"The purity that I am," *he said,* "Intelligence that effortlessly
consumes all creation, without anything affecting or altering
it in return, can recognize nothing of itself in this face of lamentations, in these eyes whose light, of which they were made,
is as it were softened by the moist imminence of their tears.

"And how can he so suffer, this lovely weeper who is mine,
is of me, considering that after all I see all that he is, being in
myself the knowledge of all things, and that the only sorrow
could be to be ignorant of something?

"O my astonishment," *he said,* "charming and sorrowing Head, is there then something other than light?"

Thus he questioned himself within the universe of the fabulously pure spiritual matter of which he was composed, and in which all the ideas dwelled equally distant both from one another and from himself, in so absolute a perfection of their harmony and a promptitude of their correspondences that he himself could almost have disappeared, leaving the system of their synchronous ordinance, coruscating like a diadem, to subsist independently in the ample sublime.

And for an eternity he never ceased to know and fail to understand.

The Bath

IN THE spotless gleaming sarcophagus, gentle is the lazy water, warm perfect spouse of the body's form.

The free and weightless nude assumes a position of total rest. All is easy in liquid, the unloosed legs as motile as the buoyant arms. The man lays down his height, flowing into the longness his highness has become. He stretches to dilate his spring to the utmost; he equals his sense of his power to let it go. Delicately he shifts from point to point of support; a finger props and lifts him; and his floating forces, half melted into the massy calm of the water, dream of algae and angels. The weight of the happily inundated flesh is almost as nothing; the heat of his blood is little different from that of the enclosing water and it searches freely into every cranny of his skin. The living body can scarcely distinguish itself from the amorphous body whose substance at once replaces it if it moves. An individual is sinking into the generalized saturation about him; someone feels himself insensibly dissolve. The physical man becomes no more than a happy dream of the vague intellect. The moment admires its soft reflection and sees its own limbs limpid in the water's glass. He who observes and speaks with himself is astonished at the size and symmetry of the frame of which he disposes, and the thinking head amuses itself with a foot, apparently very far away, which magically obeys. It sees a big toe rise from the deep, then flex, or a knee emerge, then plunge again in the transparency, like an ocean island that appears and vanishes at a geological caprice. The will itself and the general freedom of the being in the idle water become one.

There is perhaps in the flat steamy air a perfume whose complex bouquet stirs memories, caressing or coloring the vague desires of the nakedness there. His eyes lose focus or close. From lack of contacts time grows weak. The mind opens its wrists in a dream.

Laura

Since dawn she has been with me, Laura, alone in a private sphere.

Solitude I name this closed system where all things are alive. At this first hour that I bank neither with my days nor with my nights, but under a quite separate account, all that is about me shares my being there. The walls of my room are a circumscription created by my will. The light of the lamp is a sort of consciousness. The unscribbled sheet before me is clear and populous as a sleeplessness. I brood over my illumined hands as though they were the pieces of some game of innumerable gambits. The whole complex of every instant is present to my senses.

*

For Laura to appear, all things must be exactly thus, all must ensure my being ideally alone. Laura demands, as she also inhabits, a silence bristling with expectations, in which at times I become what I am awaiting. She catches the whispering between my daemon and my desire. Her white face is indistinct enough, but not her gaze. What a precision of power!...Wherever my eyes settle, they carry hers with them. And if I close my lids at last, her own are widely raised and asking. The power to question of these eyes transfixes me, and sometimes it happens that I cannot bear their unwavering depth any longer.

Then it is that the too enchanting fragrance of the dress that Laura wore, of the hands and of the hair of the real Laura, the Laura who was flesh, is born again from nothing; it dumbfounds my thinking, mingled or thickened with the bitter perfume of the dead leaves one burns at autumn's end, and I fall heartlong into a magic sadness.

Work

I love you, my Work, when you are truly mine. You, whom I recognize through all your changings. You alone, indeed, are truly I, when I master the living system of my nerves or of my thinking forces, when I feel myself enter by swiftest paths into my own durations.

I possess me if you possess me, I am the master if I am your slave and tool.

As the body of the rider mounted by his idea mounts his horse and is one with it.

As the boat between sail and tiller, with the wind, against the wind.

Oh do not let yourself be carried away (as so many have boasted of being) by the only power that is not yours!

From *Poems*
(with French texts)

La Fileuse

Lilia..., neque nent

Assise, la fileuse au bleu de la croisée
Où le jardin mélodieux se dodeline;
Le rouet ancien qui ronfle l'a grisée.

Lasse, ayant bu l'azur, de filer la câline
Chevelure, à ses doigts si faibles évasive,
Elle songe, et sa tête petite s'incline.

Un arbuste et l'air pur font une source vive
Qui, suspendue au jour, délicieuse arrose
De ses pertes de fleurs le jardin de l'oisive.

Une tige, où le vent vagabond se repose,
Courbe le salut vain de sa grâce étoilée,
Dédiant magnifique, au vieux rouet, sa rose.

Mais la dormeuse file une laine isolée;
Mystérieusement l'ombre frêle se tresse
Au fil de ses doigts longs et qui dorment, filée.

Le songe se dévide avec une paresse
Angélique, et sans cesse, au doux fuseau crédule,
La chevelure ondule au gré de la caresse...

Derrière tant de fleurs, l'azur se dissimule,
Fileuse de feuillage et de lumière ceinte:
Tout le ciel vert se meurt. Le dernier arbre brûle.

The Spinner

Lilies..., neither do they spin.

Seated the spinner in the blue of the windowpane
Where melodious the garden dawdles:
She is dazed by the humming of the ancient spinning wheel.

Sated with azure, weary of threading the wheedling
Hairs that evade fingers grown so feeble,
She is dreaming, and her small head leans.

Between them the pure air and a shrub contrive
A living spring, light-suspended, delectably sprinkling
The idle girl's garden with a squandering of petals.

A stem, where the vagabond wind comes to rest,
Bows with the vain curtsey of its starry grace,
Vowing its splendid rose to the antique spinning wheel.

But the sleeping girl is spinning a lonely thread:
Mysteriously the fragile shadow braids itself
Along the length of her slender sleeping fingers, divided.

The dream goes on unwinding with an angelic
Slowness, and ceaselessly, trustful of the soft spindle,
The hair undulates obedient to the caress....

Behind such throngs of flowers, the blue hides itself,
A spinner engirdled in foliage and light:
All the green sky is dying. The last tree blazes.

Ta sœur, la grande rose où sourit une sainte,
Parfume ton front vague au vent de son haleine
Innocente, et tu crois languir. . .Tu es éteinte

Au bleu de la croisée où tu filais la laine.

Your sister, the great rose with the smile of a saint,
Scents your vague brow with the wind of her innocent
Breath, and you feel you are fainting. . . . You have faded
   out

In the blue of the window where you were spinning wool.

Narcisse parle

Narcissae placandis manibus.

Ô frères ! tristes lys, je languis de beauté
Pour m'être désiré dans votre nudité,
Et vers vous, Nymphe, Nymphe, ô Nymphe des fontaines,
Je viens au pur silence offrir mes larmes vaines.

Un grand calme m'écoute, où j'écoute l'espoir.
La voix des sources change et me parle du soir ;
J'entends l'herbe d'argent grandir dans l'ombre sainte,
Et la lune perfide élève son miroir
Jusque dans les secrets de la fontaine éteinte.

Et moi ! De tout mon cœur dans ces roseaux jeté,
Je languis, ô saphir, par ma triste beauté !
Je ne sais plus aimer que l'eau magicienne
Où j'oubliai le rire et la rose ancienne.

Que je déplore ton éclat fatal et pur,
Si mollement de moi fontaine environnée,
Où puisèrent mes yeux dans un mortel azur
Mon image de fleurs humides couronnée !

Hélas ! L'image est vaine et les pleurs éternels !
À travers les bois bleus et les bras fraternels,
Une tendre lueur d'heure ambiguë existe,
Et d'un reste du jour me forme un fiancé
Nu, sur la place pâle où m'attire l'eau triste...
Délicieux démon, désirable et glacé !

Narcissus Speaks

To placate the shades of Narcissa.

O brothers, mournful lilies, I am dying of beauty
For having desired myself in your nakedness,
And, Nymph, it is to you, O Nymph of the fountains,
I come offering vain tears to this utter silence.

   A great calm listens to me, where I listen to hope.
The voice of the springs changes, and speaks to me of
     evening;
I hear the silvery grass growing in the holy shade,
And the traitorous moon lifts up her mirror
Even into the secrets of the exhausted fountain.

And I! Flinging me down bodily in these reeds,
I am dying, O sapphire, of my own sad beauty!
I can love nothing now but the bewitching water
Where I forgot laughter and the rose of former times.

   How I rue your pure and fatal glitter,
Fountain so softly surrounded by me,
Where my eyes drank in, from a mortal azure,
My own image crowned with moistened flowers!

Ah, that image is vain, and tears are eternal!
Through the blue of the woods and their fraternal arms
A tender gleam of time ambiguous exists,
Where from an ember of day is fashioned a betrothed
Naked, on the pale space where the water draws me....
Delicious demon, desirable and icy!

Voici dans l'eau ma chair de lune et de rosée,
Ô forme obéissante à mes yeux opposée !
Voici mes bras d'argent dont les gestes sont purs !...
Mes lentes mains dans l'or adorable se lassent
D'appeler ce captif que les feuilles enlacent,
Et je crie aux échos les noms des dieux obscurs !...

Adieu, reflet perdu sur l'onde calme et close,
Narcisse...ce nom même est un tendre parfum
Au cœur suave. Effeuille aux mânes du défunt
Sur ce vide tombeau la funérale rose.

Sois, ma lèvre, la rose effeuillant le baiser
Qui fasse un spectre cher lentement s'apaiser,
Car la nuit parle à demi-voix, proche et lointaine,
Aux calices pleins d'ombre et de sommeils légers.
Mais la lune s'amuse aux myrtes allongés.

Je t'adore, sous ces myrtes, ô l'incertaine
Chair pour la solitude éclose tristement
Qui se mire dans le miroir au bois dormant.
Je me délie en vain de ta présence douce,
L'heure menteuse est molle aux membres sur la mousse
Et d'un sombre délice enfle le vent profond.

Adieu, Narcisse...Meurs ! Voici le crépuscule.
Au soupir de mon cœur mon apparence ondule,
La flûte, par l'azur enseveli module
Des regrets de troupeaux sonores qui s'en vont.
Mais sur le froid mortel où l'étoile s'allume,
Avant qu'un lent tombeau ne se forme de brume,
Tiens ce baiser qui brise un calme d'eau fatal !

Here in the water is my body of moon and dew,
Form compliant still opposed to my gaze!
Here are my silvery arms of purest gestures....
My slow hands weary in the adorable gilding
Of luring that captive bound among the leaves,
And I shout the names of unknown gods to the echoes!...

Farewell, lost image on the enclosed, calm pool,
Narcissus...the very name is a tender perfume
To the soothed heart. To the shades of the departed,
Shed on this empty tomb the funereal rose.

Be my lip the rose shedding a kiss's petals
Bringing a gradual peace to a shade beloved,
For night speaks in a whisper, far and near,
To the flower-cups filled with shadows and light slumbers.
But the moon trifles among the lengthening myrtles.

I worship you, under those myrtles, oh uncertain
Flesh, sadly offering your flower to solitude,
Wondering at yourself in the sleeping forest's mirror.
In vain I unbind myself from your sweet presence,
The deceitful hour is kind to limbs stretched on the moss,
It fills the deep wind with a solemn bliss.

Farewell, Narcissus....Die! Twilight is here,
At the heart's sighing my image undulates,
The flute, against the entombed azure, warbles
Longings of the sounding herds as they go their way.
But on the mortal chill where a star is lit,
Before the mist forms a gradual tomb,
Accept this kiss breaking the water's fatal calm!

L'espoir seul peut suffire à rompre ce cristal.
La ride me ravisse au souffle qui m'exile
Et que mon souffle anime une flûte gracile
Dont le joueur léger me serait indulgent !...

Évanouissez-vous, divinité troublée !
Et, toi, verse à la lune, humble flûte isolée,
Une diversité de nos larmes d'argent.

Hope alone can avail to cleave this crystal.
Let the ripple ravish me on the breath that banishes
And may my breath inspire some slender flute-song
Whose carefree player thinks of me kindly !...

Faint away, vanish, troubled divinity !
And pour out to the moon, humble and lonely flute,
Our silvery tears in your diversity.

La Jeune Parque

Le Ciel a-t-il formé cet amas de merveilles
Pour la demeure d'un serpent?
Pierre Corneille

Qui pleure là, sinon le vent simple, à cette heure
Seule, avec diamants extrêmes?...Mais qui pleure,
Si proche de moi-même au moment de pleurer?

Cette main, sur mes traits qu'elle rêve effleurer,
Distraitement docile à quelque fin profonde,
Attend de ma faiblesse une larme qui fonde,
Et que de mes destins lentement divisé,
Le plus pur en silence éclaire un cœur brisé.
La houle me murmure une ombre de reproche,
Ou retire ici-bas, dans ses gorges de roche,
Comme chose déçue et bue amèrement,
Une rumeur de plainte et de resserrement...
Que fais-tu, hérissée, et cette main glacée,
Et quel frémissement d'une feuille effacée
Persiste parmi vous, îles de mon sein nu?...
Je scintille, liée à ce ciel inconnu...
L'immense grappe brille à ma soif de désastres.

Tout-puissants étrangers, inévitables astres
Qui daignez faire luire au lointain temporel
Je ne sais quoi de pur et de surnaturel;
Vous qui dans les mortels plongez jusques aux larmes
Ces souverains éclats, ces invincibles armes,
Et les élancements de votre éternité,
Je suis seule avec vous, tremblante, ayant quitté

The Young Fate

Did Heaven form this mass of marvels
To be a serpent's dwelling-place?
Pierre Corneille

Who is that weeping, if not simply the wind,
At this sole hour, with ultimate diamonds?. . .But who
Weeps, so close to myself on the brink of tears?

This hand of mine, dreaming it strokes my features,
Absently submissive to some deep-hidden end,
Waits for a tear to melt out of my weakness
And, gradually dividing from my other destinies,
For the purest to enlighten a broken heart in silence.
The surf murmurs to me the shadow of a reproach,
Or withdraws below, in its rocky gorges,
Like a disappointed thing, drunk back in bitterness,
A rumor of lamentation and self-constraint. . . .
What seek you, bristling, erect? And this hand of ice,
And what shivering of an effaced leaf is it
Persists amid you, isles of my naked breast?. . .
I am glittering and bound to this unknown heaven. . . .
The giant cluster gleams on my thirst for disasters.

Omnipotent, alien, inescapable stars
Who deign to let shine in the distances of time
Something I cannot conceive—supernatural, pure;
You who plunge into mortals to the depth of tears
Those sovereign rays, weapons invincible,
The shooting glances of your eternity,
I am alone with you, shivering, having left

199

Ma couche; et sur l'écueil mordu par la merveille,
J'interroge mon cœur quelle douleur l'éveille,
Quel crime par moi-même ou sur moi consommé?...
...Ou si le mal me suit d'un songe refermé,
Quand (au velours du souffle envolé l'or des lampes)
J'ai de mes bras épais environné mes tempes,
Et longtemps de mon âme attendu les éclairs?
Toute? Mais toute à moi, maîtresse de mes chairs,
Durcissant d'un frisson leur étrange étendue,
Et dans mes doux liens, à mon sang suspendue,
Je me voyais me voir, sinueuse, et dorais
De regards en regards, mes profondes forêts.

J'y suivais un serpent qui venait de me mordre.

Quel repli de désirs, sa traîne!...Quel désordre
De trésors s'arrachant à mon avidité,
Et quelle sombre soif de la limpidité!

Ô ruse!...À la lueur de la douleur laissée
Je me sentis connue encor plus que blessée...
Au plus traître de l'âme, une pointe me naît;
Le poison, mon poison, m'éclaire et se connaît:
Il colore une vierge à soi-même enlacée,
Jalouse...Mais de qui, jalouse et menacée?
Et quel silence parle à mon seul possesseur?

Dieux! Dans ma lourde plaie une secrète sœur
Brûle, qui se préfère à l'extrême attentive.

My couch; and over the reef gnawn away by marvel
I ask my heart what pain keeps it awake,
What crime committed against me or by myself?...
...Or whether the pain dogs me from a dream sealed up
When (the lamps' gold swept out by a velvet breath)
With my dense arms pressed about my temples
I waited long and long for my soul's lightnings?
All me? Yes, me entire, mistress of my flesh,
Stiffening with a shiver all its strange extent,
And in my own tender bonds, hung on my blood,
I saw me seeing myself, sinuous, and
From gaze to gaze gilded my innermost forests.

I was tracking a snake there that had just stung me.

What a coil of lusts, his trail!...What a riot
Of riches wrenched away from my longing,
And ah, that obscure thirst for limpidity!

O trickery!...Left illumined by the pain
I felt I was found out even more than stricken....
In my soul's most treacherous place a sting is born;
That poison of mine enlightens me, knows its skill:
It pictures a virgin wound upon herself,
Jealous....But of whom, and by whom menaced?
And what silence is it speaks to my sole possessor?

Gods! In my loaded wound a secret sister burns
Who loves herself more than her watchful opposite.

«Va ! je n'ai plus besoin de ta race naïve,
Cher Serpent...Je m'enlace, être vertigineux !
Cesse de me prêter ce mélange de nœuds
Ni ta fidélité qui me fuit et devine...
Mon âme y peut suffire, ornement de ruine !
Elle sait, sur mon ombre égarant ses tourments,
De mon sein, dans les nuits, mordre les rocs charmants;
Elle y suce longtemps le lait des rêveries...
Laisse donc défaillir ce bras de pierreries
Qui menace d'amour mon sort spirituel...
Tu ne peux rien sur moi qui ne soit moins cruel,
Moins désirable...Apaise alors, calme ces ondes,
Rappelle ces remous, ces promesses immondes...
Ma surprise s'abrège, et mes yeux sont ouverts.
Je n'attendais pas moins de mes riches déserts
Qu'un tel enfantement de fureur et de tresse:
Leurs fonds passionnés brillent de sécheresse
Si loin que je m'avance et m'altère pour voir
De mes enfers pensifs les confins sans espoir...
Je sais...Ma lassitude est parfois un théâtre.
L'esprit n'est pas si pur que jamais idolâtre
Sa fougue solitaire aux élans de flambeau
Ne fasse fuir les murs de son morne tombeau.
Tout peut naître ici-bas d'une attente infinie.
L'ombre même le cède à certaine agonie,
L'âme avare s'entr'ouvre, et du monstre s'émeut
Qui se tord sur le pas d'une porte de feu...
Mais, pour capricieux et prompt que tu paraisses,
Reptile, ô vifs détours tout courus de caresses,
Si proche impatience et si lourde langueur,
Qu'es-tu, près de ma nuit d'éternelle longueur?
Tu regardais dormir ma belle négligence...

"Go, I no longer need your simple kind,
Dear Snake.... I coil, vertiginous being, on myself!
Lend me no longer your enwound confusion
And your fidelity that eludes and knows me....
My soul, a ruin's ornament, will suffice instead!
She, her torments straying over my shadow,
Can bite the witching rocks, my breasts, by night;
There she sucks for long at the milk of reverie....
So let it yield and loosen, that arm bejeweled
Menacing my spiritual lot with love....
You have no power over me that would not be less cruel,
Less desirable.... So appease, calm these waves,
Withdraw those eddyings, those foul promises....
My amazement is cut short, my eyes are opened.
I expected no less from my rich deserts
Than such a pregnancy of fire and tresses;
Their passionate distances glitter with barrenness
The further I press, dry with the thirst to see
The hopeless confines of my thought's infernos....
I know... Sometimes my weariness is a theater.
The mind is not so pure that, never idolatrous,
Its solitary ardor flaming out like a torch
Cannot dismiss the walls of its gloomy tomb.
To infinite waiting, here below, all may come.
Darkness itself yields to unfailing agony,
The grasping soul half opens, alarmed at the monster
Writhing on the threshold of a doorway of fire....
But capricious and alert though you appear,
Reptile, oh sudden coils all rippling with caresses,
Intolerance so instant, so loaded with languor,
What are you compared with my night eternally long?
You were admiring my fine, careless slumber....

Mais avec mes périls, je suis d'intelligence,
Plus versatile, ô Thyrse, et plus perfide qu'eux.
Fuis-moi ! du noir retour reprends le fil visqueux !
Va chercher des yeux clos pour tes danses massives.
Coule vers d'autres lits tes robes successives,
Couve sur d'autres cœurs les germes de leur mal,
Et que dans les anneaux de ton rêve animal
Halète jusqu'au jour l'innocence anxieuse !...
Moi, je veille. Je sors, pâle et prodigieuse,
Toute humide des pleurs que je n'ai point versés,
D'une absence aux contours de mortelle bercés
Par soi seule...Et brisant une tombe sereine,
Je m'accoude inquiète et pourtant souveraine,
Tant de mes visions parmi la nuit et l'œil,
Les moindres mouvements consultent mon orgueil.»

Mais je tremblais de perdre une douleur divine !
Je baisais sur ma main cette morsure fine,
Et je ne savais plus de mon antique corps
Insensible, qu'un feu qui brûlait sur mes bords :

Adieu, pensai-je, MOI, mortelle sœur, mensonge...

Harmonieuse MOI, différente d'un songe,
Femme flexible et ferme aux silences suivis
D'actes purs !...Front limpide, et par ondes ravis,
Si loin que le vent vague et velu les achève,
Longs brins légers qu'au large un vol mêle et soulève,
Dites !...J'étais l'égale et l'épouse du jour,
Seul support souriant que je formais d'amour
À la toute-puissante altitude adorée...

204

But I, oh Thyrsus, am in league with my own perils,
More resourceful, and more cunning I than they.
Begone! Resume the viscous track of your dark retreat!
Go and find closed eyes for your ponderous dances,
Towards other beds slide your shedding robes,
Hatch on other hearts the seeds of their suffering,
And within the circlings of your animal dream
Let troubled innocence sleep panting till dawn!
I am awake. Pale, a thing of wonder,
Moist with the tears I have not shed, I emerge
From an absence lulled by itself alone, shaped
Like a mortal woman....And breaking a tomb serene,
I lean on my arm, uneasy and yet supreme,
So much do the slightest stirrings of my visions
Between night and the eye defer to my pride."

But I shuddered at the loss of a divine sorrow!
On my hand I would kiss that tiny sting,
And I knew no more of my former insensible
Body, than a fire that burned along its rims:

Farewell, thought I, mortal ME, sister, falsehood....

Thing of harmony, ME, unlike a dream,
Firm, flexible, feminine, whose silences lead
To pure acts! Limpid brow, and swept in waves
As far as the vague tressed wind carries them,
Long light strands mingled and lifted in the breeze,
Tell me!...I was the equal and spouse of light,
Sole smiling pillar of love that I formed
For the adored omnipotence of the height....

Quel éclat sur mes cils aveuglément dorée,
Ô paupières qu'opprime une nuit de trésor,
Je priais à tâtons dans vos ténèbres d'or !
Poreuse à l'éternel qui me semblait m'enclore,
Je m'offrais dans mon fruit de velours qu'il dévore;
Rien ne me murmurait qu'un désir de mourir
Dans cette blonde pulpe au soleil pût mûrir:
Mon amère saveur ne m'était point venue.
Je ne sacrifiais que mon épaule nue
À la lumière; et sur cette gorge de miel,
Dont la tendre naissance accomplissait le ciel,
Se venait assoupir la figure du monde.
Puis dans le dieu brillant, captive vagabonde,
Je m'ébranlais brûlante et foulais le sol plein,
Liant et déliant mes ombres sous le lin.
Heureuse ! À la hauteur de tant de gerbes belles,
Qui laissait à ma robe obéir les ombelles,
Dans les abaissements de leur frêle fierté;
Et si, contre le fil de cette liberté,
Si la robe s'arrache à la rebelle ronce,
L'arc de mon brusque corps s'accuse et me prononce,
Nu sous le voile enflé de vivantes couleurs
Que dispute ma race aux longs liens de fleurs !

Je regrette à demi cette vaine puissance...
Une avec le désir, je fus l'obéissance
Imminente, attachée à ces genoux polis;
De mouvements si prompts mes vœux étaient rempl
Que je sentais ma cause à peine plus agile !
Vers mes sens lumineux nageait ma blonde argile,
Et dans l'ardente paix des songes naturels,
Tous ces pas infinis me semblaient éternels.

Ah, the dazzle on my brows blindingly gilded,
Eyelids overborne by a night of riches,
Gropingly I was praying in your golden glooms!
Porous to the eternal that seemed to enwrap me,
I offered my velvet fruit which it devours;
No hint was whispered that a death-longing
Might ripen in this blond, sunlit flesh:
My bitter savor was still unknown to me.
All I sacrificed was my naked shoulder
To the light; and on this bosom of honey
Whose tender nativity was heaven's fulfilment
There came to lull itself the shape of the world.
Then in the god's splendor, a straying prisoner,
Burningly I moved, pressed the solid ground,
Binding, unbinding my shadows beneath the linen.
Happy! Of a height with all those lovely sheaves,
I who let their umbels obey my dress,
With the abasings of their fragile pride;
And if, against the current of this freedom,
If the dress is dragged by the rebel brambles,
The arc of my sudden body reveals me pronounced
Naked in the veil swelling with living colors
In which my kind vies with the long trammels of flowers!

I half regret that vain potency....
At one with desire, I was the imminent
Obedience implicit in these smooth knees;
My wishes answered by such instant movements,
I felt my cause itself scarcely more agile!
My blond clay swam up to my lucid senses,
And in the burning calm of natural dreams
All those continual steps seemed to me eternal.

Si ce n'est, ô Splendeur, qu'à mes pieds l'ennemie,
Mon ombre ! la mobile et la souple momie,
De mon absence peinte effleurait sans effort
La terre où je fuyais cette légère mort.
Entre la rose et moi, je la vois qui s'abrite ;
Sur la poudre qui danse, elle glisse et n'irrite
Nul feuillage, mais passe, et se brise partout...
Glisse ! Barque funèbre...

                                 Et moi vive, debout,
Dure, et de mon néant secrètement armée,
Mais, comme par l'amour une joue enflammée,
Et la narine jointe au vent de l'oranger,
Je ne rends plus au jour qu'un regard étranger...
Oh ! combien peut grandir dans ma nuit curieuse
De mon cœur séparé la part mystérieuse,
Et de sombres essais s'approfondir mon art !...
Loin des purs environs, je suis captive, et par
L'évanouissement d'arômes abattue,
Je sens sous les rayons, frissonner ma statue,
Des caprices de l'or, son marbre parcouru.
Mais je sais ce que voit mon regard disparu ;
Mon œil noir est le seuil d'infernales demeures !
Je pense, abandonnant à la brise les heures
Et l'âme sans retour des arbustes amers,
Je pense, sur le bord doré de l'univers,
À ce goût de périr qui prend la Pythonisse
En qui mugit l'espoir que le monde finisse.
Je renouvelle en moi mes énigmes, mes dieux,
Mes pas interrompus de paroles aux cieux,
Mes pauses, sur le pied portant la rêverie,

If only, oh Splendor, it were not for the enemy
My shadow at my feet, mobile, supple mummy
Effortlessly skimming, portrait of my absence,
The earth where I was fleeing that weightless death.
Between the rose and me I see it lurking;
Over the dancing dust it glides, never stirring
The leafage, passes and breaks on anything....
Glide, funereal bark!...

              And I alive, erect,
Stubborn, and secretly armed with my inner void,
But one cheek on fire as though with love,
My nostril married to the wind from the orange grove,
I can give the light no more than a stranger's look....
Ah! how much may it grow in my questing night,
That secret half of my divided heart,
And my skill grow deeper from obscure probings!...
Far from pure atmospheres, I am a captive,
And overcome by the fainting away of perfumes
I can feel my statue quiver beneath the rays,
Its marble coursed by the caprices of gold.
But I know what my vanished look can see;
My darkened eye is the door to infernal abodes!
I muse, letting hours waste in the wind
With the evanescent breath of the bitter shrubs,
On the golden edge of the universe, I muse
On that taste for death that takes the Pythoness
In whom a hope howls that the world may cease.
In myself I renew my gods, my enigmas,
My pacings interrupted by words to the heavens,
My pauses, on a step bearing a reverie

Qui suit au miroir d'aile un oiseau qui varie,
Cent fois sur le soleil joue avec le néant,
Et brûle, au sombre but de mon marbre béant.

O dangereusement de son regard la proie !

Car l'œil spirituel sur ses plages de soie
Avait déjà vu luire et pâlir trop de jours
Dont je m'étais prédit les couleurs et le cours.
L'ennui, le clair ennui de mirer leur nuance,
Me donnait sur ma vie une funeste avance:
L'aube me dévoilait tout le jour ennemi.
J'étais à demi morte; et peut-être, à demi
Immortelle, rêvant que le futur lui-même
Ne fût qu'un diamant fermant le diadème
Où s'échange le froid des malheurs qui naîtront
Parmi tant d'autres feux absolus de mon front.

Osera-t-il, le Temps, de mes diverses tombes,
Ressusciter un soir favori des colombes,
Un soir qui traîne au fil d'un lambeau voyageur
De ma docile enfance un reflet de rougeur,
Et trempe à l'émeraude un long rose de honte?

Souvenir, ô bûcher, dont le vent d'or m'affronte,
Souffle au masque la pourpre imprégnant le refus
D'être en moi-même en flamme une autre que je fus...
Viens, mon sang, viens rougir la pâle circonstance
Qu'ennoblissait l'azur de la sainte distance,
Et l'insensible iris du temps que j'adorai !

That follows in a wing's mirror a varying bird,
Wagers a hundred times void against sun,
And burns, at the dark goal of my gaping marble.

Oh, dangerously a prey to the gazing self!

For already the mind's eye on its silken strands
Had watched shine and fade too many days
Whose colors and whose course I had foreseen.
The clear-eyed tedium of seeing through their changes
Gave me a sinister start over my life:
Dawn unveiled to me the whole hostile day.
Half of me was dead; and the other perhaps
Immortal, dreaming that the future itself
Was only a diamond completing the diadem
Where sorrows-to-be exchange their icy gleams
Among all the other supreme fires of my brow.

Will Time dare, out of my diverse tombs,
To resurrect some sunset favored by doves,
An evening that trails after a rag of cloud
Some flushed reflection of my docile childhood,
Dipping a long flush of shame in the emerald?

Memory, bonfire whose gold wind assaults me,
Blow and empurple my mask with the refusal
To be, in myself aflame, another than I was....
Come, blood, redden the circumstantial pallor
Made noble once by the blue of holy distance,
And the infinite slow iris of the time I loved!

Viens ! consumer sur moi ce don décoloré;
Viens ! que je reconnaisse et que je les haïsse,
Cette ombrageuse enfant, ce silence complice,
Ce trouble transparent qui baigne dans les bois...
Et de mon sein glacé rejaillisse la voix
Que j'ignorais si rauque et d'amour si voilée...
Le col charmant cherchant la chasseresse ailée.

Mon cœur fut-il si près d'un cœur qui va faiblir?

Fut-ce bien moi, grands cils, qui crus m'ensevelir
Dans l'arrière douceur riant à vos menaces...
Ô pampres sur ma joue errant en fils tenaces,
Ou toi...de cils tissue et de fluides fûts,
Tendre lueur d'un soir brisé de bras confus?

QUE DANS LE CIEL PLACÉS, MES YEUX TRACENT
    MON TEMPLE !
ET QUE SUR MOI REPOSE UN AUTEL SANS EXEMPLE !
Criaient de tout mon corps la pierre et la pâleur...
La terre ne m'est plus qu'un bandeau de couleur
Qui coule et se refuse au front blanc de vertige...
Tout l'univers chancelle et tremble sur ma tige,
La pensive couronne échappe à mes esprits,
La Mort veut respirer cette rose sans prix
Dont la douceur importe à sa fin ténébreuse !

Que si ma tendre odeur grise ta tête creuse,
Ô Mort, respire enfin cette esclave de roi:
Appelle-moi, délie !....Et désespère-moi,
De moi-même si lasse, image condamnée !

Come burn on me that dower of drained color,
Come! Let me recognize so that I may hate
That moody child, that conniving silence,
That troubled clarity that bathes in woods. . . .
And from my icy breast let there break the voice
I did not know was so hoarse, so veiled with love. . . .
The charming neck seeking the winged huntress.

Was my heart so close by a heart ready to weaken?

Was it truly I, great lashes, who thought to bury me
In the after-sweetness that laughed at your threats. . . .
O vine-stalks grazing my cheek with clutching tendrils,
Or you. . .woven of lashes and fluid columns,
Tender evening gleam broken by mingling arms?

LET MY EYES, FIXED IN HEAVEN, TRACE MY
        TEMPLE,
AND LET REPOSE ON ME AN ALTAR UNEXAMPLED!
This was the cry of all my body's stony pallor. . . .
Earth is no more to me now than a fillet of color
That slips and falls from my white dizzy brow. . . .
The whole universe quivers and gives on my stem,
The crown of thought is falling from my senses,
Death seeks to inhale this priceless rose
Whose sweetness matters to its dark purpose!

But if my tender perfume turns your hollow head,
Oh Death, breathe in at once this royal slave:
Summon me, release!. . .And drive me to despair,
So self-weary am I, a sentenced image!

Écoute...N'attends plus...La renaissante année
À tout mon sang prédit de secrets mouvements:
Le gel cède à regret ses derniers diamants...
Demain, sur un soupir des Bontés constellées,
Le printemps vient briser les fontaines scellées:
L'étonnant printemps rit, viole...On ne sait d'où
Venu? Mais la candeur ruisselle à mots si doux
Qu'une tendresse prend la terre à ses entrailles...
Les arbres regonflés et recouverts d'écailles
Chargés de tant de bras et de trop d'horizons,
Meuvent sur le soleil leurs tonnantes toisons,
Montent dans l'air amer avec toutes leurs ailes
De feuilles par milliers qu'ils se sentent nouvelles...
N'entends-tu pas frémir ces noms aériens,
Ô Sourde!...Et dans l'espace accablé de liens,
Vibrant de bois vivace infléchi par la cime,
Pour et contre les dieux ramer l'arbre unanime,
La flottante forêt de qui les rudes troncs
Portent pieusement à leurs fantasques fronts,
Aux déchirants départs des archipels superbes,
Un fleuve tendre, ô Mort, et caché sous les herbes?

Quelle résisterait, mortelle, à ces remons?
Quelle mortelle?

          Moi si pure, mes genoux
Pressentent les terreurs de genoux sans défense...
L'air me brise. L'oiseau perce de cris d'enfance
Inouïs...l'ombre même où se serre mon cœur,
Et, roses! mon soupir vous soulève, vainqueur
Hélas! des bras si doux qui ferment la corbeille...

You hear.... Wait no longer.... The newborn year
To all my blood foretells secret impulses:
Rueful the frost relinquishes its last diamonds....
Tomorrow, at a sigh of the constellated Bounties,
Spring comes to break the sealed-up fountains:
Astounding spring, laughing, raping.... Where
Can it come from? Its frankness brims with speech
So soft, earth's entrails are seized with tenderness....
The trees re-swelling and clothed in new scales,
Loaded with all those arms and endless horizons,
Brandish against the sun their resounding fleeces,
Rise into the sharp air with all their wings
Of leaves in myriads they feel new-grown....
Do you not hear those airy names trembling,
Deaf One... And in space loaded with chains,
Vibrant with living timber twisted by its summit,
The unanimous tree rowing with and against the gods,
The undulating forest whose rough trunks
Bear devoutly up to their antic brows,
At the rending departures of those proud archipelagoes,
A tender river, O Death, hidden beneath the grass?

Who could resist, mortal, such turmoils as these,
Who among mortals?

                    Pure as I am, my knees
Can feel the terrors of knees without defense....
I am broken by air. With unspeakable infant cries
The bird pierces... the very shadow where my heart shrinks,
And roses! the sigh I heave lifts you, vanquishing
Alas, the arms so soft folded about your cradle....

Oh! parmi mes cheveux pèse d'un poids d'abeille,
Plongeant toujours plus ivre au baiser plus aigu,
Le point délicieux de mon jour ambigu...
Lumière!...Ou toi, la Mort! Mais le plus prompt me
    prenne!...
Mon cœur bat! mon cœur bat! Mon sein brûle et
    m'entraîne!
Ah! qu'il s'enfle, se gonfle et se tende, ce dur
Très doux témoin captif de mes réseaux d'azur...
Dur en moi...mais si doux à la bouche infinie!...

Chers fantômes naissants dont la soif m'est unie,
Désirs! Visages clairs!...Et vous, beaux fruits d'amour,
Les dieux m'ont-ils formé ce maternel contour
Et ces bords sinueux, ces plis et ces calices,
Pour que la vie embrasse un autel de délices,
Où mêlant l'âme étrange aux éternels retours,
La semence, le lait, le sang coulent toujours?
Non! L'horreur m'illumine, exécrable harmonie!
Chaque baiser présage une neuve agonie...
Je vois, je vois flotter, fuyant l'honneur des chairs
Des mânes impuissants les millions amers...
Non, souffles! Non, regards, tendresses...mes convives,
Peuple altéré de moi suppliant que tu vives,
Non, vous ne tiendrez pas de moi la vie!...Allez,
Spectres, soupirs la nuit vainement exhalés,
Allez joindre des morts les impalpables nombres!
Je n'accorderai pas la lumière à des ombres,
Je garde loin de vous, l'esprit sinistre et clair...
Non! Vous ne tiendrez pas de mes lèvres l'éclair!...
Et puis...mon cœur aussi vous refuse sa foudre.
J'ai pitié de nous tous, ô tourbillons de poudre!

Ah, through my hair weighs with a bee's weight,
Plunging ever wilder to the sharpest kiss,
The delectable glint of my ambiguous dawn....
Light!...Or else, Death! But let the quicker seize me!...
My heart beats! It beats! My burning breast impels me!
Ah, let it swell, dilate and stretch, that hard
Too soft witness prisoned in my nets of azure....
Hard in me...yet so soft to infinity's mouth!

Dear dawning phantoms whose thirst is one with me,
Desires! Bright faces!...And you, love's lovely fruits,
Have the gods shaped me this maternal contour
And these sinuous verges, folds and hollows,
So that life might hug an altar of delight
Where, mingling the alien soul's continual changes,
Fertility, milk and blood forever flow?
No! Horror gives me insight, accursed harmony!
Every kiss is a presage of fresh agony....
I see, I see afloat, fleeing the flesh's dignity,
The embittered myriads of impotent shades....
No no, breaths, sighs, tender gazes...my fellows,
Race all athirst for me, begging you may live,
No, from me you will not have life....Be gone,
Spectres, groans the night exhales in vain,
Go and join the impalpable throngs of the dead!
I will not concede light to shadows, I keep
Remote from you a mind ominous and clear....
No! Not from my lips will you get the lightning!...
And then...my heart too refuses you its fire.
I pity all of us, oh eddyings of dust!

Grands Dieux! Je perds en vous mes pas déconcertés!

Je n'implorerai plus que tes faibles clartés,
Longtemps sur mon visage envieuse de fondre,
Très imminente larme, et seule à me répondre,
Larme qui fais trembler à mes regards humains
Une variété de funèbres chemins;
Tu procèdes de l'âme, orgueil du labyrinthe.
Tu me portes du cœur cette goutte contrainte,
Cette distraction de mon suc précieux
Qui vient sacrifier mes ombres sur mes yeux,
Tendre libation de l'arrière-pensée!
D'une grotte de crainte au fond de moi creusée
Le sel mystérieux suinte muette l'eau.
D'où nais-tu? Quel travail toujours triste et nouveau
Te tire avec retard, larme, de l'ombre amère?
Tu gravis mes degrés de mortelle et de mère,
Et déchirant ta route, opiniâtre faix,
Dans le temps que je vis, les lenteurs que tu fais
M'étouffent...Je me tais, buvant ta marche sûre...
— Qui t'appelle au secours de ma jeune blessure?

Mais blessures, sanglots, sombres essais, pourquoi?
Pour qui, joyaux cruels, marquez-vous ce corps froid,
Aveugle aux doigts ouverts évitant l'espérance!
Où va-t-il, sans répondre à sa propre ignorance,
Ce corps dans la nuit noire étonné de sa foi?
Terre trouble...et mêlée à l'algue, porte-moi,
Porte doucement moi...Ma faiblesse de neige
Marchera-t-elle tant qu'elle trouve son piège?
Où traîne-t-il, mon cygne, où cherche-t-il son vol?
...Dureté précieuse...O sentiment du sol,

Great Gods, in you I am losing my baffled way!

I shall beg no more than your feeble inklings,
For so long striving to melt on my face,
Tear most imminent, sole response to me,
Tear setting a-quiver in my mortal gaze
A whole diversity of funereal paths;
You come from the soul, pride of the labyrinth.
You bring me from the heart this extracted drop,
This extrusion of my own precious essence
Rising to immolate my phantoms on my eyes,
A fond libation of my thought's reserve!
From a grotto of fear hollowed in my depths
Mutely the salt of mystery oozes moisture.
Whence born? What labor ever solemn and new
Draws you unwilling, tear, from the bitter dark?
You mount on my mortal and mothering rungs,
A wilful burden, and rending yourself a path
Through the time I live, your long delays
Stifle me....Dumb, I drink your steady pace....
—Who summons you to the aid of my youthful wound?

But why, oh wounds, sobs, dark probings, why?
Heartless jewels, for whom do you mark this cold body,
Blind, with stretched fingers groping away from hope!
Where bound, answerless to its own self-ignorance,
This body in black night amazed by its faith?
Troublous earth...and mingled with slime, bear me
Gently, gently bear me....Will my snowy weakness
Be able to walk until it find its snare?
Where is my swan trailing, seeking his flight?
...Precious hardness....Oh feel of firm earth,

Mon pas fondait sur toi l'assurance sacrée !
Mais sous le pied vivant qui tâte et qui la crée
Et touche avec horreur à son pacte natal,
Cette terre si ferme atteint mon piédestal.
Non loin, parmi ces pas, rêve mon précipice...
L'insensible rocher, glissant d'algues, propice
À fuir, (comme en soi-même ineffablement seul),
Commence...Et le vent semble au travers d'un linceul
Ourdir de bruits marins une confuse trame,
Mélange de la lame en ruine, et de rame...
Tant de hoquets longtemps, et de râles heurtés,
Brisés, repris au large...et tous les sorts jetés
Éperdument divers roulant l'oubli vorace...

Hélas ! de mes pieds nus qui trouvera la trace
Cessera-t-il longtemps de ne songer qu'à soi?

Terre trouble, et mêlée à l'algue, porte-moi !

Mystérieuse MOI, pourtant, tu vis encore !
Tu vas te reconnaître au lever de l'aurore
Amèrement la même...
                    Un miroir de la mer
Se lève...Et sur la lèvre, un sourire d'hier
Qu'annonce avec ennui l'effacement des signes,
Glace dans l'orient déjà les pâles lignes
De lumière et de pierre, et la pleine prison
Où flottera l'anneau de l'unique horizon...
Regarde: un bras très pur est vu, qui se dénude.
Je te revois, mon bras...Tu portes l'aube...
                                        O rude

On you my tread founded its sacred surety!
But under the living, groping foot that creates it
And strikes its native treaty with terror,
This so firm earth mines at my pedestal!
Nearby, amid these steps, my precipice dreams....
The gradual rock, slippery with seaweed, aid
To vanishing (as in one's sole ineffable self)
Begins....And through a shroud the wind seems
To weave a mazy plot of marine noises,
Blend of breakers falling in ruins, and oars....
Prolonged gulps and wallowings, hurtling rattles,
Broken, re-echoed in the deep...and all the cast lots,
Wildly at odds rolling greedy oblivion....

Ah, whoever finds the print of my bare feet,
Will he cease for long to think only of himself?

Troublous earth, and mingled with slime, bear me!

Thing of mystery, ME, are you living yet!
When dawn's curtain lifts, you will recognize
Your same bitter self....
                              A mirror is rising
From the sea....And on its lip a smile of yesterday
Heralded by the weary extinction of the signs,
Already in the east fixes the faint lines
Of light and stone, and the ample prison
Where will float the ring of the single horizon....
Look: a purest arm is seen baring itself,
My arm: I see you again....You bear the dawn....

Rude

Réveil d'une victime inachevée...et seuil
Si doux...si clair, que flatte, affleurement d'écueil,
L'onde basse, et que lave une houle amortie!...
L'ombre qui m'abandonne, impérissable hostie,
Me découvre vermeille à de nouveaux désirs,
Sur le terrible autel de tous mes souvenirs.

Là, l'écume s'efforce à se faire visible;
Et là, titubera sur la barque sensible
À chaque épaule d'onde, un pêcheur éternel.
Tout va donc accomplir son acte solennel
De toujours reparaître incomparable et chaste,
Et de restituer la tombe enthousiaste
Au gracieux état du rire universel.

Salut! Divinités par la rose et le sel,
Et les premiers jouets de la jeune lumière,
Îles!...Ruches bientôt, quand la flamme première
Fera que votre roche, îles que je prédis,
Ressente en rougissant de puissants paradis;
Cimes qu'un feu féconde à peine intimidées,
Bois qui bourdonnerez de bêtes et d'idées,
D'hymnes d'hommes comblés des dons du juste éther,
Îles! dans la rumeur des ceintures de mer,
Mères vierges toujours, même portant ces marques,
Vous m'êtes à genoux de merveilleuses Parques:
Rien n'égale dans l'air les fleurs que vous placez,
Mais, dans la profondeur, que vos pieds sont glacés!

De l'âme les apprêts sous la tempe calmée,
Ma mort, enfant secrète et déjà si formée,

Waking of a victim undispatched...and sill
So gentle...bright, soothed level with the reef
By the low wave, and washed by a deadened surf!...
The darkness that sheds me, indestructible victim,
Unveils me rosy to newborn desires
On the terrible altar of all my memories.

There, the foam strives to become visible,
And there, reels swaying in a boat that gives
With every shouldering wave, an eternal fisher.
So all is about to fulfil its solemn decree
Of forever reappearing, incomparable, untouched,
And of restoring the eager cenotaph
To a state of grace in the universal laugh.

Hail! Deities in virtue of rose and salt,
And earliest playthings of the infant light,
Islands!...Hives soon to be, when the first flame
Will see that your rocks, islands I foretell,
Again feel the red flush of powerful paradises;
Summits no sooner daunted than quickened by
The fire, woods that will hum with creatures and moods,
With hymns of men loaded with heaven's just gifts,
Islands! in the murmur of the girdling sea,
Mothers still virgin, even bearing these proofs,
To me you are marvels, kneeling Destinies:
Nothing matches the flowers you lift in air,
But how icy in the depths your feet are!

Preparatives of the soul beneath the quieted temples,
My death, secret child already fully formed,

Et vous, divins dégoûts qui me donniez l'essor,
Chastes éloignements des lustres de mon sort,
Ne fûtes-vous, ferveur, qu'une noble durée?
Nulle jamais des dieux plus près aventurée
N'osa peindre à son front leur souffle ravisseur,
Et de la nuit parfaite implorant l'épaisseur,
Prétendre par la lèvre au suprême murmure...

Je soutenais l'éclat de la mort toute pure
Telle j'avais jadis le soleil soutenu...
Mon corps désespéré tendait le torse nu
Où l'âme, ivre de soi, de silence et de gloire,
Prête à s'évanouir de sa propre mémoire,
Écoute, avec espoir, frapper au mur pieux
Ce cœur, — qui se ruine à coups mystérieux,
Jusqu'à ne plus tenir que de sa complaisance
Un frémissement fin de feuille, ma présence...

Attente vaine, et vaine...Elle ne peut mourir
Qui devant son miroir pleure pour s'attendrir.

Ô n'aurait-il fallu, folle, que j'accomplisse
Ma merveilleuse fin de choisir pour supplice
Ce lucide dédain des nuances du sort?
Trouveras-tu jamais plus transparente mort
Ni de pente plus pure où je rampe à ma perte
Que sur ce long regard de victime entr'ouverte,
Pâle, qui se résigne et saigne sans regret?
Que lui fait tout le sang qui n'est plus son secret?
Dans quelle blanche paix cette pourpre la laisse,
À l'extrême de l'être, et belle de faiblesse !

And you, divine revulsions that gave me wings,
Chaste estrangements from the lustra of my lot,
Ardency, were you only a noble interlude?
None ever who ventured thus near to the gods
Dared picture on her brow their ravishers' breath,
Nor, praying for the stupor of total night,
Dared let her lips lay claim to the final murmur....

    I withstood the dazzle of death in its purity
As I formerly had withstood the sun....
My body desperate stretched its naked torso
Where the soul, crazed with self, silence, and glory
Ready to faint away from its own memory
Listens, in hope, to this heart knocking against
The pious wall, with a secret, self-destroying beat,
Till only from sheer compliance does it keep up
This thin quivering of a leaf, my presence....

Vain the suspense, vain...She cannot die
Who weeps in her own mirror from self-pity.

Oh fool, ought I not to have fulfilled
My marvelous aim, choosing for self-torture
My lucid contempt for fate's varying moods?
    Will you ever light on a death more translucent,
On a purer slope whereby to creep to perdition
Than by that long gaze of the victim laid open,
Pale, resigned, bleeding away without regret?
What matters that blood, now no more her secret?
In what a snowy calm does the purple leave her
On the furthest edge of being, lovely in weakness!

Elle calme le temps qui la vient abolir,
Le moment souverain ne la peut plus pâlir,
Tant la chair vide baise une sombre fontaine!...
Elle se fait toujours plus seule et plus lointaine...
Et moi, d'un tel destin, le cœur toujours plus près,
Mon cortège, en esprit, se berçait de cyprès...
   Vers un aromatique avenir de fumée,
Je me sentais conduite, offerte et consumée,
Toute, toute promise aux nuages heureux!
Même, je m'apparus cet arbre vaporeux,
De qui la majesté légèrement perdue
S'abandonne à l'amour de toute l'étendue.
L'être immense me gagne, et de mon cœur divin
L'encens qui brûle expire une forme sans fin...
Tous les corps radieux tremblent dans mon essence!...

Non, non!...N'irrite plus cette réminiscence!
Sombre lys! Ténébreuse allusion des cieux,
Ta vigueur n'a pu rompre un vaisseau précieux...
Parmi tous les instants tu touchais au suprême...
— Mais qui l'emporterait sur la puissance même,
Avide par tes yeux de contempler le jour
Qui s'est choisi ton front pour lumineuse tour?

Cherche, du moins, dis-toi, par quelle sourde suite
La nuit, d'entre les morts, au jour t'a reconduite?
Souviens-toi de toi-même, et retire à l'instinct
Ce fil (ton doigt doré le dispute au matin),
Ce fil dont la finesse aveuglément suivie
Jusque sur cette rive a ramené ta vie...
Sois subtile...cruelle...ou plus subtile!...Mens
Mais sache!...Enseigne-moi par quels enchantements,

She quiets the time as it comes to annul her,
The supreme moment cannot increase her pallor,
The void flesh so kisses a dark fountain !...
Ever lonelier she feels, and more remote....
In my own mind I felt my heart nearer and nearer
To such a fate, my funeral train swaying in cypress....
    Towards a future of aromatic vapor
I felt I was being led, offered up, consumed,
To the happy clouds I was promised entire !
I even saw myself changed to that misty tree
Whose majesty diaphanously lost
Surrenders to the love of infinite space.
Immense being invades me, the burning incense
Of my divine heart breathes a shape without end....
All the forms of light quiver in my essence !...

No, no !...No longer chafe that reminiscence,
Lily of darkness ! Gloomy allusion of the skies,
Your vigor could not break a precious vessel....
Amid all possible moments you touched on the ultimate....
—But who could win mastery over the very power
That is greedy, through your eyes, to contemplate
The day which chose your brow for its tower of light?

Seek at least, and declare by what sly paths
Night restored you to day from among the dead?
Recall self to self, reclaim from instinct
That thread (your golden finger vies for it with morning)
That thread whose fine-spun trace blindly followed
Has led your life again back to this shore....
Be subtle...or cruel...or more subtle still !...
Cheat, but find out !...Tell me by what wiles,

Lâche que n'a su fuir sa tiède fumée,
Ni le souci d'un sein d'argile parfumée,
Par quel retour sur toi, reptile, as-tu repris
Tes parfums de caverne et tes tristes esprits ?

Hier la chair profonde, hier, la chair maîtresse
M'a trahie...Oh ! sans rêve, et sans une caresse !...
Nul démon, nul parfum ne m'offrit le péril
D'imaginaires bras mourant au col viril ;
Ni, par le Cygne-Dieu, de plumes offensée
Sa brûlante blancheur n'effleura ma pensée...

Il eût connu pourtant le plus tendre des nids !
Car toute à la faveur de mes membres unis,
Vierge, je fus dans l'ombre une adorable offrande...
Mais le sommeil s'éprit d'une douceur si grande,
Et nouée à moi-même au creux de mes cheveux,
J'ai mollement perdu mon empire nerveux.
Au milieu de mes bras, je me suis faite une autre...
Qui s'aliène?...Qui s'envole?...Qui se vautre?...
À quel détour caché, mon cœur s'est-il fondu ?
Quelle conque a redit le nom que j'ai perdu ?
Le sais-je, quel reflux traître m'a retirée
De mon extrémité pure et prématurée,
Et m'a repris le sens de mon vaste soupir ?
Comme l'oiseau se pose, il fallut m'assoupir.

Ce fut l'heure, peut-être, où la devineresse
Intérieure s'use et se désintéresse :
Elle n'est plus la même...Une profonde enfant
Des degrés inconnus vainement se défend,

Coward whom her own warm breath could not relinquish,
Nor the fond love of a breast of perfumed clay,
By what self-recollection, reptile, did you
Resume your cavernous savor and your glooms?

Yesterday, the insidious, the masterful flesh
Betrayed me....Oh, not by a dream or caress!
No demon, no perfume proffered me the risk
Of imagined arms a-swoon on a virile neck;
Nor, in a feathery onset, did the Swan-God
Even graze my thought with his snowy fires....

And yet...he would have known the tenderest nest!
For, thanks to the smooth oneness of my limbs,
A shaded virgin, I was a worshipful offering....
But sleep grew enamored of such sweetness,
And wrapped upon myself in my hollowed hair
Weakly I surrendered my nervous sway.
Amid my own arms, I became another....
Who is estranged?...Who is vanishing?...Wallowing?...
In what blind turning did my heart melt away?
What shell echoed to the name I had given up?
Can I guess what treacherous ebb withdrew me
From my naked and untimely extremity,
And took away the sense of my huge sigh?
As a bird alights, I had to fall asleep.

It may be it was the hour when the inner
Prophetess grows worn, loses interest:
No longer is she herself....A child far within
Against the unknown descent struggles in vain,

Et redemande au loin ses mains abandonnées.
Il faut céder aux vœux des mortes couronnées
Et prendre pour visage un souffle...
                                        Doucement,
Me voici: mon front touche à ce consentement...
    Ce corps, je lui pardonne, et je goûte à la cendre.
Je me remets entière au bonheur de descendre,
Ouverte aux noirs témoins, les bras suppliciés,
Entre des mots sans fin, sans moi, balbutiés...
Dors, ma sagesse, dors. Forme-toi cette absence;
Retourne dans le germe et la sombre innocence.
Abandonne-toi vive aux serpents, aux trésors...
Dors toujours! Descends, dors toujours! Descends, dors,
    dors!
(*La porte basse c'est une bague...où la gaze*
Passe...Tout meurt, tout rit dans la gorge qui jase...
L'oiseau boit sur ta bouche et tu ne peux le voir...
Viens plus bas, parle bas...Le noir n'est pas si noir...)

Délicieux linceuls, mon désordre tiède,
Couche où je me répands, m'interroge et me cède,
Où j'allai de mon cœur noyer les battements,
Presque tombeau vivant dans mes appartements,
Qui respire, et sur qui l'éternité s'écoute.
Place pleine de moi qui m'avez prise toute,
Ô forme de ma forme et la creuse chaleur
Que mes retours sur moi reconnaissaient la leur,
Voici que tant d'orgueil qui dans vos plis se plonge
À la fin se mélange aux bassesses du songe!
Dans vos nappes, où lisse elle imitait sa mort
L'idole malgré soi se dispose et s'endort,

And pleads from far for its own surrendered hands....
The pleas of dead crowned women, give way to them,
Let the face become a breathing....
                          Gently,
I am come: my brow is at one with this consent.
     This body, I forgive it, I am tasting ash.
I am wholly given to the bliss of falling,
Exposed to dark witnesses, my arms twisted,
Among endless words muttered without my will....
Sleep, my prudence, sleep. Shape this absence;
Turn back to the seed, into dark innocence.
Give yourself up alive to the dragons, treasures....
Sleep still! Down, sleep still! Down, sleep, sleep!
(*The low door is a ring...where gauze filters....*
All dies away, laughs, in the babbling throat....
The bird sips from your mouth, you cannot see it....
Come lower, speak low....The dark is not so dark....)

Shrouds delectable, warm disarray,
Couch where I spread, question, yield to myself,
Where I set out to drown my beating heart,
Living tomb almost within my dwelling,
Breathing, on which eternity is conscious,
Shape that is filled by me and takes me whole,
Oh, form of my form, and hollow warmth
Which my returning senses knew as theirs,
Now all the pride that plunges in your folds
Is confused in the end with the low shallows of dreams!
In your sheets where smooth she simulated
Her death, the reluctant idol lies drowsing,

Lasse femme absolue, et les yeux dans ses larmes,
Quand, de ses secrets nus les antres et les charmes,
Et ce reste d'amour qui se gardait le corps
Corrompirent sa perte et ses mortels accords.

Arche toute secrète, et pourtant si prochaine,
Mes transports, cette nuit, pensaient briser ta chaîne ;
Je n'ai fait que bercer de lamentations
Tes flancs chargés de jour et de créations !
Quoi ! mes yeux froidement que tant d'azur égare
Regardent là périr l'étoile fine et rare,
Et ce jeune soleil de mes étonnements
Me paraît d'une aïeule éclairer les tourments,
Tant sa flamme aux remords ravit leur existence,
Et compose d'aurore une chère substance
Qui se formait déjà substance d'un tombeau !...
Ô, sur toute la mer, sur mes pieds, qu'il est beau !
Tu viens !...Je suis toujours celle que tu respires,
Mon voile évaporé me fuit vers tes empires...

...Alors, n'ai-je formé, vains adieux si je vis,
Que songes ?...Si je viens, en vêtements ravis,
Sur ce bord, sans horreur, humer la haute écume,
Boire des yeux l'immense et riante amertume,
L'être contre le vent, dans le plus vif de l'air,
Recevant au visage un appel de la mer ;
Si l'âme intense souffle, et renfle furibonde
L'onde abrupte sur l'onde abattue, et si l'onde
Au cap tonne, immolant un monstre de candeur,
Et vient des hautes mers vomir la profondeur
Sur ce roc, d'où jaillit jusque vers mes pensées
Un éblouissement d'étincelles glacées,

Weary, absolute woman, eyes sunk in her tears,
Since the grottoes and charms of her naked secrets
And that relic of love which possessed her body
Undid her ruin, and her mortal pact.

All-secret ark, and yet so intimate,
My night's delirium thought to snap your moorings,
But all I did was rock with my laments
Your sides thronged with day and created things!
What! coldly my eyes bewildered by so much blue
Can watch the faint, rare star there as it fades,
And this young sun of my astonishment
Seems to light up the woes of an ancestress,
Its flames so rob remorse of its existence,
Reshaping with the dawn a precious substance
That had already shaped itself to a tomb!...
Ah, lovely over all the sea, on my feet, the sun!
You are here!...I am still she whom you breathe,
My dizzy veil flies out to your empires....

...So then—vain farewells if I live—did I only
Dream?...If I come in windswept garments
To this edge, unafraid, inhaling the high foam,
My eyes drinking the immense salt laughter,
My being into the wind, in the keenest air
Receiving the sea's challenge on my face;
If the intense soul snuffs and furious swells
The sheer on the shattered wave, and if the headland
Breaker thunders, immolating a snowy monster
Come from the open sea to vomit the deeps
Over this rock, whence leaps to my very thought
A dazzling burst of icy sparks, and over

Et sur toute ma peau que morde l'âpre éveil,
Alors, malgré moi-même, il le faut, ô Soleil,
Que j'adore mon cœur où tu te viens connaître,
Doux et puissant retour du délice de naître,

Feu vers qui se soulève une vierge de sang
Sous les espèces d'or d'un sein reconnaissant !

All my skin, stung awake by the harsh shock,
Then, even against my will, I must, oh Sun,
Worship this heart where you seek to know yourself,
Strong, sweet renewal of birth's own ecstasy,

Fire to which a virgin of blood uplifts herself
Beneath the gold coinage of a grateful breast !

Cantique des colonnes

À Léon-Paul Fargue

Douces colonnes, aux
Chapeaux garnis de jour,
Ornés de vrais oiseaux
Qui marchent sur le tour,

Douces colonnes, ô
L'orchestre de fuseaux !
Chacun immole son
Silence à l'unisson.

— Que portez-vous si haut,
Égales radieuses ?
— Au désir sans défaut
Nos grâces studieuses !

Nous chantons à la fois
Que nous portons les cieux !
Ô seule et sage voix
Qui chantes pour les yeux !

Vois quels hymnes candides !
Quelle sonorité
Nos éléments limpides
Tirent de la clarté !

Si froides et dorées
Nous fûmes de nos lits
Par le ciseau tirées,
Pour devenir ces lys !

Song of the Columns

To Léon-Paul Fargue

Tender columns, whose
Hats the light garnishes,
Adorned with real birds
Walking about the brim,

Tender columns, Oh
Orchestra of spindles !
Each one sacrificing
Its silence to unison.

—What is it you bear so high,
Equals in radiance?
—To the faultless desire
Our studious graces.

We sing in one measure
How we carry the sky.
Oh voice wise and single
Singing for the eyes !

See what candid hymns,
What a sonority
Our limpid elements
Draw from clarity !

Thus cold and thus golden
Out of our beds we
Were drawn by the chisel
To become these lilies !

De nos lits de cristal
Nous fûmes éveillées,
Des griffes de métal
Nous ont appareillées.

Pour affronter la lune,
La lune et le soleil,
On nous polit chacune
Comme ongle de l'orteil !

Servantes sans genoux,
Sourires sans figures,
La belle devant nous
Se sent les jambes pures.

Pieusement pareilles,
Le nez sous le bandeau
Et nos riches oreilles
Sourdes au blanc fardeau,

Un temple sur les yeux
Noirs pour l'éternité,
Nous allons sans les dieux
À la divinité !

Nos antiques jeunesses,
Chair mate et belles ombres,
Sont fières des finesses
Qui naissent par les nombres !

Filles des nombres d'or,
Fortes des lois du ciel,
Sur nous tombe et s'endort
Un dieu couleur de miel.

From our crystal beds
We were awakened,
Claws of metal
Fashioned us alike.

To stare back at the moon,
The moon and the sun,
We were polished each one
Like the nail on the toe !

Servants unbending,
Smiles with no faces,
Beauty before us
Feels her own limbs pure.

Devoutly of a kind,
Nose hid by the bandeau,
And our rich ears
Deaf to the white load,

A temple upon eyes
Dark for eternity,
Without the gods we go
Towards divinity.

Our ancient youthfulness,
Pale flesh and noble shadows,
Takes pride in the subtleties
That are born of numbers !

Daughters of the golden numbers,
Strong in heaven's laws,
There falls and sleeps on us
A honey-colored god.

Il dort content, le Jour,
Que chaque jour offrons
Sur la table d'amour
Étale sur nos fronts.

Incorruptibles sœurs,
Mi-brûlantes, mi-fraîches,
Nous prîmes pour danseurs
Brises et feuilles sèches,

Et les siècles par dix,
Et les peuples passés,
C'est un profond jadis,
Jadis jamais assez !

Sous nos mêmes amours
Plus lourdes que le monde
Nous traversons les jours
Comme une pierre l'onde !

Nous marchons dans le temps
Et nos corps éclatants
Ont des pas ineffables
Qui marquent dans les fables...

He sleeps content, the Day
We offer every day
On the table of love
Moveless upon our brows.

Incorruptible sisters,
Half-burning, half-cool,
We took as dancing partners
Breezes and dry leaves,

And centuries in tens,
And peoples that have passed.
A deep long since it is,
Never long since enough !

Under our equal loves
Heavier than the world
We traverse the days
As through water a stone !

Our walking is in time
And our dazzling bodies
Have paces ineffable
That leave their prints in fables....

Ébauche d'un serpent

À Henri Ghéon

Parmi l'arbre, la brise berce
La vipère que je vêtis;
Un sourire, que la dent perce
Et qu'elle éclaire d'appétits,
Sur le Jardin se risque et rôde,
Et mon triangle d'émeraude
Tire sa langue à double fil...
Bête je suis, mais bête aiguë,
De qui le venin quoique vil
Laisse loin la sage ciguë!

Suave est ce temps de plaisance!
Tremblez, mortels! Je suis bien fort
Quand jamais à ma suffisance,
Je bâille à briser le ressort!
La splendeur de l'azur aiguise
Cette guivre qui me déguise
D'animale simplicité;
Venez à moi, race étourdie!
Je suis debout et dégourdie,
Pareille à la nécessité!

Soleil, soleil!...Faute éclatante!
Toi qui masques la mort, Soleil,
Sous l'azur et l'or d'une tente
Où les fleurs tiennent leur conseil;
Par d'impénétrables délices,
Toi, le plus fier de mes complices,

Silhouette of a Serpent

To Henri Ghéon

In the tree's midst, the breeze rocks
The viper whose vesture I put on;
A smile, which the tooth pricks
Lighting it up with appetites,
Ventures and roves over the Garden.
And my triangle of emerald
Juts its tongue with double file....
Beast I am, but a sharp one,
Whose venom however vile
Can far out-vie the hemlock's wisdom!

How suave is this leisurely weather!
Mortals, beware! I'm in full vigor
When, never yawning wide enough,
My jaw gapes fit to break the lock!
The blue sky in its splendor sharpens
This wyvern who disguises me
In animal simplicity;
Come unto me, ye thoughtless ones.
I am erect and all-alert,
Exactly like necessity!

Sun!...Oh Sun, you glaring error!
You who are death's own lifemask, Sun,
Under the or and azure pavilion
That tents the flowers holding council;
By way of delights impenetrable
You, my proudest accomplice,

243

Et de mes pièges le plus haut,
Tu gardes les cœurs de connaître
Que l'univers n'est qu'un défaut
Dans la pureté du Non-être !

Grand Soleil, qui sonnes l'éveil
À l'être, et de feux l'accompagnes,
Toi qui l'enfermes d'un sommeil
Trompeusement peint de campagnes,
Fauteur des fantômes joyeux
Qui rendent sujette des yeux
La présence obscure de l'âme,
Toujours le mensonge m'a plu
Que tu répands sur l'absolu,
Ô roi des ombres fait de flamme !

Verse-moi ta brute chaleur,
Où vient ma paresse glacée
Rêvasser de quelque malheur
Selon ma nature enlacée...
Ce lieu charmant qui vit la chair
Choir et se joindre m'est très cher !
Ma fureur, ici, se fait mûre;
Je la conseille et la recuis,
Je m'écoute, et dans mes circuits,
Ma méditation murmure...

Ô Vanité ! Cause Première !
Celui qui règne dans les Cieux,
D'une voix qui fut la lumière
Ouvrit l'univers spacieux.
Comme las de son pur spectacle,

And loftiest of all my snares,
You protect all hearts from knowing
That the universe is merely a blot
On the pure void of Non-being!

Great Sun, sounding the reveille
To being, and clothing it with fire,
You who fence it in a slumber
Painted about with cheating landscapes,
Fomenter of the gay phantoms
Who enslave to the eye's seeing
The uncertain presence of the soul,
I have always enjoyed the lie
You throw across the absolute,
O king of shadows made of flame!

Pour me out your brutish heat,
Where my icy idleness
May daydream of some evil or other
Appropriate to my knotted being. . . .
How dear to me these charming purlieus
That saw flesh fall and join together!
Here my fury grows mature,
I counsel it and mull it over,
I listen to me, and in my coils
Hear my meditations murmur. . . .

O Vanity! Very First Cause!
The Other who reigns in the Heavens,
With the word that was light itself
Opened the spacious universe.
As though bored with the pure theater

Dieu lui-même a rompu l'obstacle
De sa parfaite éternité;
Il se fit Celui qui dissipe
En conséquences, son Principe,
En étoiles, son Unité.

Cieux, son erreur ! Temps, sa ruine !
Et l'abîme animal, béant !...
Quelle chute dans l'origine
Étincelle au lieu de néant !...
Mais, le premier mot de son Verbe,
MOI !...Des astres le plus superbe
Qu'ait parlés le fou créateur,
Je suis !...Je serai !...J'illumine
La diminution divine
De tous les feux du Séducteur !

Objet radieux de ma haine,
Vous que j'aimais éperdument,
Vous qui dûtes de la géhenne
Donner l'empire à cet amant,
Regardez-vous dans ma ténèbre !
Devant votre image funèbre,
Orgueil de mon sombre miroir,
Si profond fut votre malaise
Que votre souffle sur la glaise
Fut un soupir de désespoir !

En vain, Vous avez, dans la fange,
Pétri de faciles enfants,
Qui de Vos actes triomphants
Tout le jour Vous fissent louange !

Of Self, God broke the barrier
Of his perfect eternity:
He became He who fritters away
His Primal Cause in consequences,
And in stars his Unity.

Skies, his blunder! Time, his undoing!
And the animal abyss agape!
What a collapse into origin,
Glitters in place of total void!...
But the first syllable of his Word
Was ME!...The proudest of the stars
Uttered by the besotted maker,
I am!...Shall be!...I illuminate
How divinity was diminished
By all the fires of the Seducer!

Radiant target of my hate
Whom I once desperately loved,
You who had to give dominion
Over Gehenna to this your lover,
See yourself in my mirroring gloom!
Faced with your own funereal image,
Glory of my darkling glass,
So profound was your distress
That when you breathed over the clay
It was a sign of hopelessness!

All in vain You, out of the mud,
Molded these infants, facile toys,
So that Your triumphant deeds
Be lauded day-long by their praise!

Sitôt pétris, sitôt soufflés,
Maître Serpent les a sifflés,
Les beaux enfants que Vous créâtes !
Holà ! dit-il, nouveaux venus !
Vous êtes des hommes tout nus,
Ô bêtes blanches et béates !

À la ressemblance exécrée,
Vous fûtes faits, et je vous hais !
Comme je hais le Nom qui crée
Tant de prodiges imparfaits !
Je suis Celui qui modifie,
Je retouche au cœur qui s'y fie,
D'un doigt sûr et mystérieux !...
Nous changerons ces molles œuvres,
Et ces évasives couleuvres
En des reptiles furieux !

Mon Innombrable Intelligence
Touche dans l'âme des humains
Un instrument de ma vengeance
Qui fut assemblé de tes mains !
Et ta Paternité voilée,
Quoique, dans sa chambre étoilée,
Elle n'accueille que l'encens,
Toutefois l'excès de mes charmes
Pourra de lointaines alarmes
Troubler ses desseins tout-puissants !

Je vais, je viens, je glisse, plonge,
Je disparais dans un cœur pur !
Fut-il jamais de sein si dur

No sooner molded and set to breathe
Than Snake applauded with a hiss
The pretty infants You had made!
Hi there, said I, you new arrivals,
You know you are human, and stark naked,
Oh snow-white sanctimonious beasts!

In the likeness of the accursed
You were made, and you I hate
As I hate the Name that creates
All these imperfect prodigies!
I am He who modifies,
I re-touch the incautious heart
With a sure, mysterious finger!...
We'll transform these tender products,
These self-effacing little snakes
Into reptiles of pure fury!

My Numberless Intelligence
Finds in the souls of human things
A playable instrument of my vengeance
Put together by your hands!
And though your Paternity,
Veiled aloft in its starry chamber,
May receive nothing but incense,
Still my overpowering charms
Can disturb its almighty designs
With the remotest of alarms!

I come, I go, I glide, I plunge
Vanishing into the pure of heart!
Was there ever a soul so tough

Qu'on n'y puisse loger un songe !
Qui que tu sois, ne suis-je point
Cette complaisance qui poind
Dans ton âme, lorsqu'elle s'aime ?
Je suis au fond de sa faveur
Cette inimitable saveur
Que tu ne trouves qu'à toi-même !

Ève, jadis, je la surpris,
Parmi ses premières pensées,
La lèvre entr'ouverte aux esprits
Qui naissaient des roses bercées.
Cette parfaite m'apparut,
Son flanc vaste et d'or parcouru
Ne craignant le soleil ni l'homme ;
Tout offerte aux regards de l'air,
L'âme encore stupide, et comme
Interdite au seuil de la chair.

Ô masse de béatitude,
Tu es si belle, juste prix
De la toute sollicitude
Des bons et des meilleurs esprits !
Pour qu'à tes lèvres ils soient pris
Il leur suffit que tu soupires !
Les plus purs s'y penchent les pires,
Les plus durs sont les plus meurtris...
Jusques à moi, tu m'attendris,
De qui relèvent les vampires !

Oui ! De mon poste de feuillage
Reptile aux extases d'oiseau,

As to leave no lodgment for a dream?
Whoever you be, whatever am I
If not the connivance that begins
In your mind when it pleases itself?
In the depths of that very pleasure
I'm the inimitable flavor
You find that you alone possess!

Eve, long since, I took by surprise
In the depths of her dawning mind,
Her lip just opened to the ideas
Inspired by the rocking roses.
That perfection greeted my gaze,
Her spacious flank overrun with golden
Light, fearless of sun or man;
All exposed to the watching air,
Her soul still stupid, as it were,
Nonplussed on the sill of the flesh.

Oh, mass of beatitude,
How lovely you are, a just reward
For the total solicitude
Of good—and even superior minds!
To make them captive of your lips
All you need do is breathe!
The purest are smitten the worst,
The toughest are the most deeply bitten....
Yes, even me, you soften the heart
From whence the vampires arose!

True! In my leafy post of vantage,
Reptile ecstatic as a bird,

Cependant que mon babillage
Tissait de ruses le réseau,
Je te buvais, ô belle sourde !
Calme, claire, de charmes lourde,
Je dominais furtivement,
L'œil dans l'or ardent de ta laine,
Ta nuque énigmatique et pleine
Des secrets de ton mouvement !

J'étais présent comme une odeur,
Comme l'arôme d'une idée
Dont ne puisse être élucidée
L'insidieuse profondeur !
Et je t'inquiétais, candeur,
Ô chair mollement décidée,
Sans que je t'eusse intimidée,
À chanceler dans la splendeur !
Bientôt, je t'aurai, je parie,
Déjà ta nuance varie !

(La superbe simplicité
Demande d'immenses égards !
Sa transparence de regards,
Sottise, orgueil, félicité,
Gardent bien la belle cité !
Sachons lui créer des hasards,
Et par ce plus rare des arts,
Soit le cœur pur sollicité;
C'est là mon fort, c'est là mon fin,
À moi les moyens de ma fin !)

While my innocent warblings wove
Their web of ruses, lovely one,
All unawares I was drinking you in!
Calm, clear, loaded with charms,
I was slily taking command
Of the eye in your bright gold fleece,
Your enigmatic nape, charged
With the secrets of your moves!

I was immanent like a scent,
The aroma of an idea
Whose deep insidious element
Nothing can quite elucidate!
And I was troubling your candor,
O flesh, just inclining to weakness
(Though never offering you a threat)
You tottered in that blaze of glory!
Soon I'll have you, I lay a bet,
Already your mood begins to vary!

(Glorious simplicity
Calls for the immensest care!
Its transparency of gaze,
Stupidity, pride, self-content,
Are guardians of the citadel!
Let us invent some risks for it,
And by this rarest of all arts
Let the pure heart be solicited;
That's my forte, that's my craft,
I make my means to fit my ends!)

Or, d'une éblouissante bave,
Filons les systèmes légers
Où l'oisive et l'Ève suave
S'engage en de vagues dangers !
Que sous une charge de soie
Tremble la peau de cette proie
Accoutumée au seul azur !...
Mais de gaze point de subtile,
Ni de fil invisible et sûr,
Plus qu'une trame de mon style !

Dore, langue ! dore-lui les
Plus doux des dits que tu connaisses !
Allusions, fables, finesses,
Mille silences ciselés,
Use de tout ce qui lui nuise:
Rien qui ne flatte et ne l'induise
À se perdre dans mes desseins,
Docile à ces pentes qui rendent
Aux profondeurs des bleus bassins
Les ruisseaux qui des cieux descendent !

Ô quelle prose non pareille,
Que d'esprit n'ai-je pas jeté
Dans le dédale duveté
De cette merveilleuse oreille !
Là, pensais-je, rien de perdu;
Tout profite au cœur suspendu !
Sûr triomphe ! si ma parole,
De l'âme obsédant le trésor,
Comme une abeille une corolle
Ne quitte plus l'oreille d'or !

So, out of a dazzling slime
Let's weave systems of gossamer
Where Eve the idle and the smooth
Involves herself in doubt and danger !
May it, under a weight of silk,
Tremble, this victim whose skin
Is used to nothing but blue air ! . . .
For of gauze there's none so fine,
No thread so invisible and strong
As the filament of my style !

Tongue, embroider, gild for her
The softest sayings that you know.
Allusions, fables, finest fancies,
A thousand chiseled silences,
Using anything that may injure :
All that may flatter and guide
Her to perdition in my designs;
Docile to the slopes restoring
To the depths of the blue lakes
The streams that shower from the skies !

Ah, what a prose unparalleled,
What wit did I spare to throw
In the dedal downy windings
Of that most delightful ear !
Nothing, thought I, is wasted there,
All works on an undecided heart !
Triumph is certain, if my speech
Besieging the treasury of the soul,
Like a bee in a flower-bell,
Never quits that ear of gold.

«Rien, lui soufflais-je, n'est moins sûr
Que la parole divine, Ève!
Une science vive crève
L'énormité de ce fruit mûr!
N'écoute l'Être vieil et pur
Qui maudit la morsure brève!
Que si ta bouche fait un rêve,
Cette soif qui songe à la sève,
Ce délice à demi futur,
C'est l'éternité fondante, Ève!»

Elle buvait mes petits mots
Qui bâtissaient une œuvre étrange;
Son œil, parfois, perdait un ange
Pour revenir à mes rameaux.
Le plus rusé des animaux
Qui te raille d'être si dure,
Ô perfide et grosse de maux,
N'est qu'une voix dans la verdure!
— Mais sérieuse l'Ève était
Qui sous la branche l'écoutait!

«Âme, disais-je, doux séjour
De toute extase prohibée,
Sens-tu la sinueuse amour
Que j'ai du Père dérobée?
Je l'ai, cette essence du Ciel,
À des fins plus douces que miel
Délicatement ordonnée...
Prends de ce fruit...Dresse ton bras!
Pour cueillir ce que tu voudras
Ta belle main te fut donnée!»

"Nothing," I prompted, "is more unsure
Than the divine pronouncement, Eve!
A live knowledge will soon burst
The enormity of that ripe fruit.
Don't heed the ancient Puritan
Who laid a curse on the briefest bite.
For if your mouth holds a daydream,
A thirst, musing upon a savor,
That just-about-to-be delight
Is melt-in-the-mouth eternity, Eve!"

She drank in my casual words,
As they built a curious edifice;
Her eye would quit an angel's flight
To turn back towards my bower.
The craftiest of animal kind
Teasing you for being so hard,
Oh traitorous one, big with evils,
Is a bodiless voice in the greenery!
—But solemn she stood, this Eve,
Under the bough, listening hard!

"Soul," I murmured, "tender retreat
Of all prohibited ecstasy,
Can you divine the sinuous love
Which from the Father I've purloined?
That very essence of Heaven
To a purpose sweeter than honey
I have delicately devised. . . .
Try this fruit. . . . Stretch your arm. . . !
To choose and pick whatever you will
Is why you were given that lovely hand!"

257

Quel silence battu d'un cil!
Mais quel souffle sous le sein sombre
Que mordait l'Arbre de son ombre!
L'autre brillait comme un pistil!
— *Siffle, siffle!* me chantait-il!
Et je sentais frémir le nombre,
Tout le long de mon fouet subtil,
Des ces replis dont je m'encombre:
Ils roulaient depuis le béryl
De ma crête, jusqu'au péril!

Génie! Ô longue impatience!
À la fin, les temps sont venus,
Qu'un pas vers la neuve Science
Va donc jaillir de ces pieds nus!
Le marbre aspire, l'or se cambre!
Ces blondes bases d'ombre et d'ambre
Tremblent au bord du mouvement!...
Elle chancelle, la grande urne,
D'où va fuir le consentement
De l'apparente taciturne!

Du plaisir que tu te proposes
Cède, cher corps, cède aux appâts!
Que ta soif de métamorphoses
Autour de l'Arbre du Trépas
Engendre une chaîne de poses!
Viens sans venir! forme des pas
Vaguement comme lourds de roses...
Danse, cher corps...Ne pense pas!
Ici les délices sont causes
Suffisantes au cours des choses!...

A silence stricken by an eyelash beat!
But such a heave of breath in the dark
Breast bitten by the Tree's shadow!
The other breast shone like a pistil.
—*Whistle, hiss!* It hummed to me.
I felt a quiver throughout the number,
The whole length of my slender whip,
Of all the coils I am burdened with,
Rippling downwards from the beryl
Of my crest to my tip of peril!

Genius! Oh tedious impatience!
Now at last the moment comes
When a step towards the new Science
Will issue from those naked feet!
The marble yearns, the gold stretches,
Those fair foundations of shadow and amber
Tremble on the brink of movement!...
She is tilting, the great urn
Whence will trickle the consent
Of the seemingly wordless one!

The pleasure that your mind proposes,
Yield, dear body, yield to its charms!
Let your thirst for transformations
All around the Tree of Death
Give birth to a chain of poses.
Come without seeming to! making paces
As vague as though loaded with roses....
Dear body, dance....With never a thought!
Here is where delights are causes
Sufficient to the course of events!...

Ô follement que je m'offrais
Cette infertile jouissance :
Voir le long pur d'un dos si frais
Frémir la désobéissance !...
Déjà délivrant son essence
De sagesse et d'illusions,
Tout l'Arbre de la Connaissance
Échevelé de visions,
Agitait son grand corps qui plonge
Au soleil, et suce le songe !

Arbre, grand Arbre, Ombre des Cieux,
Irrésistible Arbre des arbres,
Qui dans les faiblesses des marbres,
Poursuis des sucs délicieux,
Toi qui pousses tels labyrinthes
Par qui les ténèbres étreintes
S'iront perdre dans le saphir
De l'éternelle matinée,
Douce perte, arôme ou zéphir,
Ou colombe prédestinée,

Ô Chanteur, ô secret buveur
Des plus profondes pierreries,
Berceau du reptile rêveur
Qui jeta l'Ève en rêveries,
Grand Être agité de savoir,
Qui toujours, comme pour mieux voir,
Grandis à l'appel de ta cime,
Toi qui dans l'or très pur promeus
Tes bras durs, tes rameaux fumeux,
D'autre part, creusant vers l'abîme,

Ah how madly I coveted
That copulation with barrenness:
To see the pure length of that cool spine
Quiver with disobedience!...
Already surrendering its essence
Of wisdom and illusions,
Throughout itself the Tree of Knowledge
Shaken, dishevelled with visions,
Shivered its huge body that plunges
Into the sun, and sucks at nightmares!

Tree, great Tree, Shadow of Heaven,
Irresistible Tree of trees,
Who find even in marble's weakness
A way to pursue the sap's sweet courses,
You whose labyrinthine growths
Are such as constrain the darknesses
To rise and be lost in the sapphire blue
Of the everlasting morning,
—Sweet the shedding of scent or zephyr,
Or else the predestined dove—

Oh Singer, and secret drinker
Of the deepest hidden stones,
Cradling the dreamy reptile
Who tossed his reveries to Eve,
Great Being, restless with knowing,
Forever, as though to enhance your seeing,
Growing towards your urging summit,
You who promote into purest gold
Your hard boughs, your misty branches,
While digging the abyss, its opposite,

261

Tu peux repousser l'infini
Qui n'est fait que de ta croissance,
Et de la tombe jusqu'au nid
Te sentir toute Connaissance !
Mais ce vieil amateur d'échecs,
Dans l'or oisif des soleils secs,
Sur ton branchage vient se tordre ;
Ses yeux font frémir ton trésor.
Il en cherra des fruits de mort,
De désespoir et de désordre !

Beau serpent, bercé dans le bleu,
Je siffle, avec délicatesse,
Offrant à la gloire de Dieu
Le triomphe de ma tristesse...
Il me suffit que dans les airs,
L'immense espoir de fruits amers
Affole les fils de la fange...
— Cette soif qui te fit géant,
Jusqu'à l'Être exalte l'étrange
Toute-Puissance du Néant !

You can press back the infinite,
It's only made of your increase,
And every inch from tomb to nest
Feel you are the all of Knowledge!
But this old amateur of checkers,
In the sun's dry and lazy gold,
Comes a-winding in your branchage;
In his gaze your treasure flickers.
Fruits of death it will let fall,
Of desperation, and chaos!

Lovely serpent, rocked in the blue,
With all delicacy I hiss
Offering God's glory the due
Triumph of my balefulness....
Enough for me if, in the air,
The giant promise of bitter fruits
Should madden the children of clay....
—The very thirst that made you huge
Can raise to the power of Being the strange
All-probing force of Nothingness!

Les Grenades

Dures grenades entr'ouvertes
Cédant à l'excès de vos grains,
Je crois voir des fronts souverains
Éclatés de leurs découvertes !

Si les soleils par vous subis,
Ô grenades entre-bâillées,
Vous ont fait d'orgueil travaillées
Craquer les cloisons de rubis,

Et que si l'or sec de l'écorce
À la demande d'une force
Crève en gemmes rouges de jus,

Cette lumineuse rupture
Fait rêver une âme que j'eus
De sa secrète architecture.

Pomegranates

Tough pomegranates half-opening
Yielding to your intemperate seeds,
I see you as brows of sovereign minds
Bursting with their discoveries!

If the suns that you've endured,
Oh pomegranates agape,
Have made you overworked with pride
Crack open your partitioned rubies,

And if the parched gold of the rind
Responding to a certain force
Explodes in gems ruddy with juice,

That illuminating rupture
Recalls a dream to a soul I had
About its secret architecture.

Le Vin perdu

J'ai, quelque jour, dans l'Océan,
(Mais je ne sais plus sous quels cieux),
Jeté, comme offrande au néant,
Tout un peu de vin précieux...

Qui voulut ta perte, ô liqueur?
J'obéis peut-être au devin?
Peut-être au souci de mon cœur,
Songeant au sang, versant le vin?

Sa transparence accoutumée
Après une rose fumée
Reprit aussi pure la mer...

Perdu ce vin, ivres les ondes!...
J'ai vu bondir dans l'air amer
Les figures les plus profondes...

The Lost Wine

Once on a day, in the open Sea
(Under what skies I cannot recall),
I threw, as oblation to vacancy,
More than a drop of precious wine.. . .

Who decreed your waste, oh potion?
Did I perhaps obey some divine?
Or else the heart's anxiety,
Dreaming blood, spilling the wine?

Its habitual clarity
After a mist of rosiness
Returned as pure again to the sea.. . .

The wine lost, drunken the waves !. . .
I saw leaping in the salt air
Shapes of the utmost profundity.. . .

Le Cimetière marin

Μή, φίλα ψυχά, βίον ἀθάνατον
σπεῦδε, τὰν δ'ἔμπρακτον ἄντλει μαχανάν.
Pindare, *Pythiques*

Ce toit tranquille, où marchent des colombes,
Entre les pins palpite, entre les tombes;
Midi le juste y compose de feux
La mer, la mer, toujours recommencée !
Ô récompense après une pensée
Qu'un long regard sur le calme des dieux !

Quel pur travail de fins éclairs consume
Maint diamant d'imperceptible écume,
Et quelle paix semble se concevoir !
Quand sur l'abîme un soleil se repose,
Ouvrages purs d'une éternelle cause,
Le Temps scintille et le Songe est savoir.

Stable trésor, temple simple à Minerve,
Masse de calme, et visible réserve,
Eau sourcilleuse, Œil qui gardes en toi
Tant de sommeil sous un voile de flamme,
Ô mon silence !. . . Édifice dans l'âme,
Mais comble d'or aux mille tuiles, Toit !

Temple du Temps, qu'un seul soupir résume,
À ce point pur je monte et m'accoutume,
Tout entouré de mon regard marin;
Et comme aux dieux mon offrande suprême,
La scintillation sereine sème
Sur l'altitude un dédain souverain.

The Graveyard by the Sea

My soul, do not seek immortal life,
but exhaust the realm of the possible.
Pindar, *Pythian Odes.*

Quiet that roof, where the doves are walking,
Quivers between the pines, between the tombs;
Justicer Noon out there compounds with fires
The sea, the sea perpetually renewed!
Ah what a recompense, after a thought,
A prolonged gazing on the calm of gods!

What lucid toil of pure lightings consumes
Many a diamond of imperceptible foams,
And what a stillness seems to beget itself.
For while a sun hangs over the abyss,
Pure workings of an eternal cause,
Time scintillates, and the Dream is knowledge.

Store of sameness, temple sheer to Minerva,
Massively tranquil, visibly contained,
Supercilious deep, Eye keeping your secret
Of all that slumber in a veil of flame,
My own silence!...The soul's edifice...
But towering gold, Roof of a thousand tiles!

Time's temple, summed up in a breath,
Having reached this pure height, I grow used
To my marine gaze, all around,
And as my ultimate offering to the gods,
The serene scintillation over the height
Disseminates a sovereign disdain.

Comme le fruit se fond en jouissance,
Comme en délice il change son absence
Dans une bouche où sa forme se meurt,
Je hume ici ma future fumée
Et le ciel chante à l'âme consumée
Le changement des rives en rumeur.

Beau ciel, vrai ciel, regarde-moi qui change !
Après tant d'orgueil, après tant d'étrange
Oisiveté, mais pleine de pouvoir,
Je m'abandonne à ce brillant espace,
Sur les maisons des morts mon ombre passe
Qui m'apprivoise à son frêle mouvoir.

L'âme exposée aux torches du solstice,
Je te soutiens, admirable justice
De la lumière aux armes sans pitié !
Je te rends pure à ta place première :
Regarde-toi !. . . Mais rendre la lumière
Suppose d'ombre une morne moitié.

Ô pour moi seul, à moi seul, en moi-même,
Auprès d'un cœur, aux sources du poème,
Entre le vide et l'événement pur,
J'attends l'écho de ma grandeur interne,
Amère, sombre et sonore citerne,
Sonnant dans l'âme un creux toujours futur !

Sais-tu, fausse captive des feuillages,
Golfe mangeur de ces maigres grillages,
Sur mes yeux clos, secrets éblouissants,
Quel corps me traîne à sa fin paresseuse,
Quel front l'attire à cette terre osseuse ?
Une étincelle y pense à mes absents.

As a fruit dissolves into a taste,
Changing its absence to deliciousness
Within a palate where its shape must die,
Here I can savor my own future smoke,
And the sky sings to the soul consumed
The changing of the shores into a sigh.

Clear heaven, true heaven, look at me, I change !
After so much pride, after so much strange
Idleness, and yet instilled with power,
I give myself up to this shining space,
And over the houses of the dead my shadow
Passes, taming me to that frail mover.

With soul stripped to the torches of the solstice,
I can withstand you, admirable justice
Of light itself, with your pitiless blades !
I give you back pure to your primal place,
Look at yourself!. . .But to reflect the light
Bespeaks another half of mournful shade.

Ah for myself, to my own self within,
Close by a heart, at the sources of the poem,
Between emptiness and the pure event,
I await my grandeur's echo from within,
That bitter, gloomy and resounding cistern
Ringing in the soul a still future void !

Can you tell, sham prisoner of the leaves,
Gulf devouring these flimsy rails,
On my closed eyes, dazzling secrecy,
What body drags me to its lazy end,
What brow attracts it to this bony ground?
A spark within there thinks of absent ones.

Fermé, sacré, plein d'un feu sans matière,
Fragment terrestre offert à la lumière,
Ce lieu me plaît, dominé de flambeaux,
Composé d'or, de pierre et d'arbres sombres,
Où tant de marbre est tremblant sur tant d'ombres;
La mer fidèle y dort sur mes tombeaux!

Chienne splendide, écarte l'idolâtre!
Quand solitaire au sourire de pâtre,
Je pais longtemps, moutons mystérieux,
Le blanc troupeau de mes tranquilles tombes,
Éloignes-en les prudentes colombes,
Les songes vains, les anges curieux!

Ici venu, l'avenir est paresse.
L'insecte net gratte la sécheresse;
Tout est brûlé, défait, reçu dans l'air
À je ne sais quelle sévère essence...
La vie est vaste, étant ivre d'absence,
Et l'amertume est douce, et l'esprit clair.

Les morts cachés sont bien dans cette terre
Qui les réchauffe et sèche leur mystère.
Midi là-haut, Midi sans mouvement
En soi se pense et convient à soi-même...
Tête complète et parfait diadème,
Je suis en toi le secret changement.

Tu n'as que moi pour contenir tes craintes!
Mes repentirs, mes doutes, mes contraintes
Sont le défaut de ton grand diamant...
Mais dans leur nuit toute lourde de marbres,
Un peuple vague aux racines des arbres
A pris déjà ton parti lentement.

Shut in, sacred, crammed with bodiless fire,
A patch of ground offered up to the light,
Crowned with flambeaux, this purlieu pleases me,
Compact of gilt, stone, and solemn trees
Where so much marble quivers on so many shadows;
The faithful sea's asleep there on my tombs!

Glorious bitch-hound, keep out the idolater!
While solitary, smiling like a shepherd,
I graze for hours my mysterious
Sheep, the white flock of my peaceful tombs,
Keep far away from here the cautious doves,
The vain dreams, the prying angels!

Once here, the future is an idleness,
The clear-cut insect scratches at the dryness;
Everything's burned, dispelled, received in air
Into I know not what impartial essence....
Life is immense, being drunk with its own absence,
And bitterness is sweet, the mind clear.

The dead concealed lie easy in this earth
That keeps them warm, drying their mystery.
And Noon up there, Noon the motionless,
Thinks its own thought approving its own self....
Total head, and perfect diadem,
I am the secret changing in your mind.

I am all you have to contain your fears!
My doubts, my strivings, my repentances,
These are the flaw in your great diamond....
But in their darkness under a marble load
An empty people among the tree roots
Have gradually come to take your side.

Ils ont fondu dans une absence épaisse,
L'argile rouge a bu la blanche espèce,
Le don de vivre a passé dans les fleurs !
Où sont des morts les phrases familières,
L'art personnel, les âmes singulières?
La larve file où se formaient des pleurs.

Les cris aigus des filles chatouillées,
Les yeux, les dents, les paupières mouillées,
Le sein charmant qui joue avec le feu,
Le sang qui brille aux lèvres qui se rendent,
Les derniers dons, les doigts qui les défendent,
Tout va sous terre et rentre dans le jeu !

Et vous, grande âme, espérez-vous un songe
Qui n'aura plus ces couleurs de mensonge
Qu'aux yeux de chair l'onde et l'or font ici?
Chanterez-vous quand serez vaporeuse?
Allez ! Tout fuit ! Ma présence est poreuse,
La sainte impatience meurt aussi !

Maigre immortalité noire et dorée,
Consolatrice affreusement laurée,
Qui de la mort fais un sein maternel,
Le beau mensonge et la pieuse ruse !
Qui ne connaît, et qui ne les refuse,
Ce crâne vide et ce rire éternel !

Pères profonds, têtes inhabitées,
Qui sous le poids de tant de pelletées,
Êtes la terre et confondez nos pas,
Le vrai rongeur, le ver irréfutable
N'est point pour vous qui dormez sous la table,
Il vit de vie, il ne me quitte pas !

They have melted into a dense unbeing,
The red clay has drained the paler kind,
The gift of living has passed into flowers!
Where now are the singular souls of the dead,
Their personal ways, the tricks of speech they had?
The worm channels its way where tears formed.

The piercing cries of girls being tickled,
The eyes, the teeth, the moistened eyelids,
The enchanting breast that frolics with the flame,
The blood glistening in yielding lips,
The ultimate boons, the fingers that defend...
All goes to earth and back into the game!

And you, great soul, still hoping for a dream
That will be delivered from these lying colors
Which sun and wave make here for eyes of flesh?
Will you sing, when you are vaporous?
Go on! Time flies! My presence here is porous,
Holy impatience also dies the death!

Skinny immortality, black and gilt-lettered,
Hideously laurel-crowned she-comforter,
Trying to make death a maternal lap,
—A pretty fiction, and a pious ruse!—
Who cannot know, and who cannot refuse
That empty skull, the eternal grinning gape!

Fathers deep-laid, heads uninhabited,
Who under the weight of so many spade-loads,
Are earth itself and who confound our steps,
The real canker, the irrefutable worm
Is not for you asleep under the table,
He lives on life, it's me he never quits!

Amour, peut-être, ou de moi-même haine?
Sa dent secrète est de moi si prochaine
Que tous les noms lui peuvent convenir!
Qu'importe! Il voit, il veut, il songe, il touche!
Ma chair lui plaît, et jusque sur ma couche,
À ce vivant je vis d'appartenir!

Zénon! Cruel Zénon! Zénon d'Élée!
M'as-tu percé de cette flèche ailée
Qui vibre, vole, et qui ne vole pas!
Le son m'enfante et la flèche me tue!
Ah! le soleil... Quelle ombre de tortue
Pour l'âme, Achille immobile à grands pas!

Non, non!... Debout! Dans l'ère successive!
Brisez, mon corps, cette forme pensive!
Buvez, mon sein, la naissance du vent!
Une fraîcheur, de la mer exhalée,
Me rend mon âme... Ô puissance salée!
Courons à l'onde en rejaillir vivant!

Oui! Grande mer de délires douée,
Peau de panthère et chlamyde trouée
De mille et mille idoles du soleil,
Hydre absolue, ivre de ta chair bleue,
Qui te remords l'étincelante queue
Dans un tumulte au silence pareil,

Le vent se lève!... Il faut tenter de vivre!
L'air immense ouvre et referme mon livre,
La vague en poudre ose jaillir des rocs!
Envolez-vous, pages tout éblouies!
Rompez, vagues! Rompez d'eaux réjouies
Ce toit tranquille où picoraient des focs!

Love, it may be, or else self-hatred?
Its secret tooth is so my intimate
That any name you choose to give could fit!
No matter what! It sees, wants, dreams and touches,
It likes my flesh, and even on my bed
My life's possessed by that undying one!

Zeno, Zeno, the cruel, Elean Zeno!
You've truly fixed me with that feathered arrow
Which quivers as it flies and never moves!
The sound begets me and the arrow kills!
Ah, sun!...What a tortoise shadow for the soul,
Achilles motionless in his giant stride!

No, no! Up! And away into the next era!
Break, body, break this pensive mold,
Lungs, drink in the beginnings of the wind!
A coolness, exhalation of the sea,
Gives me my soul back!...Ah, salt potency,
Into the wave with us, and out alive!

Yes, gigantic sea delirium-dowered,
Panther-hide, and chlamys filled with holes
By thousands of the sun's dazzling idols,
Absolute hydra, drunk with your blue flesh,
Forever biting your own glittering tail
In a commotion that is silence's equal,

The wind is rising!...We must try to live!
The immense air opens and shuts my book,
A wave dares burst in powder over the rocks.
Pages, whirl away in a dazzling riot!
And break, waves, rejoicing, break that quiet
Roof where foraging sails dipped their beaks!

Palme

À Jeannie

De sa grâce redoutable
Voilant à peine l'éclat,
Un ange met sur ma table
Le pain tendre, le lait plat;
Il me fait de la paupière
Le signe d'une prière
Qui parle à ma vision:
— Calme, calme, reste calme !
Connais le poids d'une palme
Portant sa profusion !

Pour autant qu'elle se plie
À l'abondance des biens,
Sa figure est accomplie,
Ses fruits lourds sont ses liens.
Admire comme elle vibre,
Et comme une lente fibre
Qui divise le moment,
Départage sans mystère
L'attirance de la terre
Et le poids du firmament !

Ce bel arbitre mobile
Entre l'ombre et le soleil,
Simule d'une sibylle
La sagesse et le sommeil.
Autour d'une même place

Palm

To Jeannie

Of his formidable grace
Scarcely veiling the glory,
An angel lays on my table
Tender bread, smooth milk;
With his eyelid he makes
Me the sign of a prayer
That speaks to my seeing:
—Calm, calm, still be calm!
Know the weightiness of a palm
Bearing its profusion.

For as much as it may bend
Under its treasured abundance,
Its form is fulfilled,
Its heavy fruits are its bond.
Wonder at how it sways,
And how a gradual sinew
Dividing a moment of time
Unpretendingly apportions
The attraction of the ground
And the weight of the firmament!

Lovely mobile arbiter
Between the shadow and the sun,
It simulates the wisdom
And the slumber of a sibyl.
Still about the same place

L'ample palme ne se lasse
Des appels ni des adieux...
Qu'elle est noble, qu'elle est tendre !
Qu'elle est digne de s'attendre
À la seule main des dieux !

L'or léger qu'elle murmure
Sonne au simple doigt de l'air,
Et d'une soyeuse armure
Charge l'âme du désert.
Une voix impérissable
Qu'elle rend au vent de sable
Qui l'arrose des ses grains,
À soi-même sert d'oracle,
Et se flatte du miracle
Que se chantent les chagrins.

Cependant qu'elle s'ignore
Entre le sable et le ciel,
Chaque jour qui luit encore
Lui compose un peu de miel.
Sa douceur est mesurée
Par la divine durée
Qui ne compte pas les jours,
Mais bien qui les dissimule
Dans un suc où s'accumule
Toute l'arôme des amours.

Parfois si l'on désespère,
Si l'adorable rigueur
Malgré tes larmes n'opère

CHARMS

The ample palm tree never tires
Of summonses and farewells....
How noble it is, and tender,
How worthy to await
Only the hands of gods !

The frail gold it murmurs
Rings on the air's artless finger,
And with a silky armor
Invests the soul of the desert.
An imperishable voice
Which it gives to the sandy wind
Sprinkling it with its grains,
Serves as its own oracle,
Soothing itself with the miracle
The griefs sing to themselves.

Self-oblivious the while
Between heaven and the sand,
Every day as it still shines
Compounds another mite of honey.
This sweetness is measured out
By the divine durability
That is not counted in days
But rather disguises them
In a juice where accumulates
All the aroma of the loves.

If at times there is despair,
If the adorable strictness,
For all your tears only labors

Que sous ombre de langueur,
N'accuse pas d'être avare
Une Sage qui prépare
Tant d'or et d'autorité:
Par la sève solennelle
Une espérance éternelle
Monte à la maturité!

Ces jours qui te semblent vides
Et perdus pour l'univers
Ont des racines avides
Qui travaillent les déserts.
La substance chevelue
Par les ténèbres élue
Ne peut s'arrêter jamais,
Jusqu'aux entrailles du monde,
De poursuivre l'eau profonde
Que demandent les sommets.

Patience, patience,
Patience dans l'azur!
Chaque atome de silence
Est la chance d'un fruit mûr!
Viendra l'heureuse surprise:
Une colombe, la brise,
L'ébranlement le plus doux,
Une femme qui s'appuie,
Feront tomber cette pluie
Où l'on se jette à genoux!

Qu'un peuple à présent s'écroule,
Palme!...irrésistiblement!

Under the guise of languors,
Do not accuse of miserliness
Her Wisdom as it prepares
So much gold and so much power:
Through the sap's funereal pace
An ever-living hopefulness
Mounts towards its ripening.

These days that seem to you void
And wasted for the universe,
Have their roots of eagerness
That put the deserts to work.
That dense and hairy mass
Allotted to the shades
Never can arrest itself,
Into the world's entrails
Pursuing water in the depths
To satisfy the treetop.

Endurance, endurance,
Endurance, in the sky's blue!
Every atom of silence
Is a chance of ripened fruit!
There will come the happy shock:
A dove, a breath of wind,
An imperceptibly gentle shake,
The touch of a woman as she leans
Will release that fall of rain
That sends us down on our knees!

Let a whole people now fall,
Palm tree!...irresistibly!

Dans la poudre qu'il se roule
Sur les fruits du firmament !
Tu n'as pas perdu ces heures
Si légère tu demeures
Après ces beaux abandons ;
Pareille à celui qui pense
Et dont l'âme se dépense
À s'accroître de ses dons !

Let them wallow in the dust
On the fruits of the firmament!
For you those hours were no loss
Now you are left so light
After such lovely yieldings:
Image of a thinking mind
Where the spirit spends itself
To be increased by what it gives.

Sinistre

Quelle heure cogne aux membres de la coque
Ce grand coup d'ombre où craque notre sort?
Quelle puissance impalpable entre-choque
Dans nos agrès des ossements de mort?

Sur l'avant nu, l'écroulement des trombes
Lave l'odeur de la vie et du vin:
La mer élève et recreuse des tombes,
La même eau creuse et comble le ravin.

Homme hideux, en qui le cœur chavire,
Ivrogne étrange égaré sur la mer
Dont la nausée attachée au navire
Arrache à l'âme un désir de l'enfer,

Homme total, je tremble et je calcule,
Cerveau trop clair, capable du moment
Où, dans un phénomène minuscule,
Le temps se brise ainsi qu'un instrument...

Maudit soit-il le porc qui t'a gréée,
Arche pourrie en qui grouille le lest!
Dans tes fonds noirs, toute chose créée
Bat ton bois mort en dérive vers l'Est...

L'abîme et moi formons une machine
Qui jongle avec des souvenirs épars:
Je vois ma mère et mes tasses de Chine,
La putain grasse au seuil fauve des bars;

Je vois le Christ amarré sur la vergue!...
Il danse à mort, sombrant avec les siens;
Son œil sanglant m'éclaire cet exergue:
UN GRAND NAVIRE A PÉRI CORPS ET BIENS!...

286

Disaster

What hour hurtles at the staves of the hull
That knock of darkness on which our fate cracks?
What force untouchable plays the castanets
In our tackle with a dead man's bones?

On the prow the crumbling of cloudbursts
Washes off the smell of life and wine:
The sea raises and then re-digs tombs,
The same water hollowing piles the ravine.

Atrocious man, your heart within capsizing,
Drunkard, foreigner, astray on the sea
Whose nausea coupled to the ship
Wrenches from the soul a longing for hell,

Total man, I shudder and calculate,
Brain too lucid, capable of this moment
Where, within a phenomenal microcosm
Time is shattered like an instrument. . . .

A curse on that swine who rigged you out,
Ark of rottenness with your moldering ballast,
In your black holds, every created thing
Rattles on your dead timbers drifting East. . . .

I and the abyss make up between us
A machine juggling scattered memories:
I see my mother, and my china cups,
The greasy trull in the bars' lurid doorways.

I see Christ roped to the yardarm!
Dancing to death, foundering with his herd;
His bloodshot eye lights me to this exergue:
A GREAT SHIP GONE DOWN WITH ALL ON BOARD!...

Two Dialogues

Dance and the Soul

Eryximachus

O Socrates, I die! . . . Give me Spirit! Pour me out Ideas! . . . Bring to my nostrils your pungent enigmas! . . . This pitiless repast outdoes all conceivable appetite and all believable thirst! . . . What a fate—to succeed to good things and be the heir of a digestion! . . . My soul is nothing now but the dream dreamt by matter struggling with itself! . . . O good things, O too good things, I bid you pass! . . . Alas! since as day declined we have fallen a prey to what is best in the world, this terrible best, multiplied by duration, imposes its unbearable presence. . . . And now I perish from a mad longing for things that are dry, and serious, and utterly spiritual! . . . Let me come and sit beside you and Phaedrus; and grant that—my back deliberately turned upon those perpetually recurring viands and those inexhaustible urns—I hold out the supreme cup of my spirit to catch your words. What were you saying?

Phaedrus

Nothing as yet. We were watching our fellows eat and drink. . . .

Eryximachus

But Socrates cannot but have been meditating upon something? . . . Can he ever remain solitary with himself—and silent to his very soul! He was tenderly smiling at his daemon upon the dark borderland of this feast. What are your lips murmuring, dear Socrates?

Socrates

They say to me—gently: the man who eats is the most just of men. . . .

Eryximachus

There we have the enigma already, and the appetite of the spirit which it is destined to whet. . . .

Socrates

The man who eats, say my lips, feeds his own goods and ills. Each morsel which he feels melt away and dissipate within him brings new strength to his virtues, but also—indifferently—to his vices. It provides sustenance for his torments just as it fattens his hopes; and is divided somewhere between passions and reasons. Love needs it, as does hate; and my joy and my bitterness, my memory together with my projects, share between them like brothers the very substance of one and the same mouthful. What think you, son of Acumenos?

Eryximachus

I think that I think as you do.

Socrates

O physician that you are, I was silently admiring the acts of all these feeding bodies. Each of them, all unknowing, fairly gives its due to each chance of life, to each germ of death within itself. They know not what they are doing, but they do it like gods.

Eryximachus

I have long observed it: all that enters into man very soon comports itself as the Fates decree. It is as though the isthmus of the gullet were the threshold of capricious necessities and organized mystery. There the will ceases, and the sure empire of knowledge. That is why, in the practice of my art, I have given up all those inconstant drugs which the general run of practitioners agree to impose upon the diversity of their patients; and I keep strictly to obvious remedies. Compounded in equal parts, one for one, as their nature allows.

Phaedrus
What remedies?

Eryximachus
There are eight: hot, cold; abstinence and its contrary; air and water; rest and movement. That is all.

Socrates
But for the soul there are only two, Eryximachus.

Phaedrus
What are they?

Socrates
Truth and falsehood.

Phaedrus
How is that?

Socrates
Are they not to one another as waking is to sleeping? Do you not seek awakening and the sharpness of light when harrowed by a bad dream? Are we not resuscitated by the sun in person, and fortified by the presence of solid bodies?— Do we not, on the other hand, ask of sleep and dreams to

dispel our troubles and to suspend the sufferings which pursue us in the world of daylight? And so we flee from the one into the other, invoking day in the middle of the night; imploring darkness, on the contrary, while we have light; anxious to know, yet only too happy to ignore, we seek in what is, a remedy for what is not; and in what is not, a relief for what is. Now the real, now illusion is our refuge; and the soul has finally no other resource but the true, which is her weapon—and falsehood, which is her armor.

Eryximachus
Agreed. . . . But do you not fear, dear Socrates, a certain consequence upon that thought of yours?

Socrates
What consequence?

Eryximachus
This: that truth and falsehood tend to the same end. . . . It is one and the same thing which, according to the way it sets about it, makes us liars or truthful; and just as at times the hot and at times the cold now attack and now defend us, so the true and the false, and the opposing wills that pertain to them.

Socrates
Nothing is more certain. I cannot help it. Life itself wills it so: you, Eryximachus, know better than I that it makes use of everything. Everything helps it never to conclude. Which means that its only conclusion is itself. . . . For is not life that mysterious movement which, taking the detour of everything that happens, transforms me unceasingly into myself and brings me back, promptly enough, to the same Socrates,

so that I may find him again—so that, imagining perforce that I recognize him, I may *be*?—Life is a woman who dances and who would cease divinely to be a woman if she could obey her bound up to the skies. But as we can go on to infinity neither in dream nor in waking, so she likewise always becomes herself again; ceases to be snowflake, bird, idea; ceases, in fine, to be all that it pleases the flute that she should be; for the same Earth which sent her forth calls her back and returns her, all breathless, to her woman's nature and to her friend. . . .

Phaedrus

A miracle! . . . Marvelous man! . . . Almost a true miracle! Scarce do you open your lips, and you call into being what is needed! . . . Your images cannot remain images! . . . And lo! just as though from thy creative lips was born the bee, and bee upon bee—behold the winged choir of the famed dancers! . . . The air hums and resounds with intimations of the spectacle about to be! . . . All the torches awaken. . . . The mutterings of the sleepers are transformed; and upon the walls atremble with flames stir the vast shadows of drunkards in uneasy amaze! . . . See that troop, half-light, half-solemn!—coming in like souls!

Socrates

By the gods, the bright dancers! . . . How lively and gracious an introduction of the most perfect thoughts! . . . Their hands speak, and their feet seem to write. What precision in these beings who school themselves to make such felicitous use of their tender strength! . . . All my difficulties abandon me, and at this moment not one problem troubles me, so happily do I obey the mobility of those figures! Here certainty is a sport; it is as though knowledge has found its act, and intelligence on a sudden gives its consent to spontaneous graces. . . . See this one! . . . the slenderest and the one most absorbed in pure rightness. . . . Who is she? . . . She is deliciously hard and inexpressibly supple. . . . She yields, she borrows, and gives back the cadence so exactly that if I shut my eyes, I see her exactly with my hearing. I follow her, I find her again, I can never lose her; and if I stop my ears and look at her, so wholly is she rhythm and music that it is impossible for me not to hear the cithers.

Phaedrus
It is Rhodopis, I think, who enchants you.

Socrates
Rhodopis' ear and ankle, then, are wonderfully wed. . . . How exact she is! . . . Old time grows young again!

Eryximachus
But no, Phaedrus! . . . Rhodopis is the other, so soft, so easy for the eye to caress indefinitely.

Socrates
Who then is the slim monster of suppleness?

Eryximachus
Rhodonia.

Socrates
Rhodonia's ear and ankle, then, are wonderfully wed.

Eryximachus
I know them all, for the matter of that, and each by herself. I can tell you their names. They go very well into a

little poem which is easily remembered: Nips, Nephoë, Nema—Nikteris, Nephele, Nexis—Rhodopis, Rhodonia, Ptile. . . . As for the little boy dancer who is so ugly, they call him Nettarion. . . . But the Queen of the Choir has not yet entered.

Phaedrus

And who is it who reigns over these bees?

Eryximachus

The astonishing and extreme dancer, Athikte!

Phaedrus

How you know them!

Eryximachus

All this charming company have plenty of other names! Some come from their parents, and others from their intimates. . . .

Phaedrus

That is what you are. . . . You know them much too well!

Eryximachus

I know them much better than well, and in some sense a little better than they know themselves. O Phaedrus, am I not *the physician*?—In me, through me, all the secrets of medicine are secretly bartered for all the secrets of the dancer! They call me for everything. Sprains, spots, phantasms, heartaches, the varied accidents of their profession (including substantial ones which derive easily from a most mobile career)—and their mysterious ailments; even jealousy,

297

be it artistic or sentimental; even dreams! . . . Do you know they have only to whisper to me some dream which torments them for me to conclude, for example, that some tooth is affected?

Socrates

Admirable man, who know teeth by dreams, think you that all those of philosophers are decayed?

Eryximachus

May the gods preserve me from the bite of Socrates!

Phaedrus

But look at those arms and legs! . . . A few women are doing a thousand things. A thousand torches, a thousand ephemeral peristyles, trellises, and columns. . . . The images melt away and vanish. . . . And now we have a grove of beautiful branches, all stirred by the breezes of music! Is there any dream, O Eryximachus, that signifies more torments, or more a dangerous affection of the mind?

Socrates

But this is precisely the contrary of a dream, dear Phaedrus.

Phaedrus

But *I* dream. . . . I dream of the softness, multiplying itself indefinitely, of these encounters, and of these interchanges of virgin forms. I dream of those inexpressible contacts which take place in the soul between the beats, between the whitenesses and passes of those limbs moving in measure, and the strains of that muffled symphony on which all things seem to be painted and transported. . . . I breathe in, like some heady and composite aroma, the mingling fragrance of this female enchantment; and my presence strays bewildered in this labyrinth of graces, wherein each dancer is lost with her companion and appears again with another.

Socrates

O soul vowed to voluptuousness, see then here the contrary of a dream and the absence of chance. . . . But what, Phaedrus, is the contrary of a dream if not some other dream? . . . A dream of vigilance and tension dreamt by Reason herself!—And what would such a Reason dream?— If a Reason were to dream—a Reason hard, erect, eyes armed, mouth closed, as though mistress of her lips—would not the dream she dreamt be what we now see—this world of exact forces and studied illusions?—A dream, a dream, but a dream interpenetrated with symmetries, all order, acts, and sequences! . . . Who knows what august Laws here dream that they have put on clear countenances, and that they are of one accord in the design of manifesting to mortals in what way the real, the unreal, and the intelligible can fuse and combine as the power of the Muses dictates?

Eryximachus

It is most true, O Socrates, that the treasure of these images is beyond price. . . . Think you not that the thought of the Immortals is precisely that which we see, and that that infinity of these noble similitudes, the conversions, the inversions, the inexhaustible diversions which answer one another and are deduced from each other before our eyes, transport us into the realm of divine knowledge?

Phaedrus

How pure it is, how graceful, the little temple they now form—a rosy round—turning slowly as the night! . . . It

resolves into girls, tunics fly, and the gods seem to be changing their mind! . . .

Eryximachus
The divine thought is at present that abundance of multi-
colored groups of smiling figures; again and again it engenders those delightful patterns of movement, swirl upon
voluptuous swirl formed of two or three bodies and indissoluble henceforth. . . . One of the dancers is as im-
prisoned. Nevermore will she escape their enchanted
chains! . . .

Socrates
But what are they doing all of a sudden? . . . They mingle
confusedly, they flee! . . .

Phaedrus
They fly to the doors. They bow in welcome.

Eryximachus
Athikte! Athikte! . . . O gods! . . . The quivering Athikte!

Socrates
She is nothing.

Phaedrus
Little bird!

Socrates
A thing without a body!

Eryximachus
A thing without a price!

Phaedrus

O Socrates, it is as though she were obeying invisible figures!

Socrates

Or yielding to some noble destiny!

Eryximachus

Look! Look! . . . She begins, do you see? with a walk all divine: a simple circular walk. . . . She begins with her art at its highest; she walks naturally on the summit she has attained. This second nature is what is farthest removed from the first, but they must be so like as to be mistaken the one for the other.

Socrates

I enjoy as none other that magnificent freedom. The others now are held motionless and as though enchanted. The flute-girls listen to their own playing, but do not lose her from sight. . . . They are tied to their task, and seem to insist upon the perfection of their accompaniment.

Phaedrus

One, of pink coral, curiously bowed, blows an enormous shell.

Eryximachus

The very tall flutist with slender thighs, close-twined together, stretches out her elegant foot, tapping the beat with her toe. . . . O Socrates, what say you of the dancer?

Socrates

Eryximachus, this little being stirs one to thought. . . . It gathers to itself, it assumes a majesty which was confusedly present in all of us and imperceptibly inhabited the actors of this orgy. . . . A simple walk, and lo, she is a goddess; and we almost gods! . . . A simple walk, the simplest chain of steps! . . . It is as though she purchased space with equal and exquisite acts, and coined with her heel, as she walked, the ringing effigies of movement. She seems to reckon and count out in pieces of pure gold what we thoughtlessly spend in vulgar change of steps, when we walk to any end.

Eryximachus

Dear Socrates, she teaches us that which we do, showing clearly to our souls that which our bodies accomplish obscurely. In the light of her legs, our immediate movements appear to us as miracles. They astound us, in fine, as much as they ought to do.

Phaedrus

In which respect this dancer would, according to you, have something Socratic—teaching us, in the matter of walking, to know ourselves a little better.

Eryximachus

Just so. Our steps are so easy and familiar to us that they never have the honor to be considered in themselves, and as strange acts (unless, being infirm or crippled, we are led by deprivation to admire them). . . . Us in the simplicity of our ignorance they lead as they know how; and according to the ground, the goal, the humor, the state of the man, or even the lighting of the way, they are what they are: we lose them without a thought.

But consider the perfect progress of Athikte, over the faultless floor, which is free, fair, and hardly elastic. Upon that mirror of her forces she places with symmetry her

alternating tread; the heel pouring the body towards the
toe, the other foot passing and receiving the body, and pouring it onwards again; and so on and on; whilst the adorable
crest of her head traces in the eternal present the brow, as it
were, of an undulating wave.

As the surface is here in some sort absolute, being scru-
pulously disengaged from all causes of rhythmlessness and
incertitude, this monumental march which has but itself for
end and whence all variable impurities have disappeared
becomes an universal model.

See what beauty, what full security of soul comes of the
length of her noble strides. The amplitude of her steps accords with their number, which emanates directly from the
music. But number and length are, again, in secret harmony
with height. . . .

Socrates

You speak so well of these things, learned Eryximachus,
that I cannot but see them in agreement with your thought.
I contemplate this woman who is walking and yet gives me
the sense of the motionless. It is this equality of measure
alone that holds me. . . .

Phaedrus

She pauses, in the midst of these commensurable
graces. . . .

Eryximachus

And now you will see!

Phaedrus

She shuts her eyes. . . .

303

Socrates

She is entirely in her closed eyes, and quite alone with her soul, in the bosom of the most intimate attention. . . . She feels in herself that she is becoming some event.

Eryximachus

But wait for. . . . Silence, silence!

Phaedrus

Delicious instant. . . . This silence is contradiction. . . . How can one avoid shouting: Silence!

Socrates

Instant entirely virginal. Instant when something must break in the soul, in our expectation, in this assembly. . . . Something break. . . . And yet, it is also like a welding.

Eryximachus

O Athikte! How you excel in imminence!

Phaedrus

Music gently seems to seize her again in another way, lifts her up. . . .

Eryximachus

Music changes her soul.

Socrates

In this moment that is about to die, ye are, O Muses, mistresses all-powerful!

Delicious suspense of breath and of the heart! . . . Gravity falls at her feet—as is marked by that great veil which drops noiselessly. Her body must be seen only in movement.

Eryximachus
Her eyes have returned to the light. . . .

Phaedrus
Let us enjoy to the full this most delicate instant when she changes her purpose! . . . Just as the bird, having reached the very edge of the roof, breaks with the splendid marble, and falls into flight. . . .

Eryximachus
I like nothing so much as what is about to happen; and even in love, I find nothing that surpasses in delight the very first feelings. Of all the hours of the day, dawn is my favorite. That is why I wish to see with a tender emotion sacred movement dawn upon this living being. See! . . . It is born of that sliding glance which invincibly draws onward the head with its soft nostrils towards the shoulder shining in the light. . . . And the whole lovely fiber of her smooth, muscular body, from the nape of her neck to the heel of her foot, progressively expresses and twists itself; all is aquiver. . . . Slowly she traces a bound about to be born. . . . She forbids us to breathe until the instant she springs, responding by a sudden act to the awaited yet unawaited clash of the rending cymbals! . . .

Socrates
Oh! There at last she is, entering on the exception and penetrating the impossible! How much alike are our souls, O my friends, in the presence of this wonder, which is

equal and entire, for each of them! . . . How they drink in together what is beautiful!

Eryximachus

Her whole being becomes dance, and wholly vows itself to total movement!

Phaedrus

First she seems, with her steps charged with spirit, to efface from the earth all folly, all fatigue. . . . And see, she is fashioning a dwelling for herself, a little above things—as though making herself a nest within her white arms. . . . But at this moment would you not say that she is spinning with her feet an indefinable carpet of sensations? . . . She crosses, she uncrosses, she weaves the warp of the earth with the woof of duration. . . . O charming workmanship, most precious task of her intelligent toes which attack, which elude, which knot and unknot, which chase each other and take to flight! . . . How skillful they are, how lively, pure artificers of the delights of time lost! . . . The two feet babble together, and bicker like doves! . . . The same point of ground makes them contend, as for a grain of corn! . . . They take off together and clash in mid-air yet again! . . . By the Muses, never have feet made my lips more envious!

Socrates

Here then we have your lips envying the eloquence of these miraculous feet! Fain would you feel their wings in your words, and adorn what you say with figures lively as their leaps!

Phaedrus

I? . . .

Eryximachus

He was thinking only of covering with kisses those turtledoves of feet! . . . An effect of the passionate attention he gives to the spectacle of the dance. What more natural, Socrates, what more ingenuously mysterious? . . . Our Phaedrus is quite dazzled with those points and glittering pirouettes, which are the rightful pride of the tips of the toes of Athikte; he devours them with his eyes, his face strains towards them—and he thinks to feel upon his lips the agile onyx run! —Do not try to excuse yourself, dear Phaedrus, nor feel the very least confusion! . . . You have experienced nothing that was not both lawful and obscure, and thus conforming perfectly to the human machine. Are we not organized fantasy? And is not our living system functioning incoherency, disorder in action? Do not events, desires, ideas interchange within us in the most necessary and incomprehensible ways? . . . What cacophony of causes and effects! . . .

Phaedrus

But you have yourself very well explained what I innocently felt. . . .

Socrates

Dear Phaedrus, in truth, you were not moved without some reason. The more I look at this ineffable dancer, the more I too converse of marvels with myself. I am troubled to conceive how nature has contrived to enclose in a girl, so frail, so refined, this monster of force and of promptitude? Hercules changed to a swallow—is there such a myth? —And can this little head, compact like a young pine cone, infallibly beget the myriads of questions and answers that link her limbs, and those dizzy gropings it produces and reproduces, repudiating them incessantly, receiving them from music and giving them back at once to the light?

Eryximachus

I for my part think of the power of the insect, whose wings' myriad vibrations sustain its fanfare, weight, and courage! . . .

Socrates

She struggles in the meshes of our gaze, like a captured fly. But my curious mind pursues her on the web, and would devour what she accomplishes!

Phaedrus

Dear Socrates, can you never enjoy anything but your-self?

Socrates

O my friends, what in truth is dance?

Eryximachus

Is it not what we see? —What clearer expression of danc-ing do you want than dancing itself?

Phaedrus

Our Socrates cannot rest until he has seized the soul of all things: if not, indeed, the soul of the soul!

Socrates

But what then is dance, and what can steps say?

Phaedrus

Oh! let us enjoy yet a little, with simplicity, these fair acts! . . . To right, to left; forward, backward; upwards and downwards, she seems to be offering gifts, perfumes, incense, kisses, and her life itself, to all the points of the sphere, and to the poles of the universe. . . .

She traces roses, interlacings, stars of movement, magic precincts. . . . She leaps from circles she has scarcely closed. . . . She leaps and runs after phantoms! . . . She plucks a flower, which forthwith is simply a smile! . . . Oh! how she protests her nonexistence by an inexhaustible lightness! . . . She is adrift in the midst of sounds, she saves herself by a thread. . . . The succorable flute has rescued her! O melody! . . .

Socrates

Now it is as though all around her were nothing but specters. . . . She creates them as she flees them; but if, of a sudden, she turns about, she seems to us to be in the presence of the immortals! . . .

Phaedrus

Is she not the soul of fable, and the runaway through all the gates of life?

Eryximachus

Do you think she knows anything of it? and that she imagines she is engendering other prodigies than beats, and double beats, the highest of kicks,—all laboriously learnt during her apprenticeship?

Socrates

It is true one can undoubtedly also consider things in this light. . . . A cold eye would without difficulty see her as demented, this woman strangely uprooted, who wrests herself incessantly away from her own form, whilst her limbs—gone mad—seem to dispute earth and air; and her head, thrown back, trails on the ground her loosened hair; and one of her legs takes the place of that head; and her finger traces I know not what signs in the dust! . . . After all, why all this? —It is enough for the soul to remain motionless and to withhold itself, for it to conceive only the strangeness and disgust of this ridiculous agitation. . . . Should you but will it, O my soul, all this is absurd!

Eryximachus

You can, then, according to your mood, understand, not understand; find something beautiful or ridiculous, as you please?

Socrates

It must of necessity be so. . . .

Phaedrus

Do you mean, dear Socrates, that your reason considers dance a stranger, whose language it scorns, whose behavior seems to it inexplicable, if not shocking; if not, indeed, altogether obscene?

Eryximachus

Reason, sometimes, seems to me to be the faculty our soul possesses of understanding nothing about our body! . . .

Phaedrus

But me, Socrates, the contemplation of the dancer makes conceive many things, and many relationships between things, which on the spot become my own thought and think in some sort in Phaedrus' stead. I find lights which I should never have gained from the presence of my soul alone. . . .

Just now, for instance, Athikte seemed to me to represent

love. —What love? —Not this one, or that; not some miserable intrigue! —For sure, she was not playing the role of a lover. . . . No mime, no theater! No, no! no fictions! Why feign, my friends, when at our disposal there are measure and movement, which are what is real in the real? . . . She was love in its very being, then! —But what is love? —Of what is it made? —How define, how paint it? —Well do we know that the soul of love is the invincible difference of lovers, while its subtle matter is the identity of their desires. Dance must therefore, by the subtlety of its lines, by the divineness of its upsurgings, by the delicacy of its tiptoe pauses, bring forth that universal creature which has neither body nor features, but which has gifts, days, and destinies—that has life and death; and which is even only life and death, for desire once born knows neither sleep nor respite.

That is why the dancer alone can make love visible by her beautiful acts. Her whole self, O Socrates, was love! . . . She was toyings and tears, and unavailing feints! Charms, falls, offerings; and surprises, and yes's and no's, and steps sadly lost. . . . She was celebrating all the mysteries of absence and presence; she seemed sometimes to be hovering on the brink of ineffable catastrophes! . . . But now, as a thank offering to Aphrodite, look at her. Is she not of a sudden a very wave of the sea? —Now heavier than her body, now lighter—she bounds, as though dashed from a rock; she softly subsides. . . . She is a wave!

Eryximachus
Phaedrus will, at all costs, have her represent something!

Phaedrus
What do you think, Socrates?

Socrates

Whether she represents anything?

Phaedrus

Yes. Do you think she represents something?

Socrates

Nothing, dear Phaedrus. But everything, Eryximachus. As well love as the sea, and as life itself, and thoughts. . . . Do you not feel she is the pure act of metamorphosis?

Phaedrus

Divine Socrates, you know what simple and singular confidence I have placed, since I have known you, in your incomparable lights: I cannot hear you without believing you, nor believe you without delighting in myself as believing you. But that the dancing of Athikte represents nothing, and is not, above all things, an image of the transports and graces of love is something I find almost unbearable to hear. . . .

Socrates

I have not yet said anything so cruel! —O my friends, I am only asking you what is dance; each of you respectively appears to know; but to know it quite separately! The one tells me that it is what it is, and can be reduced to what our eyes see here; and the other holds very firmly that it represents something, and is therefore not entirely in itself, but principally in us. As for me, my friends, my uncertainty is intact! . . . My thoughts are many in number—which is never a good sign! . . . Many, confused, pressing around me with equal insistence. . . .

Eryximachus

You complain of being rich!

Socrates

Opulence renders immobile. But my desire is movement, Eryximachus. . . . I should now have need of that
delicate power which is peculiar to the bee, as it is the
sovereign good of the dancer. . . . My mind would need
that force and concentrated movement which suspends the
insect above the multitude of flowers; which make of it the
vibrant arbiter of the diversity of their corollas; which present it as it wills to this or that flower, to that rose a little
farther off; and which allow it to touch it fleetingly, to flee
it, or to penetrate it. . . . These forces suddenly remove him
from the one he has finished loving, just as they bring it back
to that flower forthwith, if he repents having left in it some
honey whose memory follows him and whose sweetness
haunts him during the rest of his flight. . . . Or I should need,
O Phaedrus, the subtle displacement of the dancer who,
gliding in among my thoughts, awakes each of them delicately in turn, making them rise from under the shadow of
my soul, and appear in the light of your minds, in the
happiest of all possible orders.

Phaedrus

Speak, speak. . . . I see the bee on your lips, and the dancer
in your gaze.

Eryximachus

Speak, O Master of the divine art of trusting the idea as it
comes to birth! . . . Ever fortunate author of the marvelous
consequences of a dialectical accident! . . . Speak! Draw the

313

golden thread. . . . Bring to us from out of the depths of your absences some living truth!

Phaedrus

Chance is on your side. . . . It changes insensibly into wisdom, as you pursue it with your voice into the labyrinth of your soul!

Socrates

Well, before anything else, I mean to consult our physician!

Eryximachus

It is as you will, dear Socrates.

Socrates

Tell me then, son of Acumenos, O Therapeut Eryximachus, you for whom most bitter drugs and obscure aromatics have so few hidden virtues that you use them not; you, then, who possessing as fully as any man alive all the secrets of art and of nature, yet never prescribe, nor commend, balms or boluses, or mysterious masticks; you who, furthermore, put no trust in elixirs, nor believe in secretly administered philters; O you who heal without electuaries, who disdain everything which—be it powders, drops, gum, curds, flakes or gems or crystals—clings to the tongue, pierces the olfactory cavities, touches the springs of sneezing or nausea, kills or quickens; tell me, then, dear friend Eryximachus, of all healers the most learned in curative substances, tell me this: know you not, from among so many that are active and efficient, from among those masterly preparations which your science contemplates as vain or detestable weapons in the arsenal of the pharmacopoeia—tell me then, do you not know some specific remedy, or some exact antidote, for that evil amongst all evils, that poison of poisons, that venom inimical to all nature? . . .

Phaedrus

What venom?

Socrates

. . . Which is called: *the weariness of living*? —I mean, understand me, not the passing weariness, the tedium which comes of fatigue, or that of which we see the germ or know the limits; but that perfect tedium, that pure tedium which does not come from misfortune or infirmity, and which is compatible with the happiest of all conditions that we may contemplate—that tedium, in fine, whose substance is none other than life itself, and which has no other second cause than the clear-sightedness of the man who is alive. This absolute tedium is in itself nothing other than life in its nakedness, when it sees itself clearly.

Eryximachus

It is most true that if our soul purges itself of all falseness, and deprives itself of every fraudulent addition to *what is*, our existence is at once endangered by this cold, exact, reasonable, and moderate consideration of human life as it is.

Phaedrus

Life blackens on contact with truth, as does the dubious mushroom—when crushed—on contact with the air.

Socrates

Eryximachus, I was asking you if there were a remedy?

Eryximachus

Why cure so reasonable an ill? No doubt there is nothing more morbid in itself, nothing more inimical to nature, than *to see things as they are*. A cold and perfect clarity is a poison impossible to combat. The real, in its pure state, stops the heart instantaneously. . . . One drop of that icy lymph suffices to relax in a soul the springs and palpitations of desire, exterminate all hopes, ruin all the gods present in our blood. The Virtues and the most noble colors pale before it, and are little by little consumed. To a handful of ashes is the past reduced, and the future to a tiny icicle. The soul appears to itself as an empty and measurable form. —Here, then, things as they are come together, limit one another, and are thus chained together in the most rigorous and mortal fashion. . . . O Socrates, the universe cannot for one instant endure to be only what it is. It is strange to think that that which is All cannot be sufficient unto itself! . . . Its dismay at being what is, has therefore made it create and paint for itself a thousand masks; there is no other reason for the existence of mortals. What are mortals for? —Their business is to *know*. Know? And what is to know? —*It is assuredly: not to be what one is.* —And so here are humans raving and thinking, introducing into nature the principle of unlimited error, and myriads of marvels! . . .

The mistakes, the appearances, the play of the dioptrics of the mind deepen and quicken the world's miserable mass. . . . The idea introduces into what is, the leaven of what is not. . . . But truth sometimes shows its hand after all, and jars in the harmonious system of phantasmagorias and errors. . . . Everything threatens to perish forthwith, and Socrates comes in person to ask of me a remedy for this desperate case of clear-sightedness and tedium! . . .

Socrates

Well, Eryximachus, since there is no cure, can you tell me, at least, what state is the most contrary to this horrible state of pure disgust, of murderous lucidity, and of inexorable clarity?

Eryximachus

In the first place I see all the madnesses that are not melancholic.

Socrates

And then?

Eryximachus

Drunkenness, and the category of illusions due to heady vapors.

Socrates

Yes. But are there no kinds of intoxication which have not their source in wine?

Eryximachus

Assuredly. Love, hate, greed intoxicate! . . . And the sense of power. . . .

Socrates

All this gives taste and color to life. But the chance of hating, or of loving, or of acquiring very great possessions is bound up with all the hazards of the real. . . . Do you not see then, Eryximachus, that among all intoxications the noblest, the one most inimical to that great tedium, is the intoxication due to acts? Our acts, and more particularly those of our acts which set our bodies in motion, may bring us into a strange and admirable state. . . . It is the state farthest removed from that wretched state in which we left the motionless and lucid observer we were imagining just now.

Phaedrus

But if, by some miracle, this observer were seized with a sudden passion for dance? . . . If he wished to cease being clear in order to become light; and if then, essaying his skill at differing infinitely from himself, he tried to change his freedom of judgment into freedom of movement?

Socrates

In that case, he would teach us, at one stroke, what we are now trying to elucidate. . . . But there is something yet which I must ask Eryximachus.

Eryximachus

What you will, dear Socrates.

Socrates

Tell me then, wise physician, who hast fathomed in thy studies and circumnavigations the science of all living things; deeply versed as thou art in the forms and freaks of nature, and renowned for the classification of remarkable beasts and plants (the harmful and benign; the anodyne and the efficacious; the surprising, the frightful, the ridiculous; the dubious; and finally those that do not exist)—say then, hast thou never heard tell of those strange animals that live and flourish in the very flame itself?

Eryximachus

Assuredly! . . . Their shape and habits, dear Socrates, have been well studied—although their very existence has been recently a matter of contestation. I have very often described them to my disciples; yet I have never had the opportunity of observing any with my own eyes.

Socrates

Well then, does it not seem to you, Eryximachus, and to you, my dear Phaedrus, that that creature that is quivering over there, fluttering adorably within our gaze, that ardent Athikte, who divides and gathers herself together again, who rises and falls, so promptly opening out and closing in, and who appears to belong to constellations other than ours—seems to live, completely at ease, in an element comparable to fire—in a most subtle essence of music and movement, wherein she breathes boundless energy, while she participates with all her being in the pure and immediate violence of extreme felicity? —If we compare our grave and weighty condition with the state of that sparkling salamander, does it not seem to you that our ordinary acts, begotten by our successive needs, and our gestures and incidental movements are like coarse materials, like an impure stuff of duration—whilst that exaltation and that vibration of life, that supremacy of tension, that transport into the highest agility one is capable of, have the virtues and the potencies of flame; and that the shames, the worries, the sillinesses, and the monotonous foods of existence are consumed within it, making what is divine in a mortal woman shine before our eyes?

Phaedrus

Admirable Socrates, look quickly: how truly you

speak! . . . Look at the palpitating one! Dance seems to issue from her body like a flame!

Socrates

O Flame! . . .

—Perhaps this girl is a fool? . . .

O Flame! . . .

—And who can tell what superstitions and idle talk make up her soul of every day?

O Flame, notwithstanding! . . . Thing live and divine! . . .

But what is a flame, O my friends, if not *the moment itself*? —What is wild and joyful and formidable in the instant itself! . . . Flame is the act of that moment which is between earth and heaven. O my friends, all that passes from the heavy state to the subtle state passes through the moment of fire and light. . . .

And flame, is it not also the proud, ungraspable form assumed by the noblest destruction? —What will never happen again happens magnificently before our eyes! —What will never happen again must happen in the most magnificent manner possible! —As the voice recklessly sings, as the flame sings wildly between matter and ether— and from matter to ether, roars and rushes furiously—is not the great Dance, O my friends, that deliverance of our body entirely possessed by the spirit of falsehood, and of music which is falsehood, and drunk with the denial of null reality? —Look at that body, which leaps as flame replaces flame, look how it spurns and betramples what is true! How it furiously, joyously destroys the very place upon which it is, and how it intoxicates itself with the excess of its changes!

But how it wrestles with the spirit! See you not that it would vie in speed and variety with its own soul? It is strangely jealous of that freedom and ubiquity which it thinks the mind possesses! . . .

Without doubt the unique and perpetual object of the soul is that which does not exist: that which was and no longer is; that which will be and is not yet; that which is possible, and impossible—all that is the soul's concern, but never, *never* that which is!

And the body, which is that which is: see it here unable to contain itself in extension! —Where is it to put itself? —Where become? —This *One* wishes to play at being *All*. It wishes to play at the universality of the soul! It wishes to atone for its identity by the number of its acts! Being a thing, it bursts into events! —It is transported! —And just as thought, when stirred, touches all substances, vibrates between time-beat and instant, o'erleaps all differences; and just as in our minds hypotheses take shape symmetrically and possibles line up and are counted—so this body exercises itself in all its parts, joins in with itself, assumes shape upon shape, and goes out of itself incessantly! . . . At last we have it here in that state comparable to flame, in the midst of the most active exchanges. . . . We can no longer speak of "movement" . . . nor distinguish any longer its acts from its limbs. . . .

That woman who was there is being devoured by innumerable figures. . . . That body, in its bursts of vigor, offers me an extreme thought: even as we demand of our soul many things for which it was not made, and require of it to illumine us, to prophesy, to divine the future, adjuring it even to discover the God—even so the body which is there wishes to attain to an entire possession of itself, and to a point of glory that is supernatural. . . . But our body fares as does the soul, for which the God, and the wisdom, and the depth demanded of it are, and can only be, moments, flashes, fragments of an alien time, desperate leaps out of its form. . . .

Phaedrus

Look, only look! . . . She is dancing yonder and gives to the eyes what here you are trying to tell us. . . . She makes the instant to be seen. . . . Through what jewels she passes! . . . She flings her gestures like scintillations! . . . She filches from nature impossible attitudes, even under the very eye of Time! . . . And Time lets himself be fooled. . . . She passes through the absurd with impunity. . . . She is divine in the Unstable, offers it as a gift to our regard! . . .

Eryximachus

Instant engenders form, and form makes the instant visible.

Phaedrus

She flees her shadow up into the air!

Socrates

We never see her but about to fall. . . .

Eryximachus

She has made all her body as smooth, as well-knit as an agile hand. . . . Only my hand can imitate that possession and ease in all her body. . . .

Socrates

O my friends, do you not feel yourselves shaken into intoxication by fits and starts, and as though by blows repeated ever more vigorously, gradually made into the likeness of all these guests, stamping and no longer able to keep their daemons silent and hidden? I feel myself invaded by extraordinary forces. . . . Or I feel that they are going forth from me, ignorant though I was that these virtues were mine. In a sonorous world, resonant and rebounding, this intense festival of the body in the presence of our souls offers light and joy. . . . All is more solemn, all more light, all more lively, all stronger; all is possible in another way; all can begin again indefinitely. . . . Nothing can resist the alternation of the strong beat with the weak. . . . Beat on, beat on! . . . Matter struck and beaten, clashing in cadence; earth well-beaten; skins and strings well-stretched, well-beaten; palms of hands, heels, striking well, beating time, forging joy and folly; and all things, caught in this rhythm of delirium, hold sway.

But joy, increasing and rebounding, tends to outbrim all measure, shakes with the blows of a battering-ram the walls which keep being from being. Men and women in cadence lead the song on to tumult. All beat and sing at once, and something grows greater and higher. . . . I hear the clash of all the glittering arms of life! . . . The cymbals crush in our ears any utterance of secret thoughts. They resound like kisses from lips of bronze. . . .

Eryximachus

Athikte, meanwhile, presents one last figure. All her body on the might of that big toe moves.

Phaedrus

Her toe, which sustains her entirely, like thumb on drum-skin drums along the ground. What attention there is in that toe; what will stiffens it and maintains it on its tip! . . . But see her now, turning, twirling round herself. . . .

Socrates

She turns round herself—and see how things eternally linked begin to separate out. She turns and turns. . . .

Eryximachus

This is truly to penetrate into another world. . . .

Socrates

This is the supreme essay. . . . She turns, and all that is visible detaches itself from her soul; all the slime of her soul is separated at the last from its most pure; men and things will form around her a shapeless whirl of lees. . . .

See. . . . She turns. . . . A body, by its simple force, and its act, is powerful enough to alter the nature of things more profoundly than ever the mind in its speculations and dreams was able to do!

Phaedrus

One would think this could last forever.

Socrates

She could die, thus. . . .

Eryximachus

Sleep, perhaps—fall into a magic slumber. . . .

Socrates

She would rest motionless in the very center of her movement. Alone, alone to herself, like the axis of the world. . . .

Phaedrus

She turns, she turns. . . . She is falling!

Socrates

She has fallen!

Phaedrus

She is dead. . . .

Socrates

She has exhausted her second reserve of strength, and the innermost hidden treasure of her frame!

Phaedrus

Gods! She may die. . . . Eryximachus, go!

Eryximachus

I do not hurry in such circumstances! If things are to come right, it is proper that the physician should not disturb them, and should arrive a very short moment before the recovery, keeping pace with the Gods.

Socrates

But we must go and see.

Phaedrus

How white she is!

Eryximachus

Let rest act to cure her of her movement.

Phaedrus

You think she is not dead?

Eryximachus

Look at this tiny breast, asking only to live. See how faintly it pulses, clinging to time. . . .

Phaedrus
I see it only too well.

Eryximachus
The bird flutters its wings a little before taking to flight again.

Socrates
She seems happy enough.

Phaedrus
What did she say?

Socrates
She said something for herself alone.

Eryximachus
She said: "How well I feel!"

Phaedrus
The little heap of limbs and scarves is stirring. . . .

Eryximachus
Come, child, shall we open our eyes? How do you feel now?

Athikte
I feel nothing. I am not dead. And yet, I am not alive!

Socrates
Whence do you return?

Athikte
Refuge, refuge, O my refuge, O Whirlwind! I was in thee, O movement—outside all things. . . .

Dialogue of the Tree

Lucretius

What are you doing here, Tityrus, lover of the shade, at ease beneath this beech, your gaze lost in the gold of the leaf-woven air?

Tityrus

I live, I wait. My flute is set between my fingers, and I make myself like this admirable hour. I would be the instrument of the general favor of things. I abandon to the earth the whole weight of my body: my eyes live up there, in the palpitating mass of light. Look how the TREE above us seems to revel in the divine ardor from which it shelters me: its desireful being, which is certainly feminine in essence, begs me to sing to it its name and give musical form to the breeze which passes through and gently harasses it. I await my soul. To wait is of great price, Lucretius. I shall feel the pure act of my lips as it comes, and all that I still ignore of myself, lover of the Beech, will quiver. O Lucretius, is it not a miracle that a shepherd, a man forgetting a flock, can pour out to the skies the fleeting form and as it were the naked idea of the Tree and of the instant?

Lucretius

There is no miracle, Tityrus, no prodigy which the mind, if it wills it so, cannot reduce to its own artless mystery. . . . I myself think your tree, and possess it in my own way.

327

Tityrus

But *you* profess to understand things: you dream you know much more about this beech than it could know itself if it had a thought which induced it to believe it could grasp itself. . . . *I* only wish to know my happy moments. Today my soul is making itself into a tree. Yesterday I felt it to be a spring. Tomorrow? . . . Shall I rise with the smoke from an altar, or soar above the plains, with the sense of power of the vulture on its slow wings—how do I know?

Lucretius

You are nothing then but metamorphoses, Tityrus. . . .

Tityrus

It is for you to say. I leave profundity to you. But since this mass of shade draws you, like an island of coolness in the midst of the fire of the day, pause and cull the instant. Let us share this good, and let us exchange between us your knowledge of this Tree and the love and praise it inspires in me. . . . I love thee, mighty Tree—I am mad about thy limbs. There is no flower, no woman, that moves me more than thou, great Being with manifold arms, or draws a tenderer fury from my heart. . . . Thou know'st it well, my Tree, that I come to embrace thee from the moment of dawn: I kiss with my own lips thy smooth and bitter bark; I feel myself the child of this our very earth. On the lowest of thy branches I hang my belt and my sack. From out thy tufted shade suddenly a great bird noisily takes flight, escaping from thy leaves, itself afraid, affrighting me. But the squirrel, without fear, runs down and scurries towards me: it comes to recognize me. Tenderly sunrise is born, and all things declare themselves. Each says its name, for fire of the new day awakens it in its turn. The nascent wind resounds high up among thy branches. It places there a spring: I note the lively air. But Thee it is I hear. O utterance confused, O language all astir, I would fuse all thy voices together! A hundred thousand moved leaves make what the dreamer whispers to the powers of dream. I reply to thee, my Tree, I speak to thee and tell thee my secret thoughts. All of my truth I tell, all of my rustic vows: thou know'st the all of me, the artless torments too of the most simple life, the life closest to thee. I look about to see if we are indeed alone, and I confide to thee what I am. Now I confess myself as hating Galatea; now when a memory drives me to rave aloud, I hold thee for her being, am turned into a transport, wishing madly to feign, and join and catch and bite something more than a dream: something that lives. . . . But at other times I make thee God. O idol that thou art—to thee, O Beech, I pray. Why not? There are so many gods in our countryside. Some of them so ugly. But thou, when the wind falls and the majesty of the Sun calms, crushes, and illumines all that is in space, thou bearest upon thy spreading limbs, upon thy numberless leaves, the burning weight of midday's mystery; time all asleep in thee endures only in the provoking buzz of the vast insect world. . . . Then thou appear'st to me a temple as it were, and no suffering or joy comes to me that I do not dedicate to thy sublime simplicity.

Lucretius

O virtuosity! Most wonderfully stirred! I listen and admire. . . .

Tityrus

No. That you cannot do. You smile about my Tree and dream about your own. My flute for you is but a plaything of the breeze, when from a mortal's lips the breeze derives its flight: it ripples through the instant, entertains the ear. What is it for the soul—so potent and profound? It is scarce more than a suspected fragrance. My voice pursues but the shadow of a thought. But great Lucretius, you—you with your secret thirst—what is the *word*, O what, when it begins to sing? It loses in that act the power to follow truth. . . . Yes, I know well the worth of what the Tree imparts. It tells me what it would that I should wish to feel. I change that which I love into yet further joys, abandoning to air what comes to me from Heaven. Nothing more, nothing less. . . . Ah no, I do not hope my pleasure should exhaust anything else but me, all simple as I am. But you, your brow weighed down by shadows which you form, in the hope of a flash that should strike down the gods, you make yourself all mind, and sealed against the light, your eyes seek in yourself the being of what is. What to the day appears, your reason rates as naught, and what our tree is stammering to the light wind, the gentle quivering of its stirred summit, its branches spreading wide—one ample hesitance—and all its winged folk warbling without a thought: what matters it all to you? You seek the Nature of Things. . . .

Lucretius

This great Tree is for you only your fantasy. You think you love it, Tityrus, but only see your charming fancy there, which you bedeck with leaves. You love only your hymn— and so please me the more. From the majestic Beech you take wherewith to sing the eddies of its form and its sonorous birds, its shade which welcomes you from the burning heart of day, and, by the Muses blest, you duly celebrate upon your fragile reed the mighty giant's charms.

Tityrus

Well, sing, yourself, in turn; to nature give decrees, to the vast earth, to bulls, to rocks, and to the sea; give to the wave its law, give to the flowers their form! Think for the universe, a monster without head, which, for itself, in man searches for reason's dream; but O do not disdain your simple listener. Open to him the wealth of truth's obscurities. What little of this beech do you know more than we?

Lucretius

Look, to begin with, well at this brute force, the powerful timber of these outstretched limbs: look at the solid matter life has made, fitted to bear the weight of northern blast and to stand firm against the cataract; the waters of the dense maternal earth, drawn from the depths for years on end, at last bring this hard substance to the light of day. . . .

Tityrus

Substance as hard as stone, and fit like it to carve.

Lucretius

Ending in branches, too, which end in leaves themselves, and then at last the mast which, fleeing far and wide, will scatter life abroad. . . .

Tityrus

I see what you would say.

Lucretius

See then in this great being here a kind of river.

Tityrus

A river?

331

Lucretius

A river all alive whose sources downward plunge and in the earth's dark mass find the pathways of their mysterious thirst. It is a hydra, O Tityrus, at grips with the rock, growing and dividing to embrace it the better; a hydra, which, becoming ever finer, impelled by the damp, dishevels into a thousand hairs so as to drink up the least presence of water that impregnates the massive night wherein are dissolved all things that have lived. There is no hideous beast of the sea more greedy and multiple than this tousle of roots, blindly certain in their progress towards the depths and dampnesses of the earth. But their advance proceeds, irresistible, with a slowness which makes it implacable as time. Into the empire of the dead, of the mole and the worm, the toil of the tree inserts the powers of a strange subterranean will.

Tityrus

What marvels, O Lucretius, you recount! . . . But shall I tell you what I think of as I listen? This treacherous tree of yours which into the deep shade insinuates its live substance through a thousand strands, and which draws up the juice of the deep-dormant earth, recalls to me . . .

Lucretius

Well, what?

Tityrus

It recalls love.

Lucretius

Why not? Into your human sense, towards your shepherd's soul, what I say penetrates and finds its echo there. Thus has my utterance, Tityrus, touched the point, the deepest knot of being, where unity resides—whence radiates through us, illumining the world with one sole thought, all the most secret store of its similitudes. . . .

Tityrus

I know not. . . . What you say is dark to me, O Lucretius.

Lucretius

Enough that I understand myself. But you, speak freely—of love, too, if you wish. Yet rather sing to me that metamorphosis. . . . How came it in your mind that a growing plant could make you dream of love, that need of pleasure? Sing.

Tityrus

Pleasure? O love is not of such a simple substance.

Lucretius

What could you wish it more than universal urge? What is it but a goad fashioned by destiny?

Tityrus

A goad! . . . And mine you say is but a shepherd's soul! . . . A goad! . . . You make of love a cowherd's tool, no more? The love that you conceive is but the love of rams and wild things of the woods. These brutes, in sudden fits, all drunken with their seed, endeavor hideously, when in the heat of rut, to give their flesh release from this live poison. They love, but without love, as chance encounter bids. A shepherd knows it well, who plays his part at times, composing at his will the female and the male, whenever he would have the kidlings of his choice.

333

Lucretius

And so—see destiny traversed by Tityrus! . . . Into the dark where fate fumbles you thrust your hands. . . . You cheat. . . .

Tityrus

And is that not the business of men, whose total sum of wit is used to torment nature, trammel up their lives, and even would baffle death?

Lucretius

Do not get lost beneath my abstract trellises. Just leave the aphorisms and reasonings to me. I'm waiting for the tree and love, which you would join. Sing to me, if you will, something your very own. Whilst to your songs my ear lends itself willingly, I fear I'll not be won by your philosophy.

Tityrus

Well, listen then. This is what comes to me:

> Unless love grow to the utmost it is naught:
> Growth is its law; it dies from being same,
> And dies in one who dieth not of love.
> Living upon a never quenchèd thirst,
> Tree in the soul whose living roots are flesh
> Who lives from living in the quick of life
> It lives from all, from bitter as from sweet,
> And from the cruel better than the kind.
> Great Tree of Love who ceaseth not to bind
> And build into my weakness strangest powers,
> A thousand moments which the heart embowers
> For thee are foliage and shafts of light!

334

But whilst thy rapture opening into flowers
In the gold sun of happiness appears,
Thy selfsame thirst, whose depth grows with the hours,
Deep in the shade, draws from the spring of tears. . . .

Lucretius

These are no verses, are they? There's a riddle here.

Tityrus

I was improvising. 'T was but the first essay of a poem to be. What you a moment back said to me of this Tree made me dream Love. Yes, Love together with the Tree can in our minds unite into one sole idea. The one and the other are something which, born of an imperceptible germ, grows ever larger and ever stronger, spreads and branches forth; but so far as it rises towards heaven (or happiness) just so much must it down descend into the dark substance of that which we unknowingly are.

Lucretius

Our earth? . . .

Tityrus

Yes. . . . And it is there, in the depths of the shades wherein melt and are mingled what there is of our human kind, and what there is of our living substance, and what there is of our memories, and of our hidden strengths and weaknesses, and finally that which is the shapeless sense of not having always been and of having to cease to be, that there is to be found what I called the "spring of tears": THE INEFFABLE. For our tears, I hold, are the expression of our powerlessness to *express*—that is, by words to rid ourselves of the oppression of what we are. . . .

Lucretius

You go far for a shepherd. Do you then always weep?

Tityrus

Yes, I can always weep. And, shepherd though I be, I have observed that there is no thought which, pursued as close as may be to the soul, does not lead us on to those wordless shores, those silent shores where alone subsist pity, tenderness, and the kind of bitterness inspired in us by that mixture of the eternal, the fortuitous, and the ephemeral: which is our lot.

Lucretius

And so that is what you meditate upon when you spend your summer nights keeping watch over your sleeping flock, whilst a whole herd of stars, goaded hither and thither upon the horizon, by the silent flash of lightning, or traversed by the unforeseen flight of meteors, seems to browse on time, and—as a herd or flock step by step crops its way—crops the future endlessly?

Tityrus

What am I to do? At that nocturnal hour, the Tree appears to think. It is a being of shade. The birds, all now asleep, leave it alone alive. It quivers to its depths: as speaking to itself. For fear inhabits it, as she inhabits us, when we are all alone at midnight with ourselves, and quite delivered up a prey to our own truth.

Lucretius

Most true indeed: for we have only ourselves to fear. The gods and destinies cannot work aught in us but by the treachery of our all-sensitive fibers. Over our lower souls they hold a coward's sway; the power they wield is not the act of Wisdom's self; divinity just finds in bodies that are weak, for final argument, the torture of the sage.

Tityrus

But is not fire the very end of the Tree? When its being becomes one mass of racking pain, it writhes; but changes itself to light and ashes pure, rather than molder, rotted by stagnant water, nibbled by vermin. . . .

Lucretius

Tityrus, if you can, choose from among these ills! Better not think on them; for what could be more useless? For ills, when ills there are, stand out clearly enough. . . . But if I were to you the comrade of your nights, both of us in the shade unseen at the Tree's foot, reduced to our two voices, to a single being, evenly crushed by the burden of so many stars, I should recount to you, sing to you what my inner contemplation of the Idea of the Plant sings and says to me.

Tityrus

I should listen to you devoutly in the night; I should lose the feeling of my ignorance; I should not understand every-thing that you said, but I should so love it, with so great a desire that it should be true, with such a rapture of spirit, that I can conceive no surer happiness, no more incorruptible moment. . . .

Lucretius

The being filled with wonder is lovely, like a flower.

Tityrus

Forgive me: I could not refrain from interrupting you as you were speaking of that Idea of the Plant. . . .

Lucretius

Do you not see that every plant is a *work* and that there is no work without an idea?

Tityrus

But I see no author. . . .

Lucretius

The author is but a detail, useless more or less.

Tityrus

You overwhelm me. . . . You make sport of Tityrus! . . . But I am a reasonable animal, and I know just like you that all things need their cause. All that exists was made; all supposes someone, man or divinity, a cause or a desire, some potency to act. . . .

Lucretius

Are you quite sure nothing can be by itself, causeless and reasonless, without preceding end?

Tityrus

Quite sure.

Lucretius

And do you sometimes dream?

Tityrus

Yes, before every dawn.

Lucretius

Just as the dawning day acts on the granite of the illustrious statue, making it resound, so Memnon-Tityrus im-

338

provises at dawn in himself, for himself, the most astounding tales. . . . But your dreams, Tityrus, are they of any worth? Do you on waking know that they were worth the dreaming?

Tityrus

There are such lovely ones. . . . Some too that are so true! . . . Some that are all-divine. . . . And others, sinister. . . . So strange they sometimes are that they seem formed to be dreamed by some other sleeper, as though they mistook the absent, and mixed defenseless souls in the night. . . . And there are cruel ones for having been too sweet: such and such bliss is rent just as it fills me, abandons me to the day upon the shores of truth. . . . My flesh is still all quivering with love, but the spirit holds back and coldly contemplates the dying palpitation of its body. . . . And the two ends of the cut reptile writhe . . . apart.

Lucretius

And so you simply were an onlooker constrained to undergo the spectacle. But who, tell me, who is the author of this drama?

Tityrus

The author. . . . I know none. I can find nobody.

Lucretius

You?

Tityrus

Assuredly not I, for these strange games of sleep cannot be played unless I be shut out from their preparing: no terrors otherwise, nor surprises, nor charms.

339

Lucretius

There is no author, then. You see it, Tityrus: a work without an author is not impossible. No poet organized these phantasms for you, and you would never from yourself have drawn delights like these nor those abysses of your dreams. . . . No author. . . . There are then things which create themselves, without a cause, and so make their own destiny. . . . That is why I reject, as being a childish need of mortal minds, the simple-minded logic which seeks to see in all an artist and his aim, both distinct from the work. Man—innocent before everything that he sees, upon the earth, or in the skies, the stars, beasts, seasons, the semblances of rules, of happy foresight or of harmony—questions: "Who made this? Who willed it?" Thinking he must compare everything with those simple objects which our hands produce: our vessels, tools, abodes, arms—all those compounds of matter and spirit which our needs engender. . . .

Tityrus

Do you think you yourself can better grasp the nature of things?

Lucretius

I try to imitate the indivisible mode. . . . O Tityrus, I think that in our substance is to be found without going too deep that identical potency which in like manner produces all life. All that the soul puts forth is very nature's self. . . .

Tityrus

What, you think everything which comes to us essential?

Lucretius

Not everything that comes to us, but the coming itself. . . . I tell you, Tityrus, between all that's alive there is

340

a bond, is a similitude, which can engender hatred quite as much as love. The like caresses or devours its like. Whether he eat a lamb or cover a she-wolf, the wolf can do no more than make or remake wolf.

Tityrus

But could you yourself make or remake Tree?

Lucretius

I have told you that I feel, born and growing in me, a Plantlike virtue, and I can merge myself in the thirst to exist of the hard-striving seed, moving towards an infinite number of other seeds throughout a plant's whole life. . . .

Tityrus

Let me stop you. . . . A question comes to me.

Lucretius

What I was going to tell (perhaps to sing) to you would have, I think, dried up the spring of words which suddenly wells up from the depths of your mind. But speak! . . . If I asked you to wait, you would inwardly—and self-contentedly—listen to yourself instead of listening to me. . . .

Tityrus

Yes, do you not think, O Wise Man that you are, that our knowledge of anything whatsoever is imperfect if it is confined to the exact notion of that thing, if it is limited to the truth, and if—having succeeded in changing the naïve view into a clear idea, the pure outcome of investigation, experiment, and all the formal observances which eliminate error or illusion—it remains satisfied with that perfection?

341

Lucretius

What more do you need than what is? And is not the true the natural frontier of the intelligence?

Tityrus

I certainly think, for my part, that reality, always in-finitely more rich than the true, comprises, on every subject and in every matter, the quantity of misunderstandings, of myths, of childish stories and beliefs which the minds of men necessarily produce.

Lucretius

And you do not wish this weed to be burned by the wise men, exhaling an odor agreeable to Minerva?

Tityrus

If you transplant it, tending it well apart, it ceases to be weed; some use can be found for it. But in my ignorance and my simplicity, here's what I have to say. Once we hold the true firmly, and no longer fear to get lost in vain whims, wisdom should retrace her steps, take up again and gather as things human all that was created, forged, thought, dreamt, and believed, all those prodigious products of this our mind, those magic and monstrous stories that spring so spontane-ously from us. . . .

Lucretius

It is certain (and indeed strange) that the true can be known to us only by the use of many artifices. Nothing is less natural!

Tityrus

I have noticed that there is not a thing in the world that has not been adorned with dreams, held for a sign, explained by some miracle, and this all the more as the concern with knowing the origins and first circumstances is more naïvely potent. And that is doubtless why a philosopher whose name I have forgotten coined the maxim: IN THE BEGINNING WAS THE FABLE.

Lucretius

Was it not I who said it? But I have said so many things that this one is as much mine as not. . . .

Tityrus

You are so rich! . . . But I return to my discourse, and by it to our TREE. . . . Do you know the *Marvelous History of the Infinite Tree?*

Lucretius

No.

Tityrus

And about the cedar tree charged with love? Nothing? In the island of Xiphos? . . .

Lucretius

I know nothing about the cedar—nothing of the island.

Tityrus

And the most astounding?

Lucretius

I know nothing about the most astounding.

Tityrus

The most astounding history of Trees is surely that of those giant apple trees, the fruit of one of which offered to whoever bit its fabulous flesh an eternal life, whilst the fruit

343

of the other, no sooner tasted, produced a strange clearness in the mind of the eater: he felt invaded by a shame attached to the things of love. A sudden redness enveloped his whole being, and he felt his nakedness as a crime and a branding. . . .

Lucretius

What strange combinations find themselves at ease together in your memory, Tityrus!

Tityrus

I love what astonishes me and only retain that which would excite but forgetfulness in the mind of a wise man.

Lucretius

And the infinite tree?

Tityrus

In the first age it was, when virgin was the earth, and man still to be born, and all the animals. The Plant was master and covered the whole face of the soil. It might have remained the sole and sovereign form of life, offering to the eyes of the gods the varied splendor of the seasons' colors. Motionless by nature of each of its individuals, it moved about in the form of species, mastering extension bit by bit. It was by the number of its seeds (which it scattered madly to the winds) that it advanced and spread in the manner of a conflagration devouring all it finds to devour; and that is what, without man and his labors, grasses and bushes would still be doing. But what we see is nothing compared with the power of conquest by leaps and bounds of winged seeds, in that heroic age of vegetable vigor. Now (hear this, Lucretius) it happened that one of those seeds, whether through the excellence of the ground into which it fell, or through the favor of the sun upon it, or through some other circumstance, grew like no other, and from a grass grew into a tree, and that tree into a prodigy! Yes! It seems as though a sort of thought and will took form in it. It was the greatest and most beautiful being under the sky, when, divining perhaps that its tree life was only tied up with its growth and that it only lived because it grew larger, there came upon it a sort of overweening and arborescent madness. . . .

Lucretius

By which this tree was a sort of mind. What's loftiest in the mind can only live through growth.

Tityrus

As an athlete, his legs set wide apart, brings his effort to bear upon the columns between which he is placed and pushes them none the less energetically with his arms distended by willing, so that tree became the focus of the most powerful urge and the most tense form of force that life has ever produced, an enormous force, though insensible at any instant, capable of gradually lifting a rock as big as a hill or of overturning the wall of a citadel. It is said that at the end of a thousand centuries, it covered with its shadow the whole of immense Asia. . . .

Lucretius

What mortal sway that shadow must have held! . . .

Tityrus

Yes, that imperial Tree made night beneath itself. No ray of sun could pierce its foliage, within whose denseness all the winds got lost, whilst its brow shook off hostile storms, as massive oxen flick away the gnats. The rivers were no more, such was the sap it drew from sky and earth at once. Rearing in the dry azure its tense solitude, it was the God Tree. . . .

Lucretius

A marvelous adventure, Tityrus!

Tityrus

Forgive me. I have thrust this story innocently athwart the deeper, wiser discourse which you were going to make me on our present theme.

Lucretius

I know not if I can speak better than a Fable. . . . I wished to speak to you of the feeling I sometimes have of being Plant myself, a Plant that thinks, but does not distinguish between its diverse potencies, nor its form from its force, its port from its place. Forces, forms, size, and volume, and duration are but a single river of existence, a tide whose liquid expires in hard solidity, whilst the dim will of growth rises and bursts, and would again become will—in the light and innumerable form of seeds. And I feel myself live the unheard-of enterprise of the Type of the Plant, invading space, improvising a dream of branches, plunging into the midst of the mire, and drinking in the heady salts of the earth, whilst in the free air it opens by degrees to the bounty of the sky, green thousands of lips. . . . As much it goes down deep, so much it rises up: it chains the shapeless, it attacks the void; it struggles that it may change all into itself, for that is its Idea! . . . O Tityrus, it seems to me I am sharing with my whole being in that meditation—powerful, active, and rigorously followed up in its design—which the Plant bids me make. . . .

Tityrus

You say the Plant meditates?

Lucretius

I say that if someone on earth does meditate, it is the Plant.

Tityrus

Meditate? . . . Perhaps the meaning of this word is obscure to me?

Lucretius

Do not trouble about that. The lack of but one word makes a phrase live the better: its opening is the vaster—it proposes to the mind to be mind a little more and so fill in the gap.

Tityrus

I am not clever enough. . . . I cannot conceive that a plant should meditate.

Lucretius

Shepherd, what you perceive of a shrub or a tree is only the outside and instant, offered up to the indifferent eye, which only skims the surface of the world. But to spiritual eyes the plant presents not just a simple object of humble, passive life, but a strange will to join in universal weaving.

Tityrus

A shepherd's all I am—spare him, Lucretius!

Lucretius

Is not to meditate to deepen oneself in Order? Just see how the blind Tree with its diverging limbs grows up about itself, faithful to Symmetry. Life in it calculates; it raises up a structure; and radiates its rhythm through branches and their twigs, and every twig its leaf, even at the very points marked by the nascent future. . . .

Tityrus

Alas, how can I follow?

Lucretius

Do not fear, listen only: when to your soul there comes the shadow of a song, a desire to create which takes you by the throat, do you not feel your voice swell to become pure sound? Do you not feel them melt—both its life and your vow—towards the sound desired, whose wave wafts you along? Ah! Tityrus, a plant is a song whose rhythm deploys a definite form and within space displays a mystery of time. Each day it raises up a little higher the burden of its twisted scaffoldings, and offers thousandfold its leaves to the sun, each one delirious at its station in air, according to what comes of breeze to it and as it believes its inspiration unique and divine. . . .

Tityrus

But you become yourself a very tree of words. . . .

Lucretius

Yes. . . . Radiant meditation fills me with rapture. . . . And in my soul I feel all words atremble.

Tityrus

I leave you in that admirable state. But I must now gather my flock again. Mind the cool of the evening—it comes so quickly.

Notes

NOTES

From Monsieur Teste,
translated by Jackson Mathews

THE EVENING WITH MONSIEUR TESTE: "La Soirée avec Monsieur Teste" first appeared in 1896, in the second and final volumes of the quarterly review *Le Centaure* (Paris). (Vol. 6, pp. 8–21.)

A LETTER FROM MADAME ÉMILIE TESTE: First published with the title "Emilie Teste: Lettre" in the review *Commerce II*, Autumn 1924. (Vol. 6, pp. 22–34.)

Various Essays

INTRODUCTION TO THE METHOD OF LEONARDO DA VINCI: "Introduction à la méthode de Léonard de Vinci" appeared in *La Nouvelle Revue*, August 15, 1895. Valéry's marginal notes were written in 1929 and 1930 with a view to the collected edition *Les Divers Essais sur Léonard de Vinci annotés et commentés par lui-même* (Paris: Editions du Sagittaire, 1931). (From *Leonardo, Poe, Mallarmé*, translated by Malcolm Cowley and James R. Lawler, Vol. 8, pp. 3–63.)

THE CRISIS OF THE MIND: Written at the request of John Middleton Murry, "La Crise de l'esprit" originally appeared in English, in two parts, in *The Athenaeum* (London), April 11 and May 2, 1919. The French text was published the same year in the August number of *La Nouvelle Revue Française*. (From *History and Politics*, translated by Denise Folliot and Jackson Mathews, Vol. 10, pp. 23–36.)

MAN AND THE SEA SHELL: "L'Homme et la coquille" was first published in *La Nouvelle Revue Française*, Feb. 1, 1937; separately, with a preface by Valéry and sixteen drawings by Henri Mondor (Paris: *N.R.F.*, 1937). (From *Aesthetics*, translated by Ralph Manheim, Vol. 13, pp. 3–30.)

POETRY AND ABSTRACT THOUGHT: "Poésie et pensée abstraite" was delivered as the Zaharoff Lecture at Oxford, Mar. 1, 1939 and published at the Clarendon Press, 1939. (From *The Art of Poetry*, translated by Denise Folliot, Vol. 7, pp. 52–81.)

MALLARMÉ: First published in *Le Point*, Lanzac par Souillac (Lot), February–April, 1944. (From *Leonardo, Poe, Mallarmé*, translated by Malcolm Cowley and James R. Lawler, Vol. 8, pp. 294–298.)

From Poems in the Rough,
translated by Hilary Corke

A B C: These three poems first appeared in *Commerce V*, Autumn, 1925. They form part of a collection of prose poems, the rest of which were still unpublished on Valéry's death; the complete series was issued in 1976 (Paris: Blaizot) under the title *Alphabet*. (Vol. 2, pp. 223–228.)

THE ANGEL: An early draft of "L'Ange" is found in one of Valéry's notebooks for November–December 1921 (*Cahiers*, 8:370). The final version is dated May 1945, two months prior to his death; it may thus be termed his last poem. It appeared first in 1946 as a *plaquette* published by the *N.R.F.* (Vol. 2, pp. 14–16.)

THE BATH: "Le Bain" was published in *La Revue du Médecin*, April 7, 1930; in Valéry's *Morceaux choisis* (1930). (Vol. 2, pp. 233–234.)

LAURA: "Laure," published in *D'Ariane à Zoé, Alphabet galant et sentimental* . . . , an album of verse and prose (Paris: Librairie de France, 1930). (Vol. 2, pp. 235–236.)

WORK: "Travail" first appeared as "Un Poème inédit de Paul Valéry" in *Arts, Spectacles*, No. 399, February 20–26, 1953. (Vol. 2, p. 249.)

From Poems (*with French texts*),
translated by David Paul

LA FILEUSE ("The Spinner"): A first version appeared in *La Conque*, September 1, 1891. (Vol. 1, pp. 2–5.)

NARCISSE PARLE ("Narcissus Speaks"): A first version appeared in *La Conque*, March 15, 1891. (Vol. 1, pp. 28–33.)

LA JEUNE PARQUE ("The Young Fate"): The original edition was published in April 1917 (*N.R.F.*), its composition having occupied Valéry from 1913 to 1917. "What I wanted above all," he later observed, "was to combine in a work the ideas I had formed about the living organism and its very functioning in so far as it thinks and feels. . . ." (Vol. 1, pp. 68–105.)

CANTIQUE DES COLONNES ("Song of the Columns"): First appeared in *Littérature*, March 1919. (Vol. 1, pp. 122–127.)

ÉBAUCHE D'UN SERPENT ("Silhouette of a Serpent"): First appeared in *La Nouvelle Revue Française*, July 1, 1921. (Vol. 1, pp. 184–205.)

LES GRENADES ("The Pomegranates"): First appeared in *Rythme et Synthèse*, May 1920. (Vol. 1, pp. 206–207.)

LE VIN PERDU ("The Lost Wine"): First appeared in *les feuilles libres*, February 1922. (Vol. 1, pp. 208–209.)

LE CIMETIÈRE MARIN ("The Graveyard by the Sea"): Originally published in *La Nouvelle Revue Française* on June 1, 1920, the poem had been conceived some three years earlier. Its scene is a remembered one—that of the graveyard at Sète, on the Mediterranean coast, where Valéry was born—but the composition took on for him the appearance of a formal challenge: ". . . the 'Cimetière marin' first came into my head in the form of a composition in stanzas of six lines, of ten syllables each. This decision enabled me fairly easily to distribute throughout my work the perceptible, affective, and abstract content it needed so as to suggest a meditation by a particular self, translated into the universe of poetry." (Vol. 1, pp. 212–221.)

PALME ("Palm"): First appeared in *La Nouvelle Revue Française*, June 1, 1919. (Vol. 1, pp. 228–235.)

SINISTRE ("Disaster"): Published in *Mélange* in 1939, the poem is described in the preface as having been written almost fifty years before. (Vol. 1, pp. 240–241.)

Two Dialogues

DANCE AND THE SOUL: "L'Ame et la danse" first appeared in *La Revue Musicale*, December 1, 1921. It was later published, together with Valéry's contemporaneous dialogue on architecture, in *Eupalinos ou l'architecte, précédé de l'Ame et la danse* (N.R.F., 1923). (From *Dialogues*, translated by William McCausland Stewart, Vol. 4, pp. 27–62.)

<small>DIALOGUE OF THE TREE</small>: "Dialogue de l'arbre" was read by Valéry
before the annual joint session of the Cinq Académies, October 25,
1943; it was published by the Institut de France that same year and,
also in 1943, in a volume with photographs by Laure Albin-Guillot,
under the title *Arbres* (Bordeaux: Rousseau Frères, 1943). Valéry
gave this dialogue the following epigraph:

Gentlemen,

    *A certain circumstance— a chance, since chance is the fashion—having
brought me back a while ago to Virgil's Eclogues (which I had not looked
at, I confess, for many years), this return to school inspired me to write,
like a school exercise, this fancy in the form of a pastoral dialogue some
of which I shall read out to you. Speeches, more or less poetical, devoted
to the glory of a Tree, are exchanged between a Tityrus and a Lucretius,
whose names I have taken without consulting them.*

P. V.

(From *Dialogues*, translated by William McCausland Stewart, Vol.
4, pp. 153–174.)

This colophon was chosen from a number of drawings by Paul Valéry of his favorite device.